MW01285467

*Gender and Sexuality in
Indigenous North America
1400–1850*

Gender and Sexuality in Indigenous North America

1400–1850

Edited by

Sandra Slater and Fay A. Yarbrough

The University of South Carolina Press

© 2011 University of South Carolina

Published by the University of South Carolina Press
Columbia, South Carolina 29208

www.sc.edu/uscpress

Manufactured in the United States of America

20 19 18 17 16 15 14 13 12 11   10 9 8 7 6 5 4 3 2 1

Library of Congress Cataloging-in-Publication Data

Gender and sexuality in indigenous North America, 1400-1850 / edited by
Sandra Slater and Fay A. Yarbrough.
    p. cm.
  Includes bibliographical references and index.
  ISBN 978-1-57003-996-6 (cloth : alk. paper)
  1. Indians of North America—Sexual behavior. 2. Indians of North America—
Psychology. 3. Gender identity—United States—History. 4. Sex role—United
States—History. 5. Indian women—United States—Social conditions. 6. Indian
women—United States—Biography. 7. Two-spirit people—United States—History.
8. Indians of North America—Social conditions. I. Slater, Sandra. II. Yarbrough,
Fay A.
E98.S48G46 2011
305.897—dc22

                                                                    2011000902

This book was printed on Glatfelter Natures, a recycled paper with 30 percent
postconsumer waste content.

Contents

Acknowledgments

The editors of this collection are grateful for the generous assistance provided by colleagues and friends as we prepared this work. The College of Charleston and the University of Oklahoma provided crucial financial support to complete this project. Our deep gratitude goes to Linda Fogle and Alex Moore at the University of South Carolina Press for believing in this project. And, to the anonymous reviewers, thank you for your invaluable suggestions for the betterment of this work.

Preparing an edited collection requires patience and support, mostly from our spouses and families. Sandra Slater would like to thank her partner, Denise Helton, for her unyielding love and support both personally and professionally. And Fay A. Yarbrough thanks Arthur Terry, Jr., Wilson, and Rivers who each remind her daily to push away from the computer.

Finally, we wish to acknowledge the millions of people of all races and cultures who faced, and continue to face, discrimination for not fitting neatly into predominant gender paradigms.

Introduction

— Fay A. Yarbrough

One cannot hark back to a time when gender roles were clear and simple or definitions of marriage were universally agreed upon. Gender roles and sexual identities have never been static, but rather constantly shift in relation to historical change and contact between groups. Questions about how societies choose to define gender identities, the meaning of sexual orientation and behavior, and what constitutes marriage continue to provoke controversy even now. This essay collection explores some of this variation in the meanings of gender, sexuality, and marriage by examining indigenous communities in North America from the colonial period through the nineteenth century. While the essays in the collection do not directly tackle current controversies, they do offer important historical background suggesting perhaps the roots of contemporary controversies and ways to address them.

Several overarching themes connect the essays in *Gender and Sexuality in Indigenous North America, 1400–1850*. The question of how Europeans manipulated native ideas about gender for their own purposes and how indigenous people responded to European attempts to impose gendered cultural practices that clashed with native thinking informs all of the work here. For instance Sandra Slater finds that conflicting definitions of masculinity could lead to violence between indigenous groups and Europeans. Conversely Dawn G. Marsh shows that Quakers' own acceptance of more egalitarian gender roles, a pattern more in line with local native groups, enabled Lenape woman Hannah Freeman to negotiate her own economic activity and land ownership with her Quaker neighbors. Likewise M. Carmen Gomez-Galisteo describes Spanish explorer Cabeza de Vaca taking on some of the roles of native women in order to improve his situation while a captive of the local indigenous population. Both Jan V. Noel and Fay A. Yarbrough demonstrate the various ways in which indigenous peoples could react to European and Euro-American pressure to change women's roles in particular in native societies. Moreover, Europeans often spoke of the act of conquest itself in gendered terms, as discussed by Slater and Gomez-Galisteo.

Many of the essays also address how indigenous people made meaning of gender and how these meanings changed over time within their own communities.

Noel describes Iroquois women's position before European contact as quite powerful and integral to the social, economic, and political life of the Iroquois people. Marsh and Yarbrough also show that some elements of native women's authority endured despite, and sometimes because of, contact with colonists and Americans. Roger M. Carpenter's essay demonstrates the variety of possible gender roles among some indigenous groups in his description of the two-spirit phenomenon, a topic also dealt with in varying degrees by Gomez-Galisteo, Slater, and Gabriel S. Estrada.

Several authors consider sexual practice as a site for cultural articulation, as well as a vehicle for the expression of gender roles. Estrada, for instance, contends that many contemporary writers employ indigenous sexual and gender histories in describing their own contemporary racial, ethnic, and sexual identities, connecting sixteenth-century indigenous sexual practice and behavior to modern Chicano/a and Mestizo/a authors and identities. Estrada's work forms a provocative conversation with Gomez-Galisteo, Slater, and Carpenter about the roles, function, and perception of two-spirited individuals in native societies, a conversation that addresses questions such as the ability of such individuals to marry or participate in warfare and ceremonial life, and choice and consent in taking on this role. Conversely Gomez-Galisteo also notes the surprising absence of sexual activity between native women and European men in Cabeza de Vaca's narrative, an omission that runs counter to many other accounts by Cabeza de Vaca's contemporaries and that may have had political implications of its own.

Finally, race is an important lens through which many of the authors here examine native history, and thus race is another theme linking the essays in this collection. Often Europeans and colonists viewed native practices, be they related to gender, sexual activity, religion, and so forth, as suspect precisely because the practitioners were a racialized "other" group. That is, allegedly promiscuous native women described by Gomez-Galisteo, or so-called deviant sexual behavior discussed by Carpenter or Estrada, or barbarous practices in warfare presented by Slater and Carpenter merely served as evidence of how different native people were from European observers. Thus Salvadora de los Santos Ramirez, according to Dorothy Tanck de Estrada, became the subject of religious interest because she was an Otomi Indian and yet behaved in such a pious manner in spite of that identity, exceeding even many European women in the colony in virtuous comportment. And sometimes natives began to formulate their own ideas about race, as Yarbrough's discussion of resistance and accommodation to American gender roles among the Choctaw Indians demonstrates.

Gender and Sexuality in Indigenous North America, 1400–1850, bridges geographical divides with essays that focus on indigenous peoples in locations ranging from Canada, the expanse of the continental United States, and Mexico. Often the contemporary boundaries separating these places are artificial and obscure the fluidity of the societies that historically occupied these spaces. And indigenous communities across these geographical territories sometimes shared similar experiences with colonialism and conquest. Scholarship on the borderlands, such as James F. Brooks's *Captives and Cousins,* demonstrates that the people living in these spaces often did not recognize the legal borders that separated them. And other essay collections, such as Tiya Miles and Sharon P. Holland's *Crossing Waters, Crossing Worlds,* which explores indigenous interactions with people of African descent from New England to the Indian Territory, also confirm the value of looking beyond traditional regional boundaries.[1]

Authors had been producing materials considering native populations for quite some time, as early as the eighteenth century, before the recent turn by scholars to discussions of this aspect, gender and sexuality, of the meeting of indigenous peoples and Europeans.[2] In the interim of the nineteenth century, other writers provided useful histories of various native groups or events.[3] By the twentieth century native groups had become the focus of intense study for anthropologists.[4] At the same time figures such as Grant Foreman and Angie Debo were producing comprehensive histories of various North American indigenous groups while Annie Heloise Abel wrote detailed studies of American Indians confronting the American Civil War.[5] In the latter twentieth century the larger field of American Indian Studies grew, in part, out of the agitation of American Indian students who participated in the activist movements of the Civil Rights Era. Such agitation led to the growth of Native American Studies departments and programs at American universities and to a proliferation in the production of histories of native peoples. Scholars attempted to illuminate native life and reveal native perspectives on interactions with Europeans and later Americans. These students and scholars demonstrated that Indians had not, in fact, "vanished," and that a process sometimes seen as the conquest and absorption of native groups by European forces was far more complex and contested.[6] And both "natives and newcomers," to borrow James Axtell's phrase, changed in these interactions.[7]

Newer scholarship increasingly placed natives and their agency at the center of the narrative.[8] Academic histories of natives no longer began and ended with European contact. Instead, anthropologists, archaeologists, and historians plumbed new sources or considered more familiar sources in new ways to describe varied and complex native societies with mature systems of governance that sometimes came into conflict long before the arrival of Europeans.[9] Some indigenous societies established extensive networks of trade and built cities.[10] And some native groups practiced a form of slavery, enslaving indigenous enemies and then, later, people of African descent.[11] Scholars depicted native peoples not as objects of study but as historical subjects, acting and reacting to circumstances and making choices.

The field of American Indian history continues to be vibrant, as scholars ask questions that complicate notions of resistance and the meaning of cultural continuity.[12] Subjects of recent scholarship include the concept of native agency, native pursuits of nationalism and national identities, relationships between indigenous peoples and people of African descent, the fight for sovereignty in indigenous communities, and the environmental consequences of federal policies for American Indians.[13] Moreover, many native groups grapple with the meaning of Indian identity writ large in the United States given the role of the federal government and the states in recognizing various Indian nations and within a larger global context that includes indigenous peoples such as the Maori of New Zealand or the Aborigines of Australia.[14]

This collection of essays captures the growing scholarly interest in the operation of notions of gender and sexuality in native societies throughout the colonial Americas and through the Civil War era.[15] Scholars posit questions such as, how did gender roles for men and women in native societies change over time and in relation to contact with Europeans? What ideas about gender remained constant for particular indigenous communities and why? What was the role of native people who occupied seemingly incongruous places within gender paradigms? The scholars' answers to these questions reveal something of the meaning of gender in native societies and for the Europeans who encountered them.

Organized chronologically, this collection begins with M. Carmen Gomez-Galisteo's essay about the malleability of notions of gender among indigenous groups and how outsiders could negotiate those ideas as a strategy for survival. While in Spanish Florida, conquistador Cabeza de Vaca found himself in the unlikely position of performing the duties of a native woman as a trader and a healer in order to avoid the fate of many adult male captives, namely death. Performing these duties also afforded Cabeza de Vaca freedom of movement and more status than that of a slave. Rather than reject these roles because they were too feminine, Cabeza de Vaca embraced them and wrote about them, not surprisingly, in a favorable light. Gomez-Galisteo also explores the gendered language used by the conquistadors to describe the act of conquest and the physical land, as well as the indigenous people they encountered. While many other explorers portrayed native women as monstrous and sexually aberrant in their promiscuity, Cabeza de Vaca depicted native women as mothers and claimed to have been sexually chaste during his New World travels, a claim that Gomez-Galisteo questions.

Like Gomez-Galisteo, Sandra Slater addresses the meanings of masculinity as they were negotiated by European explorers and natives in the early years of contact and what happened when those ideas sometimes collided. Slater posits that both native and European men built their masculine identities on several broad concepts: honor, their relationships to and with women, warfare, and sexual practice. European and native men might deem each other more or less manly based on how each group treated women, behaved in battle, or permitted or punished certain kinds of sexual behavior. Moreover, in another point of tangency with Gomez-Galisteo, Slater finds that the entire endeavor of exploration had gendered connotations in European minds who described it in terms of the male explorers displaying manly courage as they conquered the feminized "virgin" land. And explorers sometimes extended this metaphor to the inhabitants of the land. Thus, by conquering the land, European explorers imagined they had also conquered, and therefore had access to, native women. Slater's essay underscores the importance of masculinity in constructions and negotiations of identity in the New World.

In a more synthetic exploration of gender roles within a specific native group, Jan V. Noel provides a clear and thoughtful consideration of the existing literature about gender among the Haudenosaunee (also known as the Iroquois) and argues persuasively that the Haudenosaunee were not patriarchal. To the contrary, "the Haudenosaunee, at least as late as the eighteenth century, saw male and female roles in terms of reciprocal relationships that did not require power struggles." While this description of gender relationships is hard for many modern observers to accept, Noel finds that women nonetheless performed important functions in Haudenosaunee society by choosing leaders, by determining the fate of war captives, by adjudicating land disputes, by farming the land, and by participating in council meetings. Contact with Europeans, of course, affected the relations between the sexes in Iroquoia, but Noel finds that "there is considerable evidence to suggest that many mature Iroquois women maintained unusual positions even after two or three centuries of interaction with Europeans." Noel contends the Haudenosaunee offer a glimpse of the contours and possibilities of an egalitarian society.

Dorothy Tanck de Estrada and Dawn Marsh consider the lives of individual women and what their experiences can reveal about the larger societies from which these women emerged. Tanck de Estrada describes the life of one remarkable native woman in eighteenth-century New Spain who was regarded by many of her contemporaries as a saint. Salvadora de los Santos Ramirez's rise to religious importance was all the more surprising because of her status as an Otomi Indian, "judged by many," in Tanck de Estrada's words, "to be the most backwards and uncouth people in the region." Perhaps even more unusual, shortly after her death Father Antonio de Paredes, a prominent Jesuit priest, published her biography in the form of an edifying letter, a form usually reserved for "recently deceased priest[s], novice[s], or brother[s] who w[ere] thought to be exceptionally holy." Thus, while the sisters in the *beaterio* where de los Santos Ramirez lived and worked did not appear to hold her in high regard, for reasons of class according to Tanck de Estrada, the denizens of the city of Querétaro and at least one important member of the church hierarchy did. Through de los Santos Ramirez's life, Tanck de Estrada is able to illuminate gendered and cultural expectations about women in colonial Mexico.

Just as Tanck de Estrada is able to access the life of a humble Otomi Indian woman through the writings of a male contemporary, Marsh is able to recreate the life of Hannah Freeman because a man, Moses Marshall, recorded the details. In this case Marshall collected testimony about Freeman's life for administrative purposes to determine her county of residence and eligibility for the services of the poorhouse. Hannah Freeman's life serves as a window on native/colonial interactions in the eighteenth-century Pennsylvania colony. Marsh finds that those relationships were often negotiated, and natives maintained a surprising amount of control over ancestral lands. Freeman, a Lenape Indian, was a part of a mobile woman-centered family unit that followed the demand for labor in the Brandywine River Valley and fled this territory in the face of the brutality of the Paxton Boys, who massacred Conestoga Indians in 1763. Upon the family's return from exile, Freeman continued to work as a basket maker, healer, seamstress, and servant for both black and white residents of the valley. Marsh posits that Freeman, like her counterparts elsewhere, constantly strategized to preserve her connections to her traditional territories, and that white people sometimes accommodated indigenous peoples in these claims even when not bound by law to do so.

Fay A. Yarbrough exchanges the microhistorical approach of several of the essays for a broader consideration of women's roles in Choctaw society during the nineteenth century and how those roles changed during this tumultuous time, a century that included the removal of the Choctaw Indians from the southeastern United States to Indian Territory in present-day Oklahoma and their alliance with the Confederacy during the Civil War. She begins with a discussion of matrilineally determined clans and matrilocal households and their importance to Choctaw social organization. Choctaw women also traditionally derived power from their work as agriculturalists, producing the corn that was so important to sustenance and ceremonial life among the Choctaws. Over the course of the nineteenth century, however, slaves of African descent, native men, and white men would encroach on Choctaw women's role as agriculturalists. And as Choctaws turned to more formalized systems of governance in the form of a written constitution and laws, Choctaw women found some of their traditional authority eroding and their marital choices under increased scrutiny.

While the three preceding articles focus on native women and men in more familiar gendered roles, Roger M. Carpenter turns his attention to another gendered group that many, especially Europeans, found unfathomable. Carpenter sheds important light on the role of male and female two-spirits in indigenous society, particularly in warfare, and how they were perceived by native peoples and Europeans. [16] Carpenter also offers some discussion of the origins and meaning of the controversial term *berdache*. Found throughout much of Native North America during the early contact period, two-spirit people provoked reactions from European (and later American) explorers and missionaries ranging from amusement to disgust to outright bafflement. Native groups appear to have accepted two-spirit individuals of both sexes as participants in warfare, a conclusion buttressed by Slater's assertion that two-spirit individuals often performed important functions in battle as handlers of the bodies of dead warriors. Thus, while the European colonists and their descendants found two-spirit individuals particularly disturbing, native populations appeared to have a place for more than two gender identities within their gender universe.

Finally, Gabriel S. Estrada's deeply personal essay is part historiography and part provocative consideration of how writers' conclusions about indigenous sexual and gender histories are often shaped by their own racial, ethnic, and sexual identities. Like Carpenter, Estrada discusses the contentious term *berdache* and also the origins of the term *two-spirit* and why he prefers it. Moreover Estrada suggests that sixteenth-century indigenous sexual practice and behavior continue to influence how modern Chicano/a and Mestizo/a authors see themselves. Many authors find power in invoking an indigenous past or ancestry, but Estrada argues that to do so without paying careful attention to the actual histories of the people one invokes or to the historical accuracy of the invocation is problematic. Thus, for instance, different authors can examine indigenous histories of two-spirit peoples and find degradation and oppression or celebration and adulation or invisibility.

In the end we hope this collection of essays offers a preview of some of the newest scholarship in the field of native history. Trained in different disciplines in various countries, the contributors here work in several languages, apply varied methodologies, and use different sources, so the essays also serve as a lens through which to consider scholarly inquiry. Moreover, the issues the authors discuss—gender, sexuality, and identity—have continued resonance in native communities today, as well as within the larger societies of which those native communities form a part.

Notes

1. James F. Brooks, *Captives and Cousins: Slavery, Kinship, and Community in the Southwest Borderlands* (Chapel Hill: University of North Carolina Press, 2002); Tiya Miles

and Sharon P. Holland, eds., *Crossing Waters, Crossing Worlds: The African Diaspora in Indian Country* (Durham: Duke University Press, 2006).

2. James Adair, *The History of the American Indians,* ed. Kathryn E. Holland Braund (Tuscaloosa: University of Alabama Press, 2005). This text was originally published in London in 1774. Of course there are older accounts that include information about native life that were often produced by missionaries or other religious figures. See, for instance, Bartolomé de las Casas' *History of the Indies* (New York: Harper and Row, 1971) or his *Short Account of the Destruction of the Indies* (New York: Penguin, 1999), originally published in the sixteenth century.

3. James Mooney, *Myths of the Cherokee and Sacred Formulas of the Cherokee* (Nashville: C. Elder-Bookseller, 1972), reprinted from 1900 and 1891 editions, and *The Ghost-Dance Religion and Wounded Knee* (New York: Dover, 1973), reprint of the 1896 edition; H. B. Cushman, *History of the Choctaw, Chickasaw and Natchez Indians,* ed. Angie Debo (Norman: University of Oklahoma Press, 1999), originally published in 1899.

4. For instance, see the multivolume series *Columbia University Contributions to Anthropology,* 36 vols. (New York City: Columbia University Press, 1910–1956), or *University of Washington Publications in Anthropology,* 14 vols. (Seattle: University of Washington Press, 1920–1964); Frederick Webb Hodge, ed., *Handbook of American Indians North of Mexico,* 2 vols. (Washington, D.C.: Government Printing Office, 1907–1910); Fred Eggan, ed., *Social Anthropology of North American Tribes* (Chicago: University of Chicago Press, 1937), and John R. Swanton, *Source Material for the Social and Ceremonial Life of the Choctaw Indians* (Tuscaloosa: University of Alabama Press, 2001), originally published in 1931 by the Smithsonian Institution.

5. Grant Foreman, *The Five Civilized Tribes: Cherokee, Chickasaw, Choctaw, Creek, Seminole* (Norma: University of Oklahoma Press, 1934); Angie Debo, *The Rise and Fall of the Choctaw Republic* (Norman: University of Oklahoma Press, 1934), and *A History of the Indians of the United States* (Norman: University of Oklahoma Press, 1970); Annie Heloise Abel, *The American Indian and the End of the Confederacy, 1863–1866* (Lincoln: University of Nebraska Press, 1993), originally published in 1925, *The American Indian in the Civil War, 1862–1865* (Lincoln: University of Nebraska Press, 1992), originally published in 1919, and *The American Indian as Slaveholder and Secessionist* (Lincoln: University of Nebraska Press, 1992), originally published in 1915.

6. I borrow the idea of vanishing Indians from Zane Grey, *The Vanishing American* (New York: Grossett & Dunlap, 1925). For examples of studies of the complicated nature of interactions between natives and Europeans, see James Axtell, *The European and the Indian: Essays in the Ethnohistory of Colonial North America* (Oxford: Oxford University Press, 1991), and Jack Weatherford, *Native Roots: How the Indians Enriched America* (New York: Fawcett Books, 1991).

7. James Axtell, *Natives and Newcomers: The Cultural Origins of North America* (New York: Oxford University Press, 2000).

8. See Daniel K. Richter, *Facing East from Indian Country: A Native History of Early America* (Cambridge: Harvard University Press, 2001), or Robbie Ethridge, *Creek Country: The Creek Indians and Their World* (Chapel Hill: University of North Carolina Press, 2003), for examples.

9. See Jesse D. Jennings, ed., *Ancient North Americans* (San Francisco: W. H. Freeman & Company, 1983); Thomas Dillehay, *The Settlement of the Americas: A New Prehistory* (New York: Basic Books, 2001); or John S. Henderson, *World of the Ancient Maya* (Ithaca: Cornell University Press, 1981).

10. See Roger G. Kennedy, *Hidden Cities: The Discovery and Loss of Ancient North American Civilization* (New York: Penguin, 1994); Biloine Whiting Young and Melvin L. Fowler, *Cahokia: The Great Native American Metropolis* (Urbana: University of Illinois Press, 2000); or Richard A. Diehl, *Tula: The Toltec Capital of Ancient Mexico* (London: Thames and Hudson, 1981).

11. See Brooks, *Captives and Cousins;* Daniel F. Littlefield, Jr., *Africans and Seminoles: From Removal to Emancipation* (Jackson: University of Mississippi Press, 1977); Theda Perdue, *Slavery and the Evolution of Cherokee Society, 1540–1866* (Knoxville: University of Tennessee Press, 1979); Rudi Halliburton, Jr., *Red over Black; Black Slavery among the Cherokee Indians* (Westport, Conn.: Greenwood Press, 1977); or Claudio Saunt, *A New Order of Things: Property, Power, and the Transformation of the Creek Indians, 1733–1816* (Cambridge: Cambridge University Press, 1999).

12. Richard A. Grounds, George E. Tinker, and David E. Wilkins, eds., *Native Voices: American Indian Identity and Resistance* (Lawrence: University Press of Kansas, 2003).

13. Circe Sturm considers the meaning of identity for Cherokees in *Blood Politics: Race, Culture and Identity in the Cherokee Nation of Oklahoma* (Berkeley: University of California Press, 2002). Philip J. Deloria considers native identity as it confronts modernity in *Indians in Unexpected Places* (Lawrence: University Press of Kansas, 2004). For examples of the growing literature on interactions between indigenous peoples and people of African descent, see Jack D. Forbes, *Africans and Native Americans: The Language of Race and the Evolution of Red-Black Peoples* (Urbana: University of Illinois Press, 1993); Murray R. Wickett, *Contested Territory: Whites, Native Americans and African Americans in Oklahoma, 1865–1907* (Baton Rouge: Louisiana State University Press, 2000); Tiya Miles, *Ties That Bind: The Story of an Afro-Cherokee Family in Slavery and Freedom* (Berkeley: University of California Press, 2005); Gary Zellar, *African Creeks: Estelvste and the Creek Nation* (Norman: University of Oklahoma Press, 2007); and Celia E. Naylor: *African Cherokees in Indian Territory: From Chattel to Citizens* (Chapel Hill: University of North Carolina Press, 2008). Fay A. Yarbrough considers race and the quest for sovereignty in *Race and the Cherokee Nation: Sovereignty in the Nineteenth Century* (Philadelphia: University of Pennsylvania Press, 2008). For discussions of native perspectives on the environment, see Donald A. Grinde and Bruce E. Johansen, *Ecocide of Native America: Environmental Destruction of Indian Lands and Peoples* (Santa Fe: Clear Light Books, 1995), or Michael E. Harkin and David Rich Lewis, eds., *Native Americans and the Environment: Perspectives on the Ecological Indian* (Lincoln: University of Nebraska Press, 2007). Closely connected to issues of sovereignty, identity, and cultural preservation is the subject of repatriation; see Devon A. Mihesuah, ed., *Repatriation Reader: Who Owns American Indian Remains?* (Lincoln: University of Nebraska Press, 2000).

14. The Lumbee Indians of North Carolina are just one of many groups that highlight the tensions between state and federal recognition of native groups. See Karen I. Blu, *The Lumbee Problem: The Making of an American Indian People* (Lincoln: University of Nebraska Press, 1980). For some discussion of identity for the Aborigines of Australia, see Elizabeth A.

Povinelli, *The Cunning of Recognition: Indigenous Alterities and the Making of Australian Multiculturalism* (Durham: Duke University Press, 2002). For some discussion of the parallels between identity among the Maori and American Indians, see Chadwick Allen, *Blood Narrative: Indigenous Identity in American Indian and Mori Literary and Activist Texts* (Durham: Duke University Press, 2002).

15. For examples of scholarship that discusses gender and sexuality within native communities, see Matthew Basso, Laura McCall, and Dee Garceau, eds., *Across the Great Divide: Cultures of Manhood in the American West* (New York: Routledge, 2001); Craig Thompson Friend and Lorri Glover, eds., *Southern Manhood: Perspectives on Masculinity in the Old South* (Athens: University of Georgia Press, 2004), which includes an essay on masculinity among Choctaw elites by Greg O'Brien; Devon Abbott Mihesuah, *Indigenous American Women: Decolonization, Empowerment, Activism* (Lincoln: University of Nebraska Press, 2003); Theda Perdue, *Cherokee Women: Gender and Culture Change, 1700–1835* (Lincoln: University of Nebraska Press, 1998); Susan Sleeper-Smith, *Indian Women and French Men: Rethinking Cultural Encounter in the Western Great Lakes* (Amherst: University of Massachusetts Press, 2001); and Mary Ann Irwin and James F. Brooks, eds., *Women and Gender in the American West* (Albuquerque: University of New Mexico Press, 2004).

16. For more on the phenomenon of two-spirits or other genders among indigenous groups, see Will Roscoe, *Changing Ones: Third and Fourth Genders in Native North America* (New York: St. Martin's Press, 1998); Sue-Ellen Jacobs, Wesley Thomas, and Sabine Lang, eds., *Two-Spirit People: Native American Gender Identity, Sexuality, and Spirituality* (Urbana: University of Illinois Press, 1997); and Sabine Lang, *Men as Women, Women as Men: Changing Gender in Native American Cultures* (Austin: University of Texas Press, 1998).

Subverting Gender Roles in the Sixteenth Century

Cabeza de Vaca, the Conquistador Who Became a Native American Woman

— M. Carmen Gomez-Galisteo

"I became a trader and tried to ply my trade the best I could. I liked this trade, because it gave me the freedom to go wherever I wanted. I was obligated to nothing and was not a slave. Wherever I went they treated me well and fed me because I was a trader."[1] Álvar Núñez Cabeza de Vaca, the man who wrote this statement, was a conquistador, the sixteenth-century epitome of masculinity. This quotation reflects his happiness at being a trader, since this occupation allowed him a greater freedom than his situation as a captive at the hands of the Native Americans had left him. What he forgot to mention, however, is that this role with which he was so perfectly happy was a female role among the Native Americans with whom he lived. All in all, his omission notwithstanding, it had taken a long journey (in both a literal and a metaphorical sense) for Cabeza de Vaca to be able to write something such as this in his account, the testimony of his ten-year experience in America.[2]

In Cabeza de Vaca's ordeal in North America we see his process of constructing an alternative identity, which, in a way, was genderless. Cabeza de Vaca's masculine identity did not hold and was shattered because of his powerlessness and his female-gendered job. Working in a job that a Native American woman would normally hold, he could no longer be the epitome of masculinity that conquistadors were. But at the same time, though his job was a feminine one, he did not embrace a new, female identity; instead he highlighted the masculine attributes that his new identity as trader provided him, such as the freedom to travel.

The first part of this essay contextualizes Cabeza de Vaca's experiences in the Americas in light of Europeans' mental images of the New World and Native Americans, especially women. The next section analyzes Cabeza de Vaca's perceptions of Native American gendered society, paying close attention to his descriptions of the roles filled by Native American women. The final section in the essay considers the female roles that Cabeza de Vaca played during his stay in America and highlights the significance of Cabeza de Vaca's testimony for a better understanding of European perceptions of Native American gender roles and Europeans' assimilation into Native American society.

I approach gender as a socially constructed concept, and, as such, closely related to one particular society's notions about what male and female attributes are. Because of this, what in one society is true in another might not be so; trading was a low-class male occupation in sixteenth-century Spain, whereas in the Native American societies in which Cabeza de Vaca lived, trading was a female occupation, with no class markers attached.

Historical Context of the Narváez Expedition to Florida

On June 17, 1527, the expedition commanded by Pánfilo de Narváez sailed from the Spanish port of Sanlúcar de Barrameda, Cádiz. This expedition was not just another exploration venture, for its goal was to colonize the land between Río de las Palmas (eastern Mexico) and Florida. The fact that the wives of some of the soldiers in the expedition and some friars were also traveling with them marks their intention to set up a proper colony, inhabited by families and with religious services.[3] The 1527 expedition to Florida was one of the biggest and best-equipped Spanish expeditions ever, the capstone of Narváez's career in the New World.

Narváez had actively participated in the conquest of Cuba (1511–14) as second in command to Diego Velázquez, governor of the island.[4] Therefore Hernán Cortés's rebellion against Velázquez had posed a serious threat to Narváez's up-to-then glorious military prestige. Narváez tried to stop Cortés but was defeated on May 24, 1520, at the battle of Cempoala and arrested. Once released and back in Spain, Narváez became a bitter man who tried to discredit Cortés and sought his execution, as reported by Cortés's official chronicler, Francisco López de Gómara.[5] Narváez succeeded in securing a ban on Cortés's letters, which illustrated his defeat, as well as the destruction of those copies already printed.

At the same time Narváez asked the emperor to grant a petition for Florida. Originally intended just as a trading petition, in this petition he was already requesting permission to "conquer, populate, and discover everything that there is to discover in those parts."[6] Thus this new expedition to America constituted Narváez's last chance of recovering his fading fame, putting at risk his own money as well as his reputation. This, along with his emotionalism and tendency to act impulsively, might explain some of the desperate and risky decisions he made during the journey, decisions heavily questioned by Cabeza de Vaca, treasurer and second in command.[7]

Álvar Núñez Cabeza de Vaca was born in Jerez de la Frontera, Cádiz, in 1490 to a wealthy family. Little is known about his life in general or about his childhood in particular.[8] Orphaned by his parents at a very early age, he was put into the care of his maternal aunt. He was soon employed in the service of the Duke of Medina Sidonia, a leading political figure in Andalusian society. With him he fought in Italy, where the Spanish monarch was trying to preserve his claim on certain Italian territories. Back in Spain, he married María de Marmolejo by 1520.[9]

The expedition was unfortunate from the very beginning, and calamities soon befell the soldiers. These included the wrecks of two ships, resulting in the death of sixty men, as well as the desertion of almost one-quarter of the original crew. Eventually they arrived in Florida on Maundy Thursday 1528, according to Cabeza de Vaca's account.[10] Having landed in a place their pilots were unable to identify, they were completely at a loss about their exact location. Thinking they were somewhere between Pánuco or Río de las Palmas, Narváez decided to send the ships ahead of the terrestrial party.[11] This, along with his decision to go further inland to find the province of Apalache, reported by the Native Americans to contain gold, led to the ultimate loss of the terrestrial expedition, which was separated from the ships.[12]

Europeans and Native American Women

Almost starving ("we were in such a state that our bones could easily be counted and we looked like the picture of death") and with so scarce a knowledge of the American environment that survival on their own was virtually impossible, Cabeza de Vaca and the surviving members of the expedition were forced to rely on the Native Americans' hospitality, despite their suspicions of human sacrifices:[13] "I told the Christians that, if they agreed, I would ask those Indians to take us to their lodges. And some who had been in New Spain responded that we should not even think about it, because if they took us to their lodges they would sacrifice us to their idols. But seeing that we had no other recourse and that any other action would certainly bring us closer to death, I did not pay attention to what they were saying and I asked the Indians to take us to their lodges."[14]

Their absolute dependence on the Native Americans rendered the Spaniards impotent at the hands of the Native Americans, forcing them ultimately to become slaves. Cabeza de Vaca did not return to Spain until 1537, spending the intervening years in between living among different Native American groups, among whom he performed different roles until he was found by Spanish troops.

When he embarked on the expedition to Florida, Cabeza de Vaca was a newcomer to the New World with no previous experience. A man who had never set foot in America, he had to rely on hearsay when it came to the new American reality. In the fashion of his paternal grandfather, Pedro de Vera, conquistador of the Canary Islands, Cabeza de Vaca wanted to be a conquistador, a man like Cortés, taking part in the conquest of a whole empire—maybe even greater than Cortés, if rumors to that effect are to be believed.[15] Therefore it was not unwillingness on Cabeza de Vaca's part that prevented his becoming a conquistador, but the unfavorable situation.[16]

Representations of America abound from the beginning of contact between Europeans and inhabitants of America. In the words of historian Wayne Franklin, "In 1492 America was, from the European standpoint, simply an event. But in 1493 it became a collection of words."[17] Those who had been to America as well as those who had never set foot there, all enthusiastically took the task of writing about the New World upon themselves.[18] Among the most common images of the New World was that of America as the location of the "Earthly Paradise." On his third trip Columbus identified Hispaniola as such, and thus wrote to the Catholic Monarchs: "mas yo muy asentado tengo el ánima que allí donde dije, es el Paraíso Terrenal, y descanso sobre las razones y autoridades sobrescritas."[19]

Closely associated to the notion of a paradise-like America was the similarly pervasive idea of America as a virgin land, previously untouched, which soon became an all-time favorite: "The prevalence of gendered language in exploration narratives reveals an operative fantasy of the New World as a 'virgin bride,' beautiful, unspoiled, passive, and welcoming."[20] To begin with, Columbus had "exemplified his reliance on the female body to articulate the colonial venture at the very outset of his voyage when he wrote that the earth was shaped like a breast with the Indies composing the nipple."[21] Conquistadors and explorers would write about America in feminine terms and often referred to America as a maid to be deflowered by them.

Native Americans soon became central to this picture of America. Very early in narratives describing European-Native contact, European writers represented the Native Americans as the ubiquitous Other against whom Europeans could describe and define themselves—inevitably as superior. Just as Europeans had in the first place used America to help define their own national identities, which were still somewhat unstable and vague, the existence of the Native Americans contributed to Europeans' definitions of themselves.[22] Though America proved to be a much more fertile ground than other, equally unknown regions in stirring Europeans' imagination, it shared with Africa and Asia the circumstance of being "figured in European lore as libidinously eroticized. Travelers' tales abounded with visions of the monstrous sexuality of far-off lands, where, as legend had it, men sported gigantic penises and women consorted with apes, feminized men's breasts flowed with milk and militarized women lopped theirs off."[23] Descriptions of Native American women as monstrous beings or engaged in non-normative sexual relations contributed to the task of maintaining a sense of European superiority in religious and cultural terms, with Native American women coming to symbolize sexual aberration and promiscuity.[24] Europeans also credited Native

American women with the ability to seduce European men thanks to herbal juices that made their victims lose their sexual organs.[25]

The sexual behavior of Native American women was a matter of much controversy, generating a vast literature. Starting with Michele de Cuneo, a participant in Columbus's first voyage, Native American women were commonly described by conquistadors as lecherous creatures, beautiful, voluptuous, sensuous, insatiable, lust-filled, and more than willing to satisfy the Europeans' sexual needs.[26] Stories of ardent Native American women soon became commonplace in both discovery and exploration accounts of the period as well as in the writings produced by eyewitnesses of any nationality, with a few minor variations—women assigned by their rulers or even by their own fathers to Europeans to satisfy the Europeans' sexual needs, women who willingly took this task upon themselves, or women sold or given away as presents to the newcomers. At the same time Native American women were fruitfully being employed by writers trying to pursue their views and agendas.[27]

As a general rule later writers modeled their own representations of Native American women after other writers' previous descriptions, thus shaping future travelers' expectations about the kind of women they might find in the Americas.[28] So pervasive became these negative descriptions of Native American women that favorable ones were exceptional and travelers expected to meet lecherous, dangerous Native American women. Not many European observers would have described Native American women as the Italian navigator Amerigo Vespucci did: "Theyr bodies are verye smothe and clene by reason of theyr often washinge. They are in other thynges filthy and withoute shame. Thei use no lawful coiunccion of marage, and but every one hath as many women as him liketh, and leaveth them agayn at his pleasure. The women are very fruiteful, and refuse no laboure al the whyle they are with childe. They travayle in maner withoute payne, so that the nexte day they are cherefull and able to walke. Neyther have they theyr bellies wimpeled or loose, and hanginge pappes, by reason of bearinge manye children."[29]

This description by French explorer Jean de Léry is more typical of the kind of description of female Native Americans one is likely to find in New World accounts: "I have concluded that they have the same master: that is, the Brazilian women and the witches over here were guided by the same spirit of Satan; neither the distance between the places nor the long passage over the sea keeps the father of lies from working both here and there on those who are handed over to him by the just judgment of God."[30] All Native American women consequently were equal to European witches. There might have been good European women (that is, those who were not witches), but, in Léry's mind, there were no good Native American women.

Cabeza de Vaca and Native American Women

In order to analyze Cabeza de Vaca's description of Native American women, it is necessary to bear in mind that Cabeza de Vaca's relationship with the Native Americans was different from the relationships that other explorers, conquistadors, or settlers could have had with them in that Cabeza de Vaca was powerless with regard to the Native Americans. With Cabeza de Vaca questions of superiority and inferiority were blurred because, as a captive, he occupied a position of inferiority with respect to the Native Americans. A captive and a slave himself, Cabeza de Vaca could not play the role of one superior to the Native Americans. Accordingly his perception and subsequent representation of Native American women differs significantly from those of other European observers.

Although stories of a sexual sort are recurrent in most accounts, they are most notably absent from Cabeza de Vaca's text. In a society such as colonial Spanish society in the Americas, where Spaniards not only accepted miscegenation between Spanish conquistadors and native women (more often than not identified as imperial Aztec princesses so as to reflect well on the Spaniards' consorting with the Native Americans[31]) but also promoted, encouraged, and applauded it (remember Hernán Cortés and Malinche), that Cabeza de Vaca and the three companions who made it back to Spanish territory remained chaste during their time in America is most remarkable.[32] Scholars including Juan Francisco Maura have commented on this, and for readers of Cabeza de Vaca's age this omission might have been equally noted.[33]

For Cabeza de Vaca, Native American women were not sexual beings, or, at least, they were not so for the Spaniards. For Cabeza de Vaca female Native Americans were mothers rather than women, and he made reference to pregnancy and nursing, topics most unusual for a typical conquistador's account: "From the Isle of Misfortune to this land, all the Indians we encountered have the custom of not sleeping with their wives from the time they first notice they are pregnant until the child is two-years old. The children nurse at the breast until they are twelve years old, when they can look for food for themselves."[34]

In his account Cabeza de Vaca does not include any remarks about sex between Spaniards and Native American women. Even when he describes naked female bodies, he does not dwell on this matter at length, contrary to what most contemporary and later chroniclers did: "All the people of this land go about naked. Only the women cover part of their bodies with a kind of wool that grows on the trees. Young women cover themselves with deerskins."[35] In his references to Native American women, he does not portray them as lecherous but, on the contrary, as modest: "The women cover their private parts with grass and straw."[36] Even in Anglo-American captivity narratives, more conservative than Spanish conquest texts when it comes to sexual references, scenes of sex between some of the Native American women and white males are commonplace. For historian Gary L. Ebersole these captivity narratives "participate in the white male fantasy that white men are sexually irresistible to beautiful, sensuous native women."[37] Cabeza de Vaca nevertheless presented his life among Native American women in an altogether different light.

Cabeza de Vaca's physical description corresponds to the stereotypical idea of the superiority of European males. His contemporary Juan de Campo described him almost as an Adonis.[38] Without any contemporary portrait of Cabeza de Vaca of which the authenticity has been asserted beyond doubt, it is necessary to accept this description. According to Campo, Cabeza de Vaca was the epitome of masculinity, a handsome man, well-liked by women, even irresistible, and feared by men. And yet Cabeza de Vaca denied any sexual contact with Native American women. In this regard Cabeza de Vaca's omission of sex resembles Anglo-American female captives' statements denying sexual abuse (or any sort of sexual contact) with Native American men while in captivity: "Except in the most egregious examples of [captivity] narratives whose value as anti-Indian propaganda was being exploited by the press, most female captives either remained silent about any sexual abuse they may have experienced while in captivity or explicitly commented that their Indian captors respected their chastity."[39]

With regard to the fact that in his thirty-first chapter Cabeza de Vaca mentions that some women gave birth during their journey, Maura comments that it is doubtful that Cabeza de Vaca and his three companions remained in strict sexual abstinence for nine years, and he points out the possibility that some mestizos (children of mixed ancestry) might have been fathered by either Cabeza de Vaca or any other of his three companions.[40] However, Cabeza de Vaca never hinted at that possibility. In his attitude toward sexual relations, then, Cabeza de Vaca's account falls within a typically female writing strategy of chastity and denial of any sexual contact whatsoever, far from men's detailed descriptions of sexual contact between Europeans and Native American women.

But much more central to Cabeza de Vaca's *Account* than Native American women's sexuality is the question of the (female) roles he fulfilled among the Native Americans. Since for Europeans hunting was no longer a necessity for survival but an upper-class sport, they interpreted Native American men's engagement in hunting parties as sport, not as a means to provide food for their communities. Perceiving Native American men as permanently idle had the effect that, in contrast to them, Europeans perceived (and represented) Native American women as industrious, for cultivating the crops was among women's responsibilities.[41] Nevertheless, in general terms not much attention was given to the role of native women, and European newcomers to America often misunderstood gender roles within Native American societies. By filtering what they were seeing through their European-centered point of view, Europeans created the lasting stereotype of "the industrious, overburdened [Native American] woman, the slothful, pleasure-seeking [Native American] man."[42]

Cabeza de Vaca's depiction of Native Americans in general was ambivalent, alternating negative descriptions with positive remarks throughout his whole account, sometimes on the very same page.[43] Ironically, his own situation among the Native Americans was ambiguous from a gendered point of view. Because of the failure of the expedition, Cabeza de Vaca was reduced to slavery and forced to adopt female roles, circumstances that, in turn, shaped his own perceptions of Native Americans' gendered division of labor. Cabeza de Vaca for the most part shared the views of other European observers about Native American men's laziness and women's industriousness. About the Native American groups he met at the Isle of Misfortune Cabeza de Vaca stressed that "the women do the hard work."[44] When still in the hands of the first Native American group with whom Cabeza de Vaca lived, he explained that "because they worked me so hard and treated me so poorly, I decided to flee from them and go to those that live in the forests and mainland, a people called the Charruco. I could not bear the kind of life I had with them. Among many other afflictions, in order to eat I had to pull the roots from the ground under the water among the canes where they grew. My fingers were so worn by this that a light brush with a piece of straw would cause them to bleed."[45]

This was a female role, as he himself acknowledged: "Among these people men carry no loads, nor anything heavy. This is done by women and old people, who are the people they least esteem. The women are worked very hard with many tasks, and out of the twenty-four hours in a day, they rest only six. They spend the rest of the night stoking their ovens to dry those roots that they eat. At dawn they begin to dig and carry firewood and water to their dwellings and to take care of other important needs."[46]

Later, Cabeza de Vaca's living and working conditions only improved (and very much so) once he began fulfilling the female role of trader. For the Native American societies Cabeza de Vaca lived among, trading was a female activity (though Cabeza de Vaca never identified it as such), and Cabeza de Vaca was most willing to perform this task: "I liked this trade, because it gave me the freedom to go wherever I wanted. I was obligated to nothing and was not a slave."[47] Cabeza de Vaca, in not taking part in typically male activities such as warring or hunting, became like a woman; furthermore, just as Native American women did, Cabeza de Vaca could trespass both territorial and ethnic boundaries.[48]

To understand fully Cabeza de Vaca's later "feminization," it is necessary to take into account that, typical of a sixteenth-century conquistador, Cabeza de

Vaca held women in general in little regard. The Spanish women that appear in his *Account,* the wives of his companions that took part in the expedition, are far more concerned for their physical safety and social well-being than for the lives of their beloved ones. He bitterly reports (obviously relying on second-hand information, for he was at the time with the rest of the terrestrial expedition), the decision of the women aboard to consider their missing husbands dead and become the wives or mistresses of the remaining men: "They say that everyone there could clearly hear that woman tell the other women, whose husbands were going inland and exposing themselves to such great danger, that they should not count on their returning and ought to look for someone else to marry as she intended to do. She did so, and she and the other women married and cohabited with the men who remained on the ships."[49]

For all his negative portrayal of women Cabeza de Vaca was, however, happy to act as one when among Native Americans. The failure of the expedition unmanned him, forcing him to snub traditional gender divisions and adopt a female role rather than to participate in male activities such as engaging in fighting. Cabeza de Vaca could not be a conquistador, a male occupation that, moreover, denoted such cherished male virtues as bravery, courage, and physical strength. Instead he became a picker first and later on a trader, though as he was aware of these two occupations being reserved for women among Native Americans.

Cabeza de Vaca was certainly not unaware that the practice of men adopting female roles was widespread among certain Native American groups. Actually one of the most striking features of Native American life for the Spanish conquistadors in America was the existence of two-spirits, or berdaches, Native American males who cross-dressed and performed female sexual and social roles.[50] Though this figure exists in a number of civilizations, "in the context of the early American natives, the berdache was a transvested male, who had permanently taken on the dress, language, and mannerisms of the female gender in their particular society. In homosexual relationships, the berdache assumed the position of the passive role. The member of a particular culture 'became' a berdache in varying ways, some at a very young age and others, at a later stage in life, possibly following warriordom, when they were no longer capable of fighting effectively."[51]

When he first discovered the existence of these men, Cabeza de Vaca was mortified: "During the time I spent with these people I saw one wicked thing, and that was a man married to another man. These are womanish, impotent men who cover their bodies like women and do women's tasks. They shoot bows and carry heavy loads. Among these people we saw many of these womanish men, who are robust and taller than other men and who carry heavy loads."[52]

Native Americans did not see the role of berdaches as threatening to the status quo, contrary to European perceptions; berdaches helped confirm hierarchical relationships and were highly regarded. Though Europeans saw (and described) them as feminized men, for Native Americans they were two-spirit, that is, a third gender moving between the boundaries of man and spirits and also the boundaries of gender. This made berdaches go-betweens between both worlds. The very existence of the berdaches proves that in Native American societies gender was a socially constructed notion, regardless of biological sex.

Like Cabeza de Vaca, the berdaches transgressed gender boundaries, thus proving that the very concept of gender for Native American was looser and more flexible than in European society. Cabeza de Vaca, who did not participate in Native American warring activities because of his condition as foreigner (and therefore not trustworthy enough to take part in battle), could fulfill the female roles of picker or trader instead. The existence of berdaches in Native American society paved the way for Cabeza de Vaca to be able to fulfill female roles, given that transgendering was a fairly common (and socially acceptable) occurrence for Native Americans.[53]

One of the most noteworthy aspects of Cabeza de Vaca's adopting female roles is his satisfaction in having performed these roles, a most unusual circumstance for a man of his times. One would expect that a Spanish *señorito andaluz,* unused to any kind of physical labor and disrespectful of women, would feel ashamed at being reduced to a trader.[54] Since trading involved physical work and was a female role for Native Americans, it meant that this activity was not one in which Cabeza de Vaca would have willingly engaged at first. In sixteenth-century Spanish society both law and custom forbade people from the upper classes from performing any physical work, for engaging in physical labor was considered to be below their social status and therefore demeaning. Trading fell within the category of manual and base labor and accordingly was socially inappropriate for someone of Cabeza de Vaca's social standing.

Cabeza de Vaca enthusiastically embraced his new role of trader without ever expressing any remorse or shame. His self-confidence is remarkable, especially because he surely expected his account to be widely read—the whereabouts of Narváez's expedition had been a matter of much controversy that had generated a lot of talk until Cabeza de Vaca and his companions' return put an end to the "mystery." Cabeza de Vaca could have chosen to conceal his having performed an actual job, but he did not and instead included this information in his account. That he saw nothing to be ashamed of is most unusual for a sixteenth-century man. In fact, Cabeza de Vaca expressed his happiness at having become a trader.

A possible explanation for this seemingly contradictory situation is that Cabeza de Vaca managed to distance himself from idle Native American men and instead sided with industrious Native American women. They might be women, but their industriousness somehow redeemed them in Cabeza de Vaca's mind. The fact that in Spain the occupation of trader, though not suitable for a man of his social status, was not associated with women might have also contributed to Cabeza de Vaca's eagerness to portray himself as a trader. Had trading been a female role in Spain as well, Cabeza de Vaca might have been more reluctant to describe himself as a trader. Furthermore, given that he had suffered captivity and other torments at the Native Americans' hands, Cabeza de Vaca would be entitled to rewards from the emperor; while enhancing his own image he perpetuated and propagated the negative portrayal of Native American men as cruel and fond of torture. In this context, that Cabeza de Vaca was forced to work was another of the many torments that the Native Americans inflicted on him, thus making him a man deserving rewards for his services in America.

Cabeza de Vaca's ambiguity about the gendered roles he played during his stay in America continues throughout his narrative. When Cabeza de Vaca eventually fled from the Native Americans for whom he traded, this did not mean that he had left feminine roles behind him. In fact, he next adopted the role of healer, which I argue was a female one. In his flight Cabeza de Vaca eventually reunited with three other surviving members of the expedition. Forced by their circumstances, the four began to perform healings: "On that island I have spoken of, they wanted to make us physicians, without testing us or asking for any degrees, because they cure illnesses by blowing on the sick person and cast out the illness with their breath and their hands. So they told us to be useful and do the same. We laughed at the idea, saying they were mocking us and that we did not know how to heal. They in turn deprived us of our food until we did as they ordered. In brief, we were in such need that we had to do it, putting aside our fear that anyone would be punished for it."[55]

Historian Mariah Wade, on the other hand, identifies the role of healer as an exclusively male one and thus describes Cabeza de Vaca as a hybrid who performed both male and female gender roles; however, Wade fails to acknowledge that Cabeza de Vaca was a captive forced to heal in order to survive. It is useful to consider Cabeza de Vaca's text within the larger context of captivity narratives written by Europeans in North America since Cabeza de Vaca's situation among the Native Americans is better understood when taking into account his role as a captive. *The Account* shares many of the conventions, strategies, and characteristics of the captivity narrative genre.[56] In their study of captivity narratives literary scholars Kathryn Zabelle Derounian-Stodola and Arthur James Levernier find that captive European women made use of their knowledge and skills in order to survive and protect themselves and their children.[57] Whereas male European captives were usually killed during or immediately after an Indian attack, women and children were kept alive to be ransomed and had to negotiate their position within Native American society in the meantime. The knowledge European women often made use of was their knowledge of healing, as illustrated by the autobiographical captivity narrative *The Story of My Capture and Escape* (1904) by Helen Tarble. Similarly Cabeza de Vaca, unmanned and reduced to a situation comparable to that of female European captives, had to make use of healing techniques in order to negotiate his and his companions' survival. Cabeza de Vaca's healing abilities cannot be understood as a male activity related to shamanism but, rather, as a (female) strategy to negotiate his survival, especially since his skills were reduced to a few prayers in Latin and making the sign of the cross on the Native Americans.[58] Moreover, Cabeza de Vaca stressed their being forced to perform healings, denying any willing agency on their part.

Though he did not fully regain his status as a free man until he and his companions were found by Spanish troops, Cabeza de Vaca was most reluctant in his account to present his situation as that of a captive slave and instead eagerly strove to portray himself as a trader. Cabeza de Vaca did not mind that to achieve a status different from that of a slave he had to adopt a female role (be it as a picker, healer, or trader). Although it is paradoxical that a man who held women in so little regard was so happy to be treated like one, it is more paradoxical that when he described his experience in the Americas and sought to disguise his situation as a slave, he did so by fulfilling the female roles of picker and trader and using healing skills generally employed by female captives. While most European travelers identified America with the female in their writings, the Native Americans forced Cabeza de Vaca to adopt female roles in America. In Cabeza de Vaca's case he identified himself with the female, rather than identifying the New World with the feminine.

Conclusions

Cabeza de Vaca's case is far from being unique when it comes to his captive status.[60] In Spanish colonial America numerous Native Americans and Spanish women and children participated in the captive-exchange system up to the point that there existed a "borderlands politic economy."[60] These Spanish captives had to learn to negotiate a role for themselves, moving between the opposing forces of exploitation and negotiation.[61] What makes Cabeza de Vaca's case unique is that he traded with himself. Rather than letting others negotiate with him, Cabeza de Vaca negotiated his own role, not in being sold and bought but in using his own terms to establish his position within Native American groups. Cabeza de Vaca resorted to cross-cultural negotiation and performing female roles in order to avoid the fate that awaited most men.[62]

To abandon his captive status and be free to a certain extent, Cabeza de Vaca played female roles, but in his writings he felt compelled to conceal the gender division represented by trading in Native American society. Furthermore, in his *Account* Cabeza de Vaca emphasized over and over again the relative freedom that his being a trader and no longer a slave allowed him. Cabeza de Vaca sought to make readers see him in a different light from that of a slave or a captive kept constantly under the watch of the Native Americans. His unwillingness to present himself as a slave is a fairly common occurrence. Literary critic Leslie A. Fiedler in *The Return of the Vanishing American* (1968) describes the tendency of male captives to refuse to speak of their captivity in terms of bondage. According to Fiedler, "the male imagination, for better or worse, tends to transform the tale of captivity into one of adoption, to substitute the male dream of joining the Indians for the female fantasy of being dragged off by them," and this is just what Cabeza de Vaca was doing in presenting himself as a trader or healer—in short, as anything but a captive.[63]

Reinterpreting his trading position to conceal his bonded situation, early in his narrative Cabeza de Vaca turns away from the discourse of a captive slave to present his situation among the Native Americans in another way. According to historian June Namias, European men could describe their experiences among Native Americans as anything from torture and death to adoption and acceptance;[64] Cabeza de Vaca chose to describe his relationship with the Indians as one of relative freedom first and then of superiority, as a person greatly respected and admired by the Native Americans because of his curing abilities.[65] Although Cabeza de Vaca had no qualms about becoming a trader during his stay with Native Americans, once back in Spanish society he concealed its humiliating aspect while highlighting its advantages. Cabeza de Vaca thus abandoned the tale of captivity to present himself as a member of Native American society.

Perhaps most telling is the fact that, in light of the interrelatedness of the concepts of gender identity and sexuality, these two are disassociated in Cabeza de Vaca's retelling of his experiences in the Americas. While embracing this genderless identity as trader—not a conquistador but not a woman either—he either hid the matter of sexuality altogether or he outright denied it, claiming sexual abstinence for almost a decade-long period.

Literary critic Richard Poirie in *A World Elsewhere* asserts that "the classic American writers try through style temporarily to free the hero (and the reader) from systems, to free them from the pressures of time, biology, economics, and from the social forces with are ultimately the undoing of American heroes and quite often of their creators."[66] Cabeza de Vaca created a new America wherever he set his eyes upon the land, for his were the first European eyes to behold that area. Cabeza de Vaca became so free from conventional western mores, from traditional European gender roles, that he was able to become a woman or, at the very least, perform the roles of one. Cabeza de Vaca's text is a classical American text of survival, of exercising one's mastery upon the American land and becoming one with one's surroundings, but, in contrast to other classical American writers, he transgressed the gender barrier as well. In this regard, not only does Cabeza de Vaca's text become a classic text in American letters, but a pioneering one as well for its representation of gender, identity, and Native American women.

Notes

1. Álvar Núñez Cabeza de Vaca, *The Account: Álvar Núñez Cabeza de Vaca's Relación*, ed. Martin A. Favata and José B. Fernández (Houston: Arte Público Press, 1993), 64–65.

2. One of Cabeza de Vaca's duties in his role of treasurer of the Narváez expedition was to write an official report (a *relación*) to inform Emperor Charles V of the goals, achievements, and circumstances of the journey and the expedition. However, the failure of the expedition prevented his account from being similar to other official reports. First published in Zamora in 1542, its original title was *La Relación que dio Alvar Núñez Cabeça de Vaca de lo acaescido en las Indias en la armada donde iva por governador Pámphilo de Narváez desde el año de veinta y siete hasta el año de treinta y seis que bolvió a Sevilla con tres de su compagnía* (The Account That Alvar Núñez Cabeza de Vaca Gave of What Happened in the Indies to the Army of Which Pánfilo de Narváez was Governor Since the Year Twenty-seven to the Year Thirty-six When He Went Back to Seville with Three of His Company). By the time this account was published for the second time in Valladolid in 1555, it received the title of *Naufragios y Comentarios* (Shipwrecks and Commentaries)—the *comentarios* being a report of Cabeza de Vaca's subsequent experiences as governor of the Río de la Plata province (present-day Argentina), written by a ghost writer, Pedro Hernández. In English Cabeza de Vaca's text is usually referred to as *The Account*.

3. This same situation marks their intention to convert the Native Americans to Christianity.

4. Beatriz Pastor, "Silencio y escritura: La historia de la Conquista," in *Crítica y descolonización: El sujeto colonial en la cultura latinoamericana,* ed. Beatriz González Stephan and Lúcia Helena Costigan (Caracas: Fuentes para la Historia Colonial de Venezuela, 1992), 145.

5. Despite the humiliating defeat, Narváez retained the approval of the monarch, continuing to be one of his favorites until the very end of his life. Frank Goodwyn, "Pánfilo de Narváez: A Character Study of the First Spanish Leader to Land an Expedition to Texas," *Hispanic American Historical Review* 29, no. 1 (1949): 155.

6. Rolena Adorno and Patrick Charles Pautz, *Álvar Núñez Cabeza de Vaca: His Account, His Life, and the Expedition of Pánfilo de Narváez,* vol. 2 (Lincoln: University of Nebraska Press, 1999), 11.

7. Goodwyn, "Pánfilo de Narváez," 153. Cabeza de Vaca also repeatedly claimed that he had been appointed *alguacil mayor,* or high constable, though documentary evidence proves that this title was granted to Narváez, not to him. Adorno and Pautz, *Alvar Núñez Cabeza de Vaca,* 21.

8. There is some controversy with regard to the accuracy of this date, and some authors place his birth as late as 1506. However, 1490, the date defended by Adorno and Pautz most recently, seems to be more accurate than 1506. We have to take into account that, prior to

going to America, Cabeza de Vaca had already participated in several campaigns in Italy. Had he been born in 1506, it would be highly unlikely that a man in his early twenties at the time of his embarking on the Narváez expedition would have already reached the post of treasurer, one of great responsibility and social prestige.

9. References to Cabeza de Vaca's wife are notably absent in most studies dealing with him, despite the important role she played in Cabeza de Vaca's life. Her money was used for her husband's defense once he returned, in chains, to Spain, after the failure of his Río de la Plata adventure. It is paradoxical that sixteenth-century conquistadors did not seem to appreciate their wives (or women, in general) much, but in having constantly to assert their honor (a concept closely linked to their masculinity), they had no shame in using their wives' money. Just as Cabeza de Vaca used his wife's money to pay for his legal defense, the Narváez expedition was financed with money produced by his Cuban plantations, whose management was supervised by his wife during his prolonged absences; Cortés also financed his expedition with his wife's jewels. Similarly, Hernando de Soto, the governor of Cuba and the man who was appointed the next governor of Florida, the post Cabeza de Vaca would covet (and unsuccessfully petition for), left his wife as the surrogate governor of Cuba when he embarked on the conquest of Florida in 1538.

10. The accuracy of this date is questioned by some scholars. Donald E. Sheppard, "De Vaca's Florida Landing" (2005, accessed: December 22, 2005); available from: www.florida history.com/cab-land.html; Internet. With regard to these discrepancies, we should take into account that Cabeza de Vaca did not have any kind of writing material to put down his thoughts or his experiences during his time in America, and, therefore, he was relying just on his own memories of events that had taken place ten years earlier.

11. The pilots reckoned that Pánuco was ten or fifteen miles away and Río de las Palmas was more or less at the same distance, when in fact they were more than six hundred and nine hundred miles away, respectively. Cyclone Covey, *Cabeza de Vaca's Adventures in the Unknown Interior of America* [book online] (The Crowell-Collier Publishing Co., 1961, accessed June 20, 2006); available from: http://www.ibiblio.org/eldritch/Cabeza de Vaca/ rel.htm; Internet. Alex D. Krieger, *We Came Naked and Barefoot: The Journey of Cabeza de Vaca across North America* (Austin: University of Texas Press, 2002), 25.

12. The ships would look for the expedition for a year, in vain, before returning to give news about the loss of the expedition. Narváez's wife petitioned over and over again to have new exploration parties sent to the area to search for her husband.

13. Cabeza de Vaca, *The Account,* 56.

14. Ibid., 57. Cabeza de Vaca referred to himself and the other Spaniards as "the Christians."

15. Indicative of this desire to emulate his grandfather is that, during his governorship in Río de la Plata, Cabeza de Vaca named both a port at Santa Catalina Island and a whole province "Vera." However, he never used his grandfather's last name himself, Cabeza de Vaca's own last name being that of an ancestor on his maternal side made possible because of the loose Spanish rules for child naming in the sixteenth century. Krieger, *We Came Naked and Barefoot,* 2.

16. Juan Francisco Maura, ed., *Naufragios,* 2d ed. (Madrid: Cátedra, 1996), 175.

17. Wayne Franklin, *Discoverers, Explorers, and Early Settlers: The Diligent Writers of Early America* (Chicago: University of Chicago Press, 1979), xi.

18. M. Carmen Gomez-Galisteo, "America as First Seen and Reported" (M.A. thesis, Universidad de Alcalá, 2006), 21.

19. "I have in my soul the certainty that the Earthly Paradise lays where I said it was, and I rest my claim on the reasons and authorities stated above" (translation mine). Quoted in Antonio Gutiérrez Escudero, *América: Descubrimiento de un mundo nuevo* (Madrid: Ediciones Istmo, 1990), 26.

20. "Exploring Borderlands," unit 2, *American Passages: A Literary Survey* (accessed January 10, 2006); available from: http://www.learner.org/amerpass/unit02/pdf/unit02ig .pdf; Internet. For literary theorist Louis Montrose, English representations of America as a maiden are closely related to the circumstance that England was then ruled by Elizabeth I, the Virgin Queen. Louis Montrose, "The Work of Gender in the Discourse of Discovery," *Representations,* no. 33 (1991): 3. Similarly, another female monarch, Queen Isabella of Castile, supported the Spanish discovery of America out of the revenues of her own territories, despite the opposition of her husband King Ferdinand of Aragon to Columbus's scheme.

21. Jennifer L. Morgan, "'Some Could Suckle over Their Shoulder': Male Travelers, Female Bodies, and the Gendering of Racial Ideology, 1500–1770," *William and Mary Quarterly* 54, no. 1 (1997): 170.

22. This was especially relevant because "many Elizabethan writers voice a nagging concern that—in military, commercial, and/or artistic terms—the English are a backward and peripheral nation" (Montrose, "The Work of Gender in the Discourse of Discovery," 17). To help overcome these feelings the English colonial project would decisively contribute to "shape an English Protestant identity in opposition to the Catholic powers (i.e., Spain and Portugal) involved in the colonial venture" (Thomas Scanlan, *Colonial Writing and the New World, 1583–1671: Allegories of Desire* [Cambridge: Cambridge University Press, 1999], 36).

23. Anne McClintock, *Imperial Leather: Race, Gender and Sexuality in the Colonial Contest* (New York, London: Routledge, 1995), 22.

24. Morgan, "'Some Could Suckle over Their Shoulder,'" 168. McClintock, *Imperial Leather,* 22.

25. William Brandon, *New Worlds for Old: Reports from the New World and Their Effect on the Development of Social Thought in Europe, 1500–1800* (Athens: Ohio University Press, 1986), 37.

26. Cuneo described how "while I was in the boat, I captured a very beautiful Carib woman, whom the said Lord Admiral gave to me. . I was filled with desire to take my pleasure with her and attempted to satisfy my desire. She was unwilling, and so treated me with her nails that I wished I had never begun. But . . . I then took a piece of rope and whipped her soundly, and she let forth such incredible screams that you would not have believed your ears. Eventually, we came to such terms, I assure you, that you would have thought she had been brought up in a school for whores." Quoted in Michael Hardin, "Altering Masculinities: The Spanish Conquest and the Evolution of the Latin American Machismo," *International Journal of Sexuality and Gender Studies* 7, no. 1 (2002): 16. Brandon, *New Worlds for Old,* 37.

27. This trend of having Native Americans represent European values alien to themselves did not fade with the end of the discovery or the colonial period. It is well known that at the Boston tea party Americans dressed as Native Americans. See Gail H. Landsman, "The

'Other' as Political Symbol: Images of Indian in the Woman Suffrage Movement," *Ethnohistory* 39, no. 3 (1992): 247–84, for the use suffragists made of Native American women to pursue their own political goals.

28. Morgan, "'Some Could Suckle over Their Shoulder,'" 169.

29. Quoted in "'Some Could Suckle over Their Shoulder,'" 171.

30. Quoted in Stephen Greenblatt, *Marvelous Possessions: The Wonder of the New World* (Chicago: University of Chicago Press, 1991), 15–16.

31. It should be borne in mind that Pocahontas, in the best-known case of British-Native American intermarriage (and a very rare instance), was also a princess. This practice of labeling Native American women as princesses can be traced back to the Muslim princess legend. M. Carmen Gomez-Galisteo, "Representing Native American Women in Early Colonial American Writings: Álvar Núñez Cabeza de Vaca, Juan Ortiz and John Smith" *SEDERI: Yearbook of the Spanish and Portuguese Society for English Renaissance Studies* 19 (2009): 36–37.

32. See James F. Brooks, *Captive and Cousins: Slavery, Kinship, and Community in the Southwest Borderlands* (Chapel Hill: University of North Carolina Press, 2002), 25, for Spanish policies with regard to intermarriage between Spaniards and Native Americans in colonial Spain.

33. Although Native American women followed Cabeza de Vaca and his companions in their route throughout the United States there is, nevertheless, not one single sexual reference in the whole text or any hint of the Spaniards having engaged in sexual relationships with Native American women. Maura, *Naufragios,* 175.

34. Cabeza de Vaca, *The Account,* 85.

35. Ibid., 63. What is more, throughout his account Cabeza de Vaca repeatedly stresses his own nakedness too.

36. Ibid., 105.

37. Gary L. Ebersole, *Captured by Texts: Puritan to Postmodern Images of Indian Captivity,* (Charlottesville: University Press of Virginia, 1995), 201.

38. "Animoso, noble, arrogante, los cabellos rubios y los ojos azules y vivos, barba larga y crespa, era Alvar un caballero y un capitán a todo lucir; y las mozas del Duero enamorábanse de él y los hombres temían su acero." Quoted in Trinidad Barrera, ed., *Naufragios* (Madrid: Alianza Editorial, 2005), 11. "Spirited, noble, arrogant, with blond hair and bright, blue eyes, a long, curly beard, Alvar was a gentleman and a good-looking captain; and the women from the Duero River area fell in love with him and men feared his steel" (translation mine).

39. Kathryn Zabelle Derounian-Stodola and Arthur James Levernier, *The Indian Captivity Narrative, 1550–1900* (New York: Twayne, 1993), 3.

40. Maura, *Naufragios,* 195.

41. However, agriculture, in the minds of Native Americans (both men and women), was regarded as an "unmanly" activity.

42. Nancy Oestreich Lurie, "Indian Cultural Adjustment to European Civilization," in *Seventeenth-Century America: Essays in Colonial History,* ed. James Morton Smith (Chapel Hill: University of North Carolina Press, 1959), 57.

43. One instance of this ambivalent description can be illustrated by the following quotation, in which women are described as peacemakers as well as the cause for the beginning

of the fighting: The women of the Quevenes came and mediated between them and caused them to be friends, although the women sometimes are the reason battles begin" (Cabeza de Vaca, *The Account*, 86).

44. Ibid., 59.

45. Ibid., 64.

46. Ibid., 71.

47. Ibid., 65.

48. Mariah Wade, "Go-between: The Roles of Native American Women and Alvar Núñez Cabeza de Vaca in Southern Texas in the Sixteenth Century," *Journal of American Folklore* 112, no. 445 (1999): 333.

49. Cabeza de Vaca, *The Account*, 121.

50. Anthropologists have found evidence of the existence of berdaches in approximately one hundred twenty North American tribes. Wendy Susan Parker, "The Berdache Spirit" (accessed: July 23, 2008); available from: http://www.nu-woman.com/berdache.htm; Internet. The reverse practice of women passing as men, though far less common, was also possible. The term *berdache* comes from the Persian *berdaj,* a boy who was a passive homosexual partner. The Europeans first learned of the existence of the *berdaj* during the Crusades.

51. Megan Langford, "The Berdache of Early American Conquest" (9 May 1998; accessed: 22 July 2008); available from: http://academic.reed.edu/English/Courses/English 341gs/FinalPaper/MeganL/berdache_web.html; Internet.

52. Cabeza de Vaca, *The Account*, 90.

53. See Richard C. Trexler, *Sex and Conquest* (Ithaca: Cornell University Press, 1995), for more about berdaches and Spanish conquistadors' perceptions of them.

54. *Señorito* is a derogatory Spanish term that, by analogy to *señorita* (the equivalent of "Miss"), was coined to be applied to those young men of good families who in Andalusian society, rather than having a job or doing something productive, spent their days leisurely.

55. Cabeza de Vaca, *The Account*, 62. Cabeza de Vaca, instead of using the native practice of blowing on the sick person, replaced it with performing the Christian sign of the cross and saying prayers in Latin. The reason why Cabeza de Vaca chose to underrate his curing abilities and never assume for himself the label of saint or god was that at that time the Spanish Inquisition was at its most powerful and would have condemned Cabeza de Vaca for blasphemy or another similar charge had he called himself a miracle worker.

56. Wade, "Go-between," 339. An interpretation of Cabeza de Vaca's account as a captivity narrative, exploring the similarities between the genre of captivity narratives and *The Account,* is provided by M. Carmen Gomez-Galisteo, "The Conquistador Who Wrote a Captivity Narrative: Cabeza de Vaca's *Naufragios* as a Captivity Narrative," *Americana: E-Journal of American Studies in Hungary* 4, no. 2 (2008) (accessed: February 9, 2009); available from: http://americanaejournal.hu/vol4no2/gomez-galisteo; Internet.

57. Derounian-Stodola and Levernier, *The Indian Captivity Narrative,* 143.

58. Cabeza de Vaca, *The Account,* 62.

59. See M. Carmen Gomez-Galisteo, "Leaving the New World, Entering History: Álvar Núñez Cabeza de Vaca, John Smith and the Problems of Describing the New World," *RAEI: Revista Alicantina de Estudios Ingleses* 22 (2009): 115–26.

60. James F. Brooks, "'This Evil Extends Especially . To the Feminine Sex': Negotiating Captivity in the New Mexico Borderlands," *Feminist Studies* 22, no. 2 (1996): 280.

61. Ibid., 280–81, 299.

62. European males were usually sacrificed soon after their capture. In contrast, European women who were not ransomed successfully acculturated and married into Native American families, and their children became Native Americans. As they negotiated a new identity and new social and cultural roles for themselves, captives also provoked lasting changes within their host society (Ibid., 301–2). Illustrative of the fate that usually awaited male captives is the case of another of the members of the Narváez expedition, Juan Ortiz. Ortiz, age eighteen, was captured along with three companions by Chief Hirrihugua of the Calusa Indians in present-day Florida. His companions were sacrificed immediately after capture, though Ortiz was spared for a ritual death, from which he was pardoned only after the chief's daughter's pled in his favor. He was found by the Hernando de Soto expedition, which he joined as an interpreter, but died in American territory during the course of the expedition.

63. Quoted in Derounian-Stodola and Levernier, *The Indian Captivity Narrative,* 39.

64. June Namias, *White Captives: Gender and Ethnicity on the American Frontier* (Chapel Hill: University of North Carolina Press, 1993), 51.

65. Cabeza de Vaca tells how "all these people came to us to be touched and blessed. . . . Everyone, sick or healthy, wanted to be blessed. . . . We enjoyed a great deal of authority and dignity among them" (*The Account,* 104).

66. Quoted in Nina Baym, "Melodramas of Beset Manhood: How Theories of American Fiction Exclude Women Authors," *American Quarterly* 33, no. 2 (1981): 137.

"Nought but women"

Constructions of Masculinities and Modes of Emasculation in the New World

⟶ SANDRA SLATER

Over the course of the early modern period of European history, adventurers and profiteers saw the lure of the New World. Men sought to achieve wealth or glory; most desired both. European men arrived in North America with a distinctly European sense of identity that directly contradicted the masculine identities and gender relations enacted by natives. Native and European men challenged one another's understandings of manhood, and the resulting conflicts demonstrated the powerful effect each had on the other. The goal of presenting oneself as the dominant man, or in most cases the dominant masculinity, characterized much of these early encounters. This essay specifically looks at instances in which both native and European men attempted to undermine the masculinities of one another and how these moments of contact directly impacted the course of events in the New World. Furthermore, understanding gendered dynamics of native masculinities helps to illuminate their direct contradictions of European ideals and shows how these collisions of identities may have impacted the impetus for Europeans to Christianize through conquest. Warfare provides the most obvious example of this contestation of power, but other more subtle incidents reveal the intricacies of these exchanges. Native and European men both sought to bolster their own masculinity through the emasculation of their enemies. Sometimes using women's role in society, rape, verbal or physical assaults, or even attitudes toward homosexuality and the two-spirited natives, European men displayed their determination to place themselves as the dominant masculinity, accruing the most power and authority. This essay examines the moments in which these contests reveal themselves most distinctly and the contextualized attitudes that created the impetus for conflict. It asserts that while Europeans and natives possessed distinct masculinities prior to contact, it is only when studying their interactions that ideas about masculine identities can clearly be understood. These interactions shed light on conceptions of self and the ubiquitous "other."

Definitions of "masculinity" vary among historians, anthropologists, and sociologists. For the purpose of this research, masculine identities emerge from a variety of socioeconomic influences. Personal history, national influence, environment, expectation, religion, and economics all contribute to one's personal construction of self. Because these are multiple identities, they require language that recognizes their plurality (i.e., masculinities). Individuals usually perform their constructed masculine identities in relation to dominant tropes of appropriate manhood. It is through these performances and sometimes articulations of what men deem appropriate or dominant masculinities that cultural constructions of masculine identities can be gleaned. More important, conflicts between men over what constituted the best masculine performance illuminate both individual and cultural constructions and the influence both can have on potential conflict.[1]

Old World Masculinities

The world in which early modern European men lived demanded highly dichotomized performances of gender. Women as guardians of the home should project the utmost chastity, humility, and piety. Their obedience to their husbands and the male authorities within the politic and the church required women to maintain a very narrow identity of submission. For men, power and authority characterized their existence, particularly for noblemen and military leaders. They controlled their homes, wives, and families, and inhabited an intensely religious world that fortified their position of power both in public and private. Men of high birth and those who sought to attain prominence demonstrated confidence, honor, physical strength, bravery, and pious authority. Christianity, both Protestant and Catholic, considered the reverence for male authority paramount to the order of the church and society. Men fought literally and figuratively for the empowerment of their country and church. Men who traveled to North America in the sixteenth and early seventeenth centuries began their conquests on the fields of Europe and the Middle East, eagerly seeking to exert the dominance of their king and church. The religious wars of Europe and the Crusades of the Middle Ages provided a strong precedent for the mentality that led men to America to convert the natives and claim those fertile lands in the name of the country and king.

For many Europeans the possession and display of courage defined successful masculinity. According to the *Dictionnaire de L'Académie Française* (1694) the term *courage* in French connoted meanings similar to present-day "courage" in English. However, in the definition of *courage* special emphasis was given to the state of the soul and its willingness to explore something unknown, which would explain its significance to explorers.[2] Discrepancies existed as to its uses and its ability to be used as a negative epithet in conjunction with *effemine* or "effeminate" in English. Samuel de Champlain considered its possession essential to the character of a good sailor or explorer who, in the face of danger, "must display manly courage, make light of death though it confronts you, and in a steady voice and with cheery resolution urge all to take courage and do what can be done to escape the danger, and thus dispel fear from the most cowardly bosoms."[3] The experiences of navigation and the perils of the adventure of exploration entailed a degree of this "manly courage" for which many explorers gained great fame. Marc Lescarbot praised the virtue of courage and the rewards gained from its possession in the following passage: "And when all is well considered, it may truly be called pulling out thorns to take in hand such enterprises, full of toils and of continual danger, care, vexation and discomfort. But virtue and the courage which overcomes all such obstacles make these thorns to be but gilly-flowers and roses to those who set themselves to these heroic deeds in order to win glory in the memory of men, closing their eyes to the pleasures of those weaklings who are good for nothing but to stay at home."[4]

Courage, as linked to danger, heroism and glory, became amplified in the New World where danger was inescapable. Those who failed to exhibit courage received insults that degraded them as being feminine or unmanly. It is clear from the written accounts that the enactment of courage was expected from all New World men, not just Frenchmen. As reported by Lescarbot, Savignon, a native youth who learned French and lived in France for a time, mocked men who refused to engage in physical fights as "nought but women [who] had no courage."[5] For the natives, chiefs and particularly warriors embodied shining examples of manhood. Glimpses of admiration for courageous and manly native warriors and chiefs appear in the texts. Whenever natives perceived French courage, the explorers grew in esteem and vice versa. Displays of courage garnered respect.

England, at the dawn of its exploration of the North American continent, experienced unique circumstances that deeply affected explorers' expectations and experiences in the New World. The English literature from this period demonstrates a heightened awareness of gender identity and a people grappling with the paradox of a female queen, Elizabeth I. Historians and theorists studying the construction of gendered identities in early modern England insist that during the reign of Elizabeth I men felt both threatened and pressured to create a masculine identity that reflected their superior strength and fortitude. For Mark Breitenberg this "male, heterosexual jealousy—the anxiety and violence engendered in men by a patriarchical economy that constructs masculine identity as dependent on the coercive and symbolic regulation of women's sexuality"—led to the formation of male identities that attempted urgently and vehemently to enforce traditional gender norms.[6] This "anxious masculinity" can be seen in early modern England in the preoccupation with regulating women's sexuality and power. This attitude is paradoxical, given the role of Elizabeth I as queen and head of state. Men grappled with this reality differently.

According to historians, the ascension of Elizabeth I to the English throne revived debates about the nature of women, their disposition, and potential to govern and about how female authority affected men and the dominant gender paradigm that had long reinforced white male supremacy in England.[7]Although occupying a traditionally masculine role as head of state, Elizabeth I was able to reinvent herself as a virtuous queen married to the English nation. This seeming androgyny relied on discourses of women's role and appropriate femininity to survive. Sir Walter Raleigh felt it necessary to declare to the natives of Guiana that he served a queen "who was the great cacique of the north, and a virgin."[8] At all times Elizabeth embodied the male political figure and the female dutiful wife, chaste and pure, wife to nation and mother to citizens.[9] Nanette Saloman highlights this dichotomy in her discussion of Elizabeth I's royal portraits. Rejecting the convention of a court-appointed artist, Elizabeth I employed a variety of painters to capture her image. In Saloman's discussion this "absence [of a single male painter] may be better understood in terms of Elizabeth's own determined avoidance of a powerful 'master' to shape her image artistically, just as she had assiduously avoided a master as a mate."[10] Interestingly, Elizabeth I insisted that her portraits reflect her innocence, modesty, and youth, never allowing a portrait to reflect her aging person. Latter portraits included contemporary wardrobe and jewels but relied upon earlier likenesses for her physically ageless form. This constructed identity was essential to her projection of a virgin queen, powerful and innocent.

As new worlds entered the psychological scope of possibilities, the Old World struggled to adapt. Within English culture, negotiations of gender norms and behaviors reflected this tumultuous period of social and global alteration. Looking at pamphlets devoted to the perceived threats to traditional expectations of gender, Michael S. Kimmel discusses the ways in which "masculinity was seen to be in crisis" in the seventeenth and early eighteenth centuries. As women recognized the possibilities of their sex via Elizabeth I, men retaliated by assaulting these gains. Rather than seeking changes in their own status, men of this era sought to contain the aspirations of women. Challenges to women's authority derived from politicians and social commentators who denounced these advances as detrimental to society as a whole. Using natural law as a reference point, men marginalized women who behaved outside the prescribed roles ordained by biology and theology.[11] Threatened by "new claims against the inherited gender hierarchy, men's conceptual universe is shaken, and many will scramble, both rhetorically and institutionally, to reassert the traditional gender hierarchy and reestablish patriarchal authority."[12] Within this context Englishmen felt a responsibility to assert their masculine authority and dominance not only over women but also over seemingly weaker persons and places.

Gender in the Natural World

Nature also heavily informed the English discussion of women's role in the world. Literary and philosophical minds of the Renaissance and the early modern period likened women to various natural occurrences or entities such as the moon and water. Men identified women, who were supposedly both fluid and fickle, with the changing of the moon and the cool flow of water.[13] The idea of Mother Nature as a secretive but powerful force also shrouded the identity of women in mystery. Unclaimed nature associated with women was wild, sensual, mysterious, and diametrically opposed to civilization, reason, Christianity, and male domination. It is not surprising that many men used gendered metaphors to discuss nature and the role of explorers in taming the feminine lands that attracted them across the sea.

For explorers the idea of a female head of state and uncharted territories translated into their interpretations of themselves as conquerors. The land became feminized and their incursions into its secretive depths adopted a sexual tone evident in their writings. Metaphors of "deflowering" or taking the "virgin lands" abound.[14] These issues of gender subjugation began from the colonies' inception and informed not only the colonists' conception of their role and responsibility, but also the ways in which men encountered the land, understood themselves, and formed an identity that incorporated both English ideals and the wildness of North America.

Sir Walter Raleigh's writings offer fascinating insight into the mentality of male explorers and what it meant to them to find new unspoiled lands and make them their own. He wrote of Guiana that she was a "country that hath yet her maidenhead, never sacked, turned, nor wrought, the face of the earth hath not been torn, not the virtue and salt of the soil spent by manurance."[15] Guiana represented the ideal woman embodied in land. She was chaste, unsoiled, and pure, waiting patiently for the arrival of the English. Her virtue lay in having "never been entered by any army of strength, and never conquered by and Christian prince," a truly pure maid.[16] This idealized image stands in contrast to the depiction of European nations as soiled and taxed, used for centuries for war and domination. Guiana offered a paradise of virginity. Its appeal lay in its location accessible by "one entrance by the sea" so that "whosoever shall first possess it, he shall be found inaccessible for any enemy."[17] This singular entrance served as path to total possession, but also a metaphoric opportunity to deflower Guiana with penetration.

Given the heavily gendered discourse surrounding the land of the New World, it is not a stretch to say that as the Europeans penetrated North America's maidenhead, they also conquered women.[18] To own the land implied the ownership of its inhabitants. Assigning native women to a subservient gender alone would not have produced such violence. Race, religion, and biological sex worked collectively to justify their objectification and violation. Rape, particularly in the New World, was an assertion of power and dominance. The narratives of history are replete with stories of conquests that describe women as possessions. The Spanish Dominican friars often expressed concern about the way in which conquistadores sexually assaulted native women without regard to them as human beings. In their theory of hypermasculinity, Donald L. Mosher and Silvan S. Tomkins consider "callous sexual attitudes" one of the critical actions of men exerting their power over women.[19] This is particularly true in situations where native women were sexually available and willing to engage in intercourse with the Europeans, but instead were violently taken.

Michele de Cuneo, an Italian voyager with Columbus to the Caribbean, recorded a detailed description of his rape of a native woman. Viewing her as lusty and the actions as a form of conquest, recognition of sexual assault is exchanged for an account of seduction. He wrote:

> While I was in the boat, I capture a very beautiful Carib woman, who the Lord Admiral [Columbus] gave to me. When I had taken her to my cabin she was naked—as was their custom. I was filled with my desire to take my pleasure with her and attempted to satisfy my desire. She was unwilling, and so treated me with her nails that I wished I had never begun. But—to cut a long story short—I then took a piece of rope and whipped her soundly, and she let forth such incredible screams that you would not have believed your ears. Eventually we came to such terms, I assure you, that you would have thought she had been brought up in a school for whores.[20]

Several elements here illustrate the male psyche of explorers. That Columbus "gave" this woman to Cueno assumes that Columbus as admiral owned her. As an inhabitant of the land he conquered, he could dispose of her how he saw fit. This commodification of sexuality belies the very humanity of the people being conquered and also the role women occupied in advancing the masculine endeavor of conquest. Cuneo romanticized this sexual violence and interpreted it as an amorous challenge. He did not view this rape as anything beyond a game with his possession. According to Stephanie Wood, "Cuneo twists the rape into a scene of seduction, titillating his European male audience back home, knowing full well that the 'Carib' woman's version of events would never come to the fore."[21]

Emasculation as Power

Assaults on native women resulted in an emasculation of their husbands, fathers, and brothers who found it difficult to protect them. An experience in Hispaniola powerfully demonstrates the tension between men who used the women as pawns and acts of aggression. Guillermo Coma commented: "Bad feeling arose and broke out into warfare because of the licentious conduct of our men towards the Indian women, for each Spaniard had five women to minister to his pleasure the husbands and relatives of the women, unable to take this, banded together to avenge this insult and eliminate this outrage."[22] When Columbus returned to the fort he found it burned and all the remaining Spanish soldiers dead.

Women themselves often acted in ways to thwart the sexual advances of the Spanish. The *Florentine Codex* reveals that many women of Mexico City "covered their faces with mud and put on ragged blouses and skirts" in an effort to seem less appealing to the conquistadores who desired "beautiful women, with yellow bodies."[23] This behavior indicates quite clearly that native women feared sexual assault and sought ways to foil their attackers. It also serves to contradict scholarship that insists that the sexual promiscuity of native women made them more willing to engage in sexual activity with the Spanish. Whether these tactics successfully deterred the Spanish is hard to say. What is certain is that conquistadores viewed native women as free for the taking whether they consented or not.

Historians have been mixed in their portrayal of sexual violence against native women by the French. To what degree it was practiced is much debated, but sources indicate that it was present. Twentieth-century historian Marcel Trudel records an incident in which Robert Grave, son of François Grave, was "accused by the Indians of having abused and raped one of their women."[24] Trudel blames the sexual violence on the nudity exhibited among Souriquois, Montagnais, Algonquins, and Huron women "for whome the flesh was permissible pleasure and therefore were shocked at the behaviour of the French."[25] Observations by Recollect Le Caron seem to confirm the "abuses and thousand kinds of vile deeds" executed by the Frenchmen.[26] Although the reasons for the imprisonment of crew members were rarely recorded, it is possible that the presence of criminals among the crew exacerbated the fear of rape. Some had violent histories and naturally would have been chosen for a sea voyage based on physical strength and fortitude, so their potential threat would not have gone unnoticed.[27]

Fortunately the prevalence of sexual violence was not necessarily the case in New France. The religious observers present left little indication that these were frequent occurrences or that sexual conquest was a part of exploration. Frenchmen chose to assert their dominance through protection and gallant civilization, assuming that the inherent weaknesses and vulnerability of women necessitated male defense. Christian attitudes toward the protection of women seemingly tempered inclinations toward sexual assault by Champlain and Cartier. Sources indicate that they viewed native women more as victims of their society and in need of masculine protection than as wanton deviants. Jesuits priests wrote an account of a man, Monsieur Abraham, accused of rape who received the second sentence of execution by the French in America.[28] Two years later Paul Ragueneau put in writing that "Courville [was] arrested as a prisoner, *propter raptum imminentem* of Madamoislle Dauteuil."[29] Occasionally these sexual assaults extended to child abuse as well. In November 1667 a "man was hanged for having ravished a little girl eleven years of age."[30] Taken as a whole, these accounts depict the French similarly to the Spanish in Mesoamerica. However, it must be noted that these accounts are the only ones in existence, compared with the dozens recorded from the Spanish presence further south.

Old and New England

English gentlemen also brought expectations from courtly society to the New World. Karen Ordahl Kupperman emphasizes that for early travelers "their criterion for civility was the degree to which the Indians recognized male-female distinctions and a hereditary hierarchy and maintained these demarcations by outward signs."[31] This obsession with social order derived largely from a fear that English society was breaking down and that markers of class and position in society continued to become blurred. Richard Brathwait commented on confusing modes of dress that disregarded social conventions of rank and gender. Noblemen representing the apex of English masculinity suddenly seemed effeminate in dress while women "suting their light feminine skirts with manlike doublets" appeared more masculine.[32]

Working on understandings of English conceptions of manhood, Elizabeth A. Foyster has posited honor as the most defining characteristic of successful English masculinity in the early modern period.[33] Within the concept of honor exist many subcategories and expectations of behavior and values that reflect this overarching idea. Among those were honesty, sobriety, and mastery of one's home and wife. The last provided the most overt examples of failed men. To be called a cuckold was the worst possible offense to a man, implying not only that was he failing to control his wife but also that her sexual needs required another male. Women's bad behavior reflected poorly on men whose success depended upon an understanding of their role as head of household with responsible subordinate wives. Although Susan Amussen in her writings on rape in early modern England contends that rape was not part of the English performance of manly behavior, she argues that sexuality was crucial to understandings of honorable and dishonorable men and those social conventions of rape assisted in these notions.[34] Rather than exerting force upon women, English men sought to woo women through their skill, wit, and charm, thus making physical aggression wholly unnecessary. This is not to say that rape was not an occurrence, but it was instead understood as the act of a lesser man, unable to succeed at the art of seducing women.[35]

In New England, as in early modern England, reputation defined one's social success. Defamation at the hands of a thorough gossip network often shed light on masculine shortcomings, such as infidelity, unethical business practices, and dishonesty in either social or economic relationships. Foyster argues that men continually maintained their reputations through assertions of masculinity and control of both self and women.[36] She asserts that this designation of women as the primary determinate of successful men empowered women. This is echoed in Terri L. Snyder's *Brabbling Women*.[37] Snyder found that women in early colonial Virginia demonstrated remarkable power through speech. Extensive networks of gossip and defamation found their way not only to kitchen tables but also to court rooms, as men and women eagerly sought to redeem their reputations for lying, promiscuity, stealing, and a bevy of other offenses. In this way gossip acted as a social control with women as the predominant patrollers.

This scorn extended to members of the clergy who failed to embody their highest virtues. The Reverend John Lyford arrived in Plymouth in 1623. Initial impressions praised his "reverence and humility."[38] Like a man truly about God's work, Lyford "wept and shed many tears, blessing God that had brought him" to America.[39] Right away he confessed to "his former disorderly walking and his being entangled with many corruptions" but God had delivered him from his sinful past.[40] Suspicious of his behaviors and relying heavily upon local gossip, Governor William Bradford ordered Lyford's letters be secretly opened before being sent to England. Among his many communications Bradford found criticisms made against the colonies and separatists. He copied and kept or sent copies of the originals. At trial, Lyford remained silent when Bradford asked if he thought him evil for opening his private correspondence. Declaring it his right as magistrate, Bradford produced the incriminating letters and read them aloud. The court convicted Lyford and allowed him six months probation to prove his character otherwise. He seized this opportunity to beg forgiveness from the court and the community at large. Bradford records that he "confessed his sin publicly in the church."[41] His speech to the congregation recited his many failings and the "pride, vain-glory, and self-love" that induced him to such slanders.[42] He expressed joy that such evil writings had been stayed by Bradford and that his deeds had been called out before the community. The theatrics of his confession and petition for forgiveness moved some "tenderhearted men," and his conviction was forgiven.[43] The fact that he sent another letter to England within two months affirming the content of the letters casts doubt on his recantation.

The second episode of punishment for the Rev. Mr. Lyford extended well beyond his public conduct. His wife "was so affected with his doings as she could no longer conceal her grief and sorrow" and began to share details of their marriage.[44] She began telling secrets to her friends, some of the church deacons, and then anyone who would hear her tales of woe. She testified that he "had a bastard by another before they were married," which he denied in order to convince her to marry him. The indiscretions continued and he brought the bastard home for her to rear, begging her pardon. He seduced their housemaids and brought shame upon their household. Evidence at the trials indicated that while ministering in Ireland he overcame and defiled a young woman who sought his counsel in the days before her wedding.[45] Convicted and publicly humiliated, Lyford moved to Salem and then to Virginia.

Several elements of this story warrant attention. First, the concept of private property so beloved by settlers of New England evidently did not extend to letters and other means of correspondence. That Bradford found useful information for Lyford's censure in private letters does little to redeem this notion of community spying. Second, the power of the community and gossip again contributed to Lyford's demise, using the testimonies of his wife against him. His wife admitted that she feared what would become of her were they to be expelled from Plymouth. Using the declaration of God to David that wives too would bear the sins of their husbands, his wife distanced herself from him as soon as possible. She declared that it was her conscience and the fear that, if exiled from the colony, she might succumb to sexual assault at the hands of Indians that caused her to come forward. There is little doubt that her plight would have received sympathy. She appealed directly to Puritan men's masculine sense of obligation toward women and their responsibility for protecting them. Furthermore, she cleverly engaged the community gossip networks to her advantage. By impugning her husband's fidelity and reputation, she brought upon him the wrath of the larger society but saved herself. That she failed to come forward at his first trial where he was forgiven makes her motivations suspect. Was she genuinely contrite or desperate? With the second trial and ejection almost certain, she took measures to guard her own reputation and protection within the community.

Native Americans and Conflicts of Gender

Ultimately female power in native society as interpreted by Europeans was a reflection of the inadequacy of Native American men, who were less masculine for failing to exert authority over the women in their tribes. While Europeans admired the strength and fortitude of native women, they criticized the laziness of the men.[46] Explorers saw the hunting, and gaming lifestyle of the men as comparable to the aristocratic forms of leisure in Europe and therefore supposed native men to be idle. English observers freely criticized the gender system of Chesapeake Indians. John Smith denounced the fact that while men spent their time "fishing, hunting, [in] wars, and such manlike exercises," the women often did the rest of the work including the necessary agriculture.[47] This contradicted English assumptions about women's place in society and the home. The role of women and the gender systems present in native Chesapeake society incurred scorn from the English who, in George Percy's words, perceived that "their women doe all their drugerie [while] the men takes their pleasure in hunting and their warres, which they are in continually one Kingdome against another."[48] John Smith concurred with Percy. Smith described the ways that "men bestowe their times in fishing, hunting, wars, and such manlike exercises, scorning to be seene in any woman like exercise, which is the cause that the women be verie painefull and the men often idle. The women and children do the rest of the worke."[49] Ironically this criticism mirrored the ways English gentlemen behaved in the New World. Because the gentlemen were unable to fend for themselves or provide sustenance, English captains harshly condemned their idleness. These criticisms are a direct corollary to Smith's denunciation of Indian men whose pursuits mirrored those of English gentlemen. The result was the engagement of women in masculine enterprises. Native men's failure also operated as an outlet to assert English masculinity via Englishmen's respect toward gentlewomen. Women who possessed valued masculine characteristics, such as strength and a dedicated work ethic, could no longer be women but were desexualized through the rendering of them as masculine.

This contradictory portrayal of native women by explorers caused inconsistent labeling. Their writings reflected ambivalence. Native women simultaneously embodied wanton sexual deviance and women in need of male protection. They controlled their own sexuality within native society through multiples suitors, husbands, and lovers. Native women's sexual authority and freedoms often shocked and appalled explorers who brought with them expectations of patriarchal authority and Christian conventions. While this affronted French explorers, they nonetheless preserved the right to choose by offering protection against unwanted sexual advances. Women could only exert choice and power when they fell under the jurisdiction of French protection. Within the heavily dichotomized minds of Europeans, women could not simultaneously be both masculine and feminine. In an attempt to reconcile this paradox explorers oscillated between their characterizations. Gender relations between the French and the native women were fraught with European expectations of Christian womanhood, concerns over the ways in which women's power in native society threatened ideas of masculine authority and power, and the difficulties they had in reconciling the sexual lasciviousness they perceived in native women with the skill and love they exhibited as mothers.[50] The disparate dimensions of French and native womanhood extended beyond the virgin/whore dichotomy that was prevalent among Europeans.[51]

Champlain's quadrant drawing illustrating native womanhood reveals both the complexities of gender and the strength that these "powerful women of extraordinary stature" displayed.[52] The first rendering is of a young bare-breasted girl with flowing hair, decorated with wampum representing the sexuality and allure of native womanhood. In contrast to, or as a complement to her, a fully clothed woman holds a baby in one hand and an ear of corn in the other, signifying reproduction, pure motherhood, and the fertility of woman, as well as suggesting a correlation between woman as reproducer and the earth as a fertile maid. The lower drawings are much more interesting and surprising. They present the two women in slightly masculine forms, one ambiguously painted from behind, highlighting a muscular back as she works, the other attired in crude military suit designed for warfare with all vestiges of femininity disguised.[53] These, perhaps more than the familiar renderings above, suggest the gendering of native women as simultaneously feminine and masculine or defiant of categorization according to early modern capabilities. This last rendering invites comparison with the other drawings by Champlain of native men engaged in warfare completely nude. These are inconsistent renderings and reveal much more of Champlain's personality than the reality of native dress in combat. Certainly in native society women assumed responsibilities that in European society would have been masculine, yet they still possessed feminine allure and reproductive capabilities.

For Champlain and the Great Lakes natives, war provided an opportunity to prove their "manly courage," bravery, and heroism. The Ochteguins (Hurons) and Algonquians, "men skilled in war and full of courage," came to Champlain to enlist French aid against the Iroquois.[54] He jumped at the opportunity "of showing them by results more than they could expect from [him]," thus exceeding their expectations of his skill.[55] They faced an enemy described as "two hundred, in appearance strong, robust men" who possessed "a gravity and calm" which impressed Champlain.[56] With much bravado Champlain claimed that at the outset of the war and with only *one* shot he killed two of the three head chiefs, thus proving the "courage and readiness" he admired in himself.[57] His drawing depicting this scene further amplifies his courage and skill in battle. Drawing the natives on both sides nude, he inserts himself between the two groups, mortally wounding the two chiefs all the while placing himself at the head of his Indian alliance and at the forefront of danger.[58] This affirms the value of courage and also European perceptions of themselves as more courageous and therefore manlier, entitled to authority over their native allies.[59] Champlain and other Europeans who engaged in alliance with natives in battles seem completely oblivious to their own roles as mercenaries in tribal warfare.

Several days after this initial encounter, an alliance of Huron, Montagnais, and Algonquians prepared to once again go on the warpath. While Champlain chose to join their party, the natives "shouted to those [French] who stayed behind that they were woman-hearted, and knew no other kind of fighting but the war on peltry," as fur trading denoted a compromise in masculinity.[60] This statement reinforced Champlain's own perceptions of his superior masculinity by validating his manly courage. This chastisement of seemingly feminine men who lacked courage was designed to undermine their confidence in their own abilities and courage and therefore assign them a subservient masculine identity. A "courageous young man of St. Malo named Des Prairies," a fur trader nearby, heard the echoes of battle and chastised those French who had not followed Champlain into battle. Other traders rushed to the aid of the brave Champlain, and Champlain, in gratitude, stepped aside "so that the new-comers might have their share of this pleasure" of taking down the Iroquois fort.[61] War was a stage for the performance of masculinity but also an enjoyable opportunity to prove oneself.[62]

The Great Lakes natives similarly created a culture of masculinity centered on warriors and chiefs who were warriors. This reverence for war and warriors echoed the French glorification of courage and strength in battle. Records from the narratives indicate that elaborate sepulchers were made only for the warriors, and "for other men they put in no more than they do for women, as being useless people. Hence but few of these tombs are found amongst them."[63] Once again this confirms the association of femininity and womanhood as the antithesis of the courageous warrior. Women and uncourageous men were universally termed as "useless people."

In matters of warfare Champlain and Lescarbot recounted the brutality practiced upon those unfortunate enough to be captured by the Iroquois. Dismembering a body as practiced by Hurons and Montagnais, as well as Iroquois, was seen as an insult to the dignity of the living and detrimental to the successful transition of the living to the afterlife.[64] Champlain observed an incident designed not only to torture a war captive, but to debase his masculinity as well by setting fire to his penis, or *membrum virile.* He wrote:

> Meanwhile our Indians kindled a fire, and when it was well lighted, each took a brand and burned this poor wretch a little at a time in order to make him suffer the greater torment. Sometimes they would leave off, throwing water on his back. Then they tore out his nails and applied fire to the ends of his fingers and to his *membrum virile.* Afterwards they scalped him and

caused a certain kind of gum to drip very hot upon the crown of his head. Then they pierced his arms near the wrists and with sticks pulled and tore out his sinews by main force, and when they saw they could not get them out, they cut them off. This poor wretch uttered strange cries, and I felt pity at seeing him treated in this way. Still he bore it so firmly that sometimes one would have said he felt scarcely any pain.[65]

Champlain admired the courage and bravery the captive demonstrated in the face of these incredible tortures.[66] Hoping to set an example for the natives, he refused to participate and demanded the man be shot and released from his suffering. He explained himself to the natives in terms of his own Christianity piety. Champlain placed himself as superior both in his Christianity and in his pious mercy toward others. The native reaction was not recorded, but it is doubtful that a culture so predicated on displays of manliness would view Champlain's mercy as benevolence rather than weakness.

As for the tribes of the Great Lakes, capturing enemies in Mesoamerica symbolized success and cunning as a warrior and man. The successful capture of an enemy was a rite of passage necessary for all Aztec men. A warrior engaged in battle at Zacatlán "took a captive with the help of others and became a man."[67] Those who completed this sacrament received accolades that included access to hairstyles and dress that reflected their status as adequate warriors. Assistance from seasoned warriors constituted a mentorship of behavior that young men, eager to prove themselves, welcomed. Conversely the greatest shame of a warrior was capture. Death in battle was noble, but capture symbolized weakness and fear, an unwillingness to fight to the death in order to preserve one's position in battle and society. This important paradigm of captivity served to distinguish successful warriors from those who failed. To capture was clearly a sign of the triumph of one male over another, of one masculine warrior society over the other. Subsequently this domination and the ability of warriors to capture others buttressed their honor and position in society, both of which depended heavily upon this ritual performance of masculine conquest. However, not all men ranked equally. Accolades depended upon the ability and masculine force of those captured. Huastecs, considered by Aztecs to be less manly and not as strong as Aztecs, allowed for little honor for Aztec captors. A single warrior of Atlixco or Uexotzinco, considered brave and mighty, counted for more than a multitude of Huastecs.[68]

Two honorable options accompanied warfare for Aztecs: death in battle or death as a prisoner. According to Warwick Bray and using the various codices, "A captured Mexican was expected to face death without flinching. Lyric poetry addresses the nobility of military death. One Mexican poet declared, 'There is nothing like death in war, nothing like the flowery death so precious to Him who gives life; far off I see it: my heart yearns for it.'"[69] If an Aztec warrior was killed in battle, his soul was believed to go straight to the Eastern Paradise or the House of the Sun. Even after death Aztec warriors spent their after lives engaged in mock battles after the sun arose. It was said that the "souls of the warriors greeted [the sun] by clashing their swords and lances against their shields."[70] Interestingly, enemy warriors who died nobly and sacrificed prisoners could rejoin their comrades in salutation to the sun and redemption.[71]

Honor demanded that he should not try to escape, and any nobleman who fled and returned to his own people was put to death, for, said Alonso de Zorita, a Spanish judge in the Indies, "they said that since he had not been man enough to resist and die in battle he should have died a prisoner, for this was more honorable than to return home as a fugitive."[72] The shame that accompanied fear in battle or capture could easily cause death to an individual and also humiliation to all Aztecs and the coward's family.

Suicide offered another example of failed Aztec masculinity. The *Codex Chimpalopoca* recounts the story of Teuchtlahucatzin, the *tlacochalcatl* (Nahua for chief) of Tenochtitlan who failed as a man in the eyes of the Aztec. Contemporaries recounted that Teuchtlahucatzin

> committed suicide. It was because he was filled with fear when the ruler Chimalpopocatzin was killed, thinking that perhaps they were going to make war on Tenochca, who would perhaps be defeated. And so he sacrificed himself by swallowing poison. And when this became known, when it was found out, then the Tenochca prince and nobles were angry. And because of it, the Mexica called a meeting. They came together and held council and pronounced the decree that none of his sons, his nephews, or his grandsons would gain honor and nobility. Rather they would belong to them as vassals forever. And that is what happened. For even though his descendents were able warriors and fighters, none gained nobility and honor.[73]

This story highlights the Aztec expectations of masculinity in their warrior society. To be courageous in life and battle typified male existence. To fear a potential enemy and commit suicide was a great shame that affected not only the memory of the dead but also the future generations associated with his name. Contemporaries understood Teuctlahucatzin as a shameful coward. Committing suicide not only humiliated him; this act also offended all Aztec men who shared this shame. Although he avoided potential capture by his enemies, his reluctance to engage in battle and the fear that suicide underscored depicted him as offensive to the accepted ideas of Aztec masculinity.

Challenges to Aztec masculinity by other Central American tribes provoked deadly retribution. Neighboring tribes, aware of the rise of Aztec domination and military strength in the decades prior to European arrival, feared conquest. The Indians of Cuyoacán sought to engage the Mexicans in battle in an effort to defeat them quickly instead of waiting for them to attack. In a clever ruse the Cuyoacán invited several prominent Aztec warriors to a banquet. When the Aztecs arrived the Cuyoacán forced them to wear women's clothing, thus simultaneously provoking the battle they so desired and also emasculating and humiliating the Aztec. The Aztecs returned shortly thereafter reinforced with many troops who handily defeated the Cuyoacán. By feminizing them the Cuyoacán adeptly forced the Aztecs to assert and prove their masculinity through warfare.

The English similarly understood warfare as an arena of displaying courage and manliness. The Pequot War in New England captures the point when the English began to view themselves as warriors rather than simply settlers. The demands of the wilderness and the violent encounters with the Pequot nation produced behavior usually thought contrary to Puritan piety and restraint. Difficulties with the Pequot nation preceded the escalation of violence that occurred in 1634, but prolonged encounters began only after Captains John Endecott and John Underhill arrived at the Pequot Harbor and demanded that the Pequot fight the English in a European-style formation. The Pequots refused and the English destroyed the village in retaliation. Captain Underhill described the waste as they "burnt and spoyled both houses and corne in great abundance."[74] In retaliation the Pequots attacked Fort Saybrook and intermittent sieges continued over several months in the later summer of 1636. Underhill described the verbal assaults of the Pequots against the English as they "came neere Seabrooke fort, and made many proud challenges, and dared them out to fight."[75] The English fired their guns and the Indians disappeared only to return again. This time they challenged the masculinity of the Englishmen, once again using clothing as a source of conflict. Underhill, a witness to this incident, recalled the scene: "Other put on the English clothes, and came to the Fort jeering of them, and calling, come and fetch your English mens clothes againe; come out and fight if you dare: you dare not fight, you are all one like women, we have one amongst us that if he could kill but one of you more, he would be equall with God, and as the English mans God is, so would hee be." The Pequot warrior realized the potency of his insults, simultaneously challenging the masculine prowess of the English soldiers and also the power of their God. This directly undermined their faith in themselves and their divinity. It was the latter that most offended the devout Puritans.

Unlike his countrymen, Lion Gardiner also criticized some of the English behavior, though not the violence. The main offense came from two men in his company who, fearful of death at the hands of Pequots, "ran away and left their guns behind them."[76] These "cowards" drew "lots which of them should be hanged."[77] It is unclear whether their cowardice required punishment because it reflected poorly on them as soldiers or because their fear insinuated their lack of faith in God's ability to deliver them from their enemies. Given the Puritan emphasis on divine intervention and protection, the latter is more likely.

Two-spirits and the Masculine Order

Although native women's exercising of authority and wantonness and native men's power in warfare often challenged European men's sense of masculine authority, nothing posed so complicated a threat as homosexuality. Europeans, particularly given the Christian teachings of sexuality in the early modern period, understood homosexuality to be the work of the devil and a practice enjoyed by evil men who rejected the goodness of Christ. Colonial authorities documented the presence of such men with the greatest scorn. The "hermaphrodites," "berdache," or two-spirited people served to challenge understandings of male identity in both colonial and native society in a way that their European counterparts—who occupied a marginal and heavily condemned place in society—did not.[78]

That Europeans lacked a similar category of gender often contributes to the confusion in depictions of perceived "sodomites" or "social deviants." Homosexuality as a condemned practice varied throughout Europe, but there are some consistencies. The recipient of penetration either orally or anally became feminized in European society and often the perpetrator or "man" in the sexual act received little criticism. In actuality he had performed his masculinity while the recipient had compromised his masculinity and adopted the degraded sexual posture of a woman. The female player often acquired the label of "sodomite," thus incurring not only the wrath of society but of God as well. Homosexuality particularly offended the Catholic and Protestant faiths because of its lack of reproductive purpose and also because it compromised men's role as head of the household, the church, and the faith.

Occasionally Europeans encountered peoples that did not fit easily within either category as masculine or feminine. Homosexuality provoked severe scorn from religious officials and laymen alike. En route to America, Higginson recalled that the Puritans discovered "five beastly Sodomitical boys which confessed their wickedness, not to be named."[79] Given the severity of this act, the Puritans "referred them to be punished by the Governor who afterwards sent them back to be punished in Old England, as the crime deserved."[80] The boys reappear in the Company Records of Massachusetts Bay, and it is clear that no one knew quite how to punish them. In 1629, after they returned from New England to England, the court could not decide whether to refer their case to the judge of the Admiralty or issue a warrant.[81] They reappear in the records several days later, and the court decided they should be "legally discharged" from the company responsible for the colonies.[82] The colonies could not be affiliated with such crimes.

Assertions of homosexuality often accompanied overarching racial discourses. In early modern Spain, Jews and Arabs frequently received the label of "sodomite" part and parcel with their expulsion from Spain in the late fifteenth century. Spanish authorities vehemently denied that homosexuality existed within their realm and any appearances of the abominable act had been the product of foreign invaders and influence. This gave the Spanish the moral authority to expel and also to invade. Early Spanish arrivals in the Americas brought with them their suspicions and paranoia concerning illicit sexuality between men. Michael J. Horswell insists that the Spanish brought their criticism of homosexuality as part of the "rhetorical armaments employed to justify the invasion and colonization of the Andes."[83] The variant existences of two-spirits throughout Mesoamerica "threatened the moral order of the Old World and embodied the anxiety related to the inherent instability of hegemonic Iberian masculinity."[84] Juan Ruiz de Arce revealed his disgust with the peoples of Ecuador. He wrote "es gente muy bellaca son todos sométicos no ay principal que no trayga quarto o cinco pajes muy galances. Estos tiene pro mancebos."[85] His blatant claim that they are "all sodomites" bolsters the moral imperative of colonization.

Hernán Cortéz, perhaps a more relevant subject for this project, equally condemned the entire population of Mexico as "sodomites." "We have learnt and been informed for sure that they are all sodomites and use that abominate sin," he claimed. His contemporary and fellow conquistador Bernal Díaz del Castillo echoed these concerns, writing "all the rest were sodomites, especially those who lived on the coasts and in warm lands; so much so that young men paraded around dressed in women's clothes in order to work in the diabolical and abominable role."[86] He associated transvestitism with homosexuality and the compromised masculinity these men must embody. If they dressed in women's clothing, then they must be recipients of penetration and thus become womanly.

Gonzalo Fernández de Oviedo wrote most emphatically that all indigenous America practiced "sodomy." Within his lengthy denigration lies the overarching concern that these two-spirits posed a threat to appropriate masculinity and threatened the prevailing moral and social order adhered to by Europeans. He lamented that "they wear strings of beads and bracelets and the other things used by women as adornment; and they do not exercise in the use of weapons, nor do anything proper to men, but they occupy themselves in the usual chores of the house such as to sweep and wash and other things customary for women."[87] Debauched sexuality came second to debased masculinity. These men not only defiled themselves by sexually receiving other men but also adopted the habits of women, thus rejecting their inherent masculinity. That two-spirit men rejected the glories of warfare in favor of housework outraged European men who could not envision a masculine pursuit more splendid or noble than war.

The French encountered homosexuality as an act of emasculation in war. In Florida under the command of René de Laudonnière, a soldier witnessed how the Outina "never left the place of battle without piercing the mutilated corpses of their enemies right through the anus with an arrow."[88] This overtly sexual practice intentionally enacted "sodomy" and the emasculation of their enemies. To lose in battle was to lose one's masculinity and right to dominance. Clearly the enemies being sodomized assumed the role of women and therefore the submissive role. Renowned artist Theodor de Bry depicted this practice in his illustrations of early America. According to de Bry, the "hermaphrodites" or men who dressed as women in the Florida tribes were relegated to tasks involving the sick or deceased.[89] However, upon closer inspection it becomes clear that the "hermaphrodites" of Florida played a vital role in warfare that was not necessarily demeaning or ostracizing.

The hermaphrodites depicted by Laudonnière and Jean Ribault existed outside the realm of European understanding and, as such, could not possibly hold any true value to society. The Frenchmen failed to understand the gender dynamics of Outina society. Association with dead warriors connoted honor rather than shame. Death in battle, one of the noblest pursuits in Mesoamerica, and most likely in Florida, received the greatest accolades from society. That the hermaphrodites or berdache carried the dead warriors from the battlefield indicated a prestigious rather than subordinate existence. The French impressions indicated that the hermaphrodites, "considered odious by the Indians," lived on the periphery of society. Gordon Sayre contradicts this directly, insisting that "by taking on women's roles, berdache were not demeaning themselves, because women and women's' work were not seen as inferior to men's."[90] What Sayre does not take into account is the vast literature that clearly indicates that femininity and appearances of womanhood placed two-spirits at a subservient level. Although their work and livelihood received no scorn, their very identity placed them at a lesser manhood because of their adoption of feminine characteristics of dress and behavior.

Shortly after the arrival of Europeans in Central America, religious officials enacted laws against the practice of homosexuality and transvestitism. Franciscan Gerónimo Mendieta, a follower of Motolinía, expanded upon Moltolinía's laws, writing: "Those who committed the nefandous sin, active and passive, were executed. And every now and then, judicial officials went to search them out, and inquired about them, so as to finish them off with death. For they were well aware that this so nefandous sin was against nature, because it is not found among the brute animals. Bestiality, however, was not found among the aboriginals. A male who went about dressed in women's clothes, and a woman who went about dressed in male clothes, both received death sentences."[91]

Richard C. Trexler insists that Moltolinía acted in 1643 in part to return Aztec society to the old ways when both passive and active participants received condemnation. Moreover, concern over reproduction led to the enactment of the portion of the law concerning women who assume male identities in dress.[92] Perhaps more than a concern for reproduction was the fear and paranoia of masculinities being compromised through female adoption of maleness while at the same time men willingly adopted attitudes and dress of femininity. This gender crisis greatly disturbed the Europeans far more than the natives.

The notion of punishing the active participant in homosexuality was new. When Balboa published *De Orbe Novo* in 1516, he recalled the presence of "men dressed as women and practicing sodomy," and he "quickly threw some forty of these transvestites to the dogs," the first record of Spanish punishment of homosexuality on the American continent. The interesting part is the fact that the active partners received no punishment, while those men who were passive died for their crimes against God and nature. The concept of the passive person being the only delinquent in homosexual intercourse is not new. Well into the twentieth century in America, men actively engaged in homosexual conduct but so long as they were the active rather than the passive participants, they innocently retained their heterosexuality. Only the recipient who performed the womanly act of receiving penetration compromised his God-given masculinity and as a sinner received public condemnation and scorn.

Two-spirited peoples represent only one of many challenges the New World provided to European constructions of masculinities. Resistant to acknowledging a potentially viable and revered masculinity in native cultures set Europeans on a path of destruction, as threats to masculinity contributed to and increased violence in the New World. In many ways the entire contestation between natives and Europeans can be understood as a battle for masculine domination with women and effeminate men caught in the crosshairs as useful pawns for the exertion of power and dominance. What cannot be denied is the importance Europeans ascribed to successful enactment of their masculinities and the real and perceived threats to these precious identities embodied by the New World.

Notes

1. Some useful works of theories of gender and masculinity studies are Joan W. Scott, *Gender and the Politics of History* (New York: Columbia University Press, 1989); Judith Butler, *Undoing Gender* (New York: Routledge, 2004); Judith Butler, *Gender Trouble: Feminism and the Subversion of Identity* (New York: Routledge, 2006); Judith Butler, *Bodies That Matter: The Discursive Limits of Sex* (New York: Routledge, 1993); R. W. Connell, *Masculinities* (Berkeley: University of California Press, 2005); R. W. Connell, *Gender and*

Power: Society, the Person, and the Sexual Politics (Palo Alto: Stanford University Press, 1987); Pierre Bourdieu, *Masculine Domination* (Palo Alto: Stanford University Press, 2002).

2. *Dictionnaire de L'Académie Française,* first edition (1694). Online: http://colet .uchicago.edu/cgi-bin/dico1look.pl?strippedhw=courage&dicoid=ACAD1694.

3. Samuel de Champlain, *Treatise on Seamanship and the Duty of a Good Seaman, Works of Champlain,* ed. H. P. Biggar (Toronto: University of Toronto Press, 1971), 6: 268. The French *courage masle* which has been translated as manly courage is imbued with more meaning than simply being attributed to a man. The *Dictionnaire de L'Académie Française* (1694) excluded female from the attribute and designated it as a characteristic of the strong and noble; those who intended to rule.

4. Marc Lescarbot, *The History of New France,* ed. W. L. Grant (Toronto: Champlain Society, 1907–14), 2: 256–67.

5. Ibid., 22.

6. Mark Breitenberg, "Anxious Masculinity: Sexual Jealousy in Early Modern England," *Feminist Studies* 10, no. 2 (Summer 1993): 377.

7. Kathleen M. Brown, *Good Wives, Nasty Wenches & Anxious Patriarchs: Gender, Race, and Power in Colonial Virginia* (Chapel Hill: University of North Carolina Press, 1996) 13.

8. Sir Walter Raleigh, "Discovery of Guiana," in *Hakluyt: Voyages and Discoveries* (New York: Penguin, 1972), 388.

9. Brown, *Good Wives, Nasty Wenches & Anxious Patriarchs,* 21.

10. Nanette Saloman, "Position Women in Visual Convention: The Case of Elizabeth I," *Attending to Women in Early Modern England,* ed. Betty S. Travitsky and Adele F. Seeff (Newark: University of Delaware Press, 1994), 65.

11. Michael S. Kimmel, "From Lord and Master to Cuckold and Fop: Masculinity in 17th Century England," in *The History of Men: Essays on the History of American and British Masculinities* (Albany: State University of New York Press, 2005), 125–42.

12. Ibid., 140.

13. Brown, *Good Wives, Nasty Wenches & Anxious Patriarchs,* 19.

14. Brown, in *Good Wives, Nasty Wenches & Anxious Patriarchs,* has analyzed this discourse within the context of Colonial Virginia. For Brown the anxious masculinities that presented themselves during the sixteenth century manifested themselves fully in the seventeenth and eighteenth through the acquisition of land and power for the plantation class. The continuity of male anxiety is fascinating when considering its origins.

15. Raleigh, "Discovery of Guiana," 408.

16. Ibid.

17. Ibid.

18. See Louis Montrose, "The Work of Gender in the Discourse of Discovery," *Representations,* no. 33 (1991).

19. Donald L. Mosher and Silvan S. Tomkins, "Scripting the Macho Man— Hypermasculine Socialization and Enculturation," *Journal of Sex Research* 25, no. 1 (February 1988): 60.

20. Quoted in Stephanie Wood, "Sexual Violation in the Conquest of the Americas," *Sex and Sexuality in Early America,* ed. Merril D. Smith (New York: New York University Press, 1998): 11.

21. Ibid.

22. Ibid., 13.

23. Ibid., 17.

24. Marcel Trudel, *The Beginnings of New France, 1524–1663* (Toronto: McClelland and Stewart, 1973), 155.

25. Ibid.

26. Ibid.

27. Hierosme Lalemant, "Journal of the Jesuit Fathers in the Year 1649," in *The Jesuit Relations and Allied Documents: Travels and Explorations of the Jesuit Missionaries in New France, 1610–1791,* ed. Reuben Gold Thwaites (Cleveland: Burrows Bros. Co, 1898), vol. 34, 39–41. Subsequent references to this edition of *The Jesuit Relations* will use the abbreviation *JR.*

28. Paul Ragueneau, "Relation de ce qui s'est passé en la Nouvelle France, en annes 1650 & 1651," 28 October 1651, *JR* 36: 121.

29. François Le Mercier, "Relation de ce qvi s'est passé en la Novvelle France, les années mil fix tens foixante fix, & mil fix tens foixante fept," *JR* 50: 217.

30. Karen Ordahl Kupperman, "Presentment of Civility: English Reading of American Self-Presentation in the Early Years of Colonization," *William and Mary Quarterly,* 3d ser., 54, no. 1 (January 1997): 194.

31. Ibid.; Richard Brathwait, *The English Gentlewoman, drawne out to the full Body* (London, 1631) A4, B3v, 10.

32. Elizabeth A. Foyster, *Manhood in Early Modern England: Honour, Sex, and Marriage* (Longman: New York, 1999).

33. Susan Amussen, *An Ordered Society: Gender and Class in Early Modern England* (Oxford and New York, 1998).

34. Foyster, *Manhood in Early Modern England,* 10.

35. Ibid., 55.

36. Terri L. Snyder, *Brabbling Women: Disorderly Speech and Law in Early Virginia* (Ithaca: Cornell University Press, 2003).

37. William Bradford, *History of Plymouth Plantation,* ed. Charles Deane (Boston: Massachusetts Historical Society, 1856), 147.

38. Ibid., 148.

39. Ibid.

40. Ibid., 157.

41. Ibid., 158.

42. Ibid.

43. Ibid., 166.

44. Ibid., 168.

45. Jacques Cartier, *Shorte and Briefe Narration (Cartier's Second Voyage),* 1535–1536 (New York: Charles Scribner's Sons, 1906), 185; Champlain, *Voyages* (1619), vol. 3, 137.

46. John Smith, "Description of Virginia and Proceedings of the Colonie by Captain John Smith, 1612," 101.

47. George Percy, 18.

48. John Smith, "A True Relation, 1612," 101.

49. Lescarbot, vol. 3, 86–88; Champlain, *Voyages* (1619), vol. 3, 141–42. Carol Devens, "Separate Confrontations: Gender as a Factor in Indian Adaptation to European Colonization in New France," *American Quarterly* 38, no. 3 (1986): 467–68.

50. Pauline Turner Strong, "Feminist Theory and the 'Invasion of the Heart' in North America," *Ethnohistory* 43, no. 4 (Autumn 1996) : 683–712: 685.

51. Champlain, *Voyages* (1619), vol. 3, 136.

52. Ibid., plate VI. This rendering further suggests that nudity was not the condition in which natives fought wars and adds to the likelihood that Champlain's drawings of men were out of appreciation for form rather than as interpretation of reality.

53. Champlain, *Voyages* (1613), vol. 2, 70–71.

54. Ibid., 80–81. Although Champlain sought assistance among his own people, only two were eager to join the alliance against the Iroquois.

55. Ibid., 98.

56. Ibid., 99, 98.

57. Ibid., plate V.

58. Champlain was particularly forceful in asserting his own authority over the natives in battle and in social situations. While subtle, he clearly considered himself to be the leader over war expeditions and alliance chiefs.

59. Champlain, *Voyages* (1613), vol. 2, 123, 126.

60. Ibid., 135.

61. For the natives to invite Champlain on the warpath was a sign of affection and respect for his courage; Ibid., 284.

62. Champlain, *Voyages* (1632), vol. 4, 179.

63. Ibid, 210–11.

64. Champlain, *Voyages* (1613), vol. 1, 101–102; Champlain, *Voyages* (1632), vol. 3, 101. The story is confirmed by Lescarbot, vol. 3, 13–14.

65. Lescarbot, vol. 3, 13–14; Champlain, *Voyages* (1613), vol. 1, 137.

66. John Bierhorst, trans., *History and Mythology of the Aztecs: The Codex Chimalpopoca* (Tucson: University of Arizona Press, 1992), 86.

67. Warwick Bray, *Everyday Life of the Aztecs* (New York: Dorset Press, 1968), 194.

68. Ibid., 35

69. Ibid., 70.

70. Ibid., 71.

71. Ibid., 195.

72. Bierhorst, *History and Mythology of the Aztec,* 83.

73. John Underhill, *Nevves from America* (London, 1638; reprint, New York: De Campo Press, 1971), 7.

74. Ibid., 15.

75. Ibid.

76. Ibid., 16.

77. Europeans noted sexually divergent identities pejoratively, using the term *berdache* or *hermaphrodite* to denote what we now identify as two-spirits or Native Americans who claim both the male and female genders as part of their nature. For more information on the evolution of these identities, see Sabine Lang's *Men as Women, Women as Men: Changing Gender in Native American Cultures* (Austin: University of Texas Press, 1998); Will Roscoe,

Changing Ones: Third and Fourth Genders in Native North America (New York: St. Martin's Press, 1998).

78. Francis Higginson, *New Englands Plantation; or, A Short And True Description Of the Commodities and Discommodities of That Country* (London: T. & R. Cotes, 1630), 231.

79. Ibid.

80. Ibid., 90.

81. Ibid., 94.

82. Michael J. Horswell, *Decolonizing the Sodomite: Queer Tropes of Sexuality in Colonial Andean Culture* (Austin: University of Texas Press, 2005), 68.

83. Ibid.

84. Juan Ruiz de Arce, "Relación de servicios en Indias," 32. Reprinted in Michael J. Horswell, *Declonoizing the Sodomite: Queer Tropes of Sexuality in Colonial Andean Culture* (Austin: University of Texas, 2005). This translates: These ruinous people are all sodomites. There is not a chief among them who does not carry with him four or five gallant pages. He keeps these as concubines.

86. Bernal Díaz del Castillo, 32, reprinted in Horswell.

87. Quoted in Horswell, *Decolonizing the Sodomite,* 74.

87. Theodor de Bry, *Grand Voyages: Early Expeditions to the New World* (Francoforti ad Moenum, 1590–1596). Art reprinted in Jay Levenson, ed., *Circa 1492: Art in the Age of Exploration* (Yale University Press, 1991), 31.

88. René de Laudonniére, *Three Voyages,* Charles E. Bennett, ed. (Gainesville: University of Florida Press, 1975), 13, 70, 132; Jacques le Moyne de Morgues, Drawing entitled *Hermaphrodites as Laborers,* in *The Narrative of Jacques le Moyne de Morgues, an artist who accompanied the French Expedition to Florida under René Laudonnière in the year 1564,* which appears in *The New World: The First Pictures of America,* rev. ed., ed. Stefan Lorant (New York: Duell, Sloan and Pearce, 1965).

89. Gordon Sayre, "Native American Sexuality in the Eyes of the Beholders, 1535–1710," in *Sex and Sexuality in Early America,* ed. Merril D. Smith (New York: New York University Press, 1998), 50.

90. Reprinted in full in Richard C. Trexler, *Sex and Conquest: Gendered Violence, Political Order, and the European Conquest of the Americas* (Ithaca: Cornell University Press, 1995) 158–59.

91. Ibid.

Revisiting Gender in Iroquoia

⌒ Jan V. Noel

Although the unusual authority of women among the Iroquois (Haudenosaunee) has been acknowledged by various observers over the centuries, others have raised doubts. Of late, however, aboriginal, feminist, and environmental movements are leading to fresh scrutiny of Haudenosaunee accomplishments. New work by aboriginal and other scholars reasserts a truly unusual gender balance in the political organization of the Haudenosaunee in eighteenth-century settlements in northern New York and their kin living at the Catholic mission near Montreal. This was attended by a remarkably equitable distribution of wealth, including the food and shelter that were primarily provided by women. There is also growing evidence that female elders and clan mothers carried maternal responsibilities well beyond supervision of the longhouses and fields that stood in the "clearings." Not only were they involved in choosing and deposing chiefs; there is also considerable evidence that some served as active councilors and diplomats in ways that affected major decisions about land, war, and relations with neighboring peoples. By extending female agency to the councils of state, the Haudenosaunee created an illuminating model of what governance can mean in a society without patriarchy.

For those who are curious about gender among North America's First Nations, one group has caused fascination across the centuries. Among explorers, officers, missionaries, and the scholars who came in their wake, views have varied about precisely how much authority Iroquoian matrons or clan mothers possessed.[1] The twenty-first century brings developments that will interest all those who follow this debate. There are now major revisionist works on the subject, from a scholar who is herself Iroquois (or to use the indigenous term, Haudenosaunee) who asserts that conventional scholarship is freighted with patriarchal assumptions; and from a French Canadian anthropologist.[2] There are language issues here: perhaps because some recent analysis is written in French and some makes extensive use of oral traditions, fresh perspectives have not received the reviews or critical attention they deserve. What does twenty-first century scholarship contribute to the debate about whether the Haudenosaunee (who assigned quite different tasks to men and women) still managed to develop a gender balance that few, if any, other societies have attained? This essay discusses new scholarship in tandem with classic studies of eighteenth-century Haudenosaunee settlements in southern Canada and northern New York. It presents evidence that those regions were home to a very rare phenomenon: a nonpatriarchal society based on a genuine equilibrium in the prestige, rights, and responsibilities of women and men.

Moving beyond Binaries

This essay presents evidence that it was quite normal for Haudenosaunee women to venture beyond the villages to assume roles in the politics, diplomacy, warfare, and trade of their people. Theirs was not the confining position that so many societies across time and space have assigned to females of caring for the young in obscurity and perhaps influencing village life through gossip or pleading, while male public figures monopolized broader horizons and bigger decisions. We shall see that the timeworn binaries of public versus private, forest versus clearings, and direct versus indirect political influence are all faulty ways of conceiving Iroquois gender.

It has long been recognized that something unusual was afoot in Iroquoia. The men supplied renowned warriors and chiefs at all levels within the League of the Five (later Six) Nations. Nonetheless, father was not "master of the house," nor was he the family's sole political representative. Haudenosaunee matrons or clan mothers spoke up in councils, and they alone directed the longhouses in which villagers of both sexes dwelt. The classic formulation is that the "clearings" (the village and outlying fields) were the domain of women, the "forests" (hunting, warfare, external diplomacy) the domain of men. Nancy Shoemaker, for example, in an insightful 1991 article entitled "The Rise or Fall of Iroquois Women"[3] documented that in the Seneca Nation women retained unusual rights over land, property, and marriage all through the nineteenth century, issuing challenges to patriarchal property systems such as their 1849 assertion that "we women have an equal right to our annuities with the men, and with the chiefs."[4] Nonetheless, influenced by the work of Elisabeth Tooker, Shoemaker relegated them to a stereotypical "sphere," supposing that, "in the language of women's history, Iroquois women probably had more influence in the private sphere than in the public." She went on to assert that "Iroquois women acquired their reputation for great political influence partly because clan mothers had the right to choose successors to office among the eligible men of their clans. Their other political activities were not as visible. Some women attended councils, but few women spoke. More often, women designated someone to speak for them." Shoemaker, with some reservations, accepted a notion of indirect or secondary influence that Tooker had expressed twenty years earlier. In Shoemaker's words, "although not at the centre of political discussions, they were diligent lobbyists.

Before or after councils, women occasionally took aside participants to make their positions clear."[5] This view echoed conservative beliefs regarding women's negligible contribution to "politics" or "the public sphere." It is true that Shoemaker raised the possibility that "the roles of wife and mother may have had a political significance not accorded women's roles in other cultures."

Elisabeth Tooker first delivered her much-republished debunking of any unusual powers for Iroquois women at a conference in 1975.[6] The paper argued that the agrarian tools and longhouses controlled by Iroquois women were flimsy, impermanent, and of little value, and that when it came to exercising political choices, that too amounted to very little. It categorically asserted that "council meetings were the work of men, and council decisions the work of men, not women. Men were the orators. Women could, of course, and did attempt to influence the opinion of men."[7] The author went on to add parenthetically: "One suspects women have always and everywhere tried to defend their own interests in ways that they could." She lamented that "occasional references in the literature to women advising chiefs and to particular men being asked to speak for women [are] taken to mean that women wielded considerable political power. Such an interpretation is not applied to comparable kinds of indirect influence women exerted in say, nineteenth-century England or America."[8] The argument was the essentialist one that women in all times and places are pretty much the same: secondary creatures who cannot occupy the real center of political life.

One suspects that this view was somewhat more plausible in the 1970s at the beginning of a period of dramatic changes that has resulted in many women holding governmental offices around the world, some at the highest level. Certainly the two new twenty-first century monographs about Iroquois women contend that theirs were not politics of the "power behind the throne" or "Please John, remember the ladies" variety. Later in this essay the Iroquois convention that required males to do the public speaking in gatherings of men (the only sex the colonizers ever sent as delegates), while women were to speak on behalf of men at female gatherings is explored. The new monographs support some of the stronger claims made in earlier literature about direct female involvement in community governance, claims made by colonial missionaries and officers from the seventeenth century onward and by several nineteenth- and twentieth-century ethnographers). A female missionary at Quebec and two male missionaries who lived for years in villages (at least one of whom attended councils) asserted that women had a direct part and a decisive voice. Occasionally that decisiveness was recorded even in transcripts of treaty negotiations recorded by male officials. One goal here is to explore how "direct" political involvement was, as well as to consider broader implications of what are generally conceded to be unusual gender arrangements in this society.

An outsider who approaches this topic must take constant care not to misread or oversimplify situations. Particular caution is needed in using terms such as *power, ownership,* and *rights* that are drawn from European traditions but have no precise parallels in aboriginal ones. To complicate matters further, interaction with colonizers caused arrangements to change over time, especially in an area so charged with meaning as gender relations. In European eyes gender relations were hierarchical; dominance was all too often integral to male honor, making a powerful woman a rival to be disarmed. In contrast there is evidence that the Haudenosaunee, at least as late as the eighteenth century, saw male and female roles in terms of reciprocal relationships that did not require power struggles. Their traditional stories avoid western binaries and valorize complex pairings (such as the two successive pairs of females and males responsible for fashioning the earth) and unusual relational lines (especially bonds with maternal aunts and uncles, considered virtual parents in a matrilineage). A nonaboriginal author seeking to grasp such viewpoints needs familiarity with aboriginal worldviews, traditions, and written accounts, and preferably linguistic fluency in the relevant languages. Certainly lacking the latter, I can only struggle to understand, remaining open to suggestion and correction. To this end I have tried to consult aboriginal sources, ranging from colonial voices to the current-day feminist Haudenosaunee scholarship of Barbara Alice Mann and the First Nations colleagues I meet in the course of my work.

As has often been pointed out, outside observers of aboriginal societies have always seen what they were prepared to see, influenced by goals that were sometimes imperialist, sometimes concerned with reforming their home societies. No one is immune to misperceptions, since there is no "view from nowhere," no completely "accurate" view of Iroquoia. Some question whether a unitary view is even a worthwhile goal. However, if one believes that some conceptions do approach past realities more closely than others, one might also believe that something happened to the western imagination in the last half century to draw us a little closer to Haudenosaunee ways of being. There are grounds for believing that western society has been moving of late in two positive directions: first, toward gender equality; second, toward a more respectful approach to the natural environment. New openness in those regards may also open our minds to elusive aspects of Haudenosaunee society.

A Composite Picture of Women in Iroquoia

Nonaboriginal writers have long disagreed about the extent of Iroquoian women's powers to govern. In the eighteenth century the Jesuit Joseph-François Lafitau identified a matriarchy while his fellow Jesuit Pierre F. X. Charlevoix thought some female councillors were just figureheads, kept in the dark about key issues.

Nineteenth-century ethnographers, of whom the best known is Lewis H. Morgan, were generally struck by women's unusual authority, but they disagreed (in Morgan's case even within his own body of work) on how extensive it was. Tooker's all-too-popular debunking of the value of female agriculture, property rights, and political roles contrasted with later, somewhat perfunctory acceptance of unusual powers by a leading Iroquoianist, Daniel Richter. In his 1992 *Ordeal of the Longhouse* Richter conceded that "the workings of female clans and village councils" had been ignored by European observers, and he acknowledged considerable political influence of women as documented by early observers, but he did not return to the subject in his 2001 *Facing East from Indian Country.* At the turn of the twenty-first century, full acknowledgement finally appeared in Roland Viau's book *Femmes de personne,* devoted exclusively to Iroquois women of the colonial era.[9] Besides weighing the evidence and summarizing the current state of knowledge about the precise *ways* this group of aboriginal mothers was empowered, we are also interested in what they did with those powers. In a rare historic group in which both men and women, all scholars agree, possessed *some* formal political powers, what social order resulted for the people as a whole?

There is considerable evidence to suggest that many mature Iroquois women maintained unusual positions even after two or three centuries of interaction with Europeans. Aboriginal writings collected from the nineteenth century onward in field studies such as those of Ely and Arthur Parker, Henry Schoolcraft, Lewis H. Morgan, Seth Newhouse, and others, outline the activities of women. To these we can add oral traditions as well as quite a number of written sources from the seventeenth and eighteenth centuries when the Haudenosaunee flourished in their settlements in present-day New York, Quebec, and (after 1784) Ontario. Up until the American Revolution they were a formidable people, courted by colonial powers in search of trade and military alliances, and a trove of information about them was gathered by explorers, missionaries, colonial officials, and travelers. One of the most knowledgeable commentators was early eighteenth-century Jesuit missionary Joseph-François Lafitau, who lived for five years among the Iroquois at the Sault Saint Louis mission group outside Montreal (also known as Caughnawaga or Kahnawake). While not of course in a precontact state, these key military allies of the French retained considerable cultural autonomy.[10] Lafitau enriched his own observations with those of earlier missionaries and reports about precontact practices. The result was a one-thousand-page ethnographic study. Lafitau's familiar summation is a foundational text for all subsequent scholars of Haudenosaunee gender. It attests female *hegemony* in so many specific areas and stands in such startling contrast to what we understand about women in most societies, that it bears repeating: "Nothing is more real than this superiority of the women. It is of them that the nation really consists; and it is through them that the nobility of the blood, the genealogical tree and the families are perpetuated. All real authority is vested in them. The land, the fields and their harvest all belong to them. They are the souls of the Councils, the arbiters of peace and of war. They have charge of the public treasury. To them are given the slaves. They arrange marriages. The children are their domain, and it is through their blood that the order of succession is transmitted."[11]

The two recent full-length books on Haudenosaunee women offer considerable support for Lafitau's astonishing claims. The extensively researched work published in 2000 by Haudenosaunee scholar Barbara Alice Mann, *Iroquoian Women: The Gantowisas,* analyzes four centuries of Euro-American and aboriginal source material, among them Iroquoian "tellings" including "women's tellings," often drawn from nineteenth- and twentieth-century writings from elders and aboriginal ethnographers.[12] One might be tempted to believe that Mann supports Lafitau's portrayal of a matriarchy, since she too assigns women superiority at councils as well as in the longhouse. However, Mann never employs terms that correspond to the concepts of *gynocracy* and *Empire of Women* that are found in Lafitau.[13] She claims the Iroquois mindset rejects the kind of binary thinking that assumes one sex or the other must prevail. Another important new voice on this question is that of award-winning Université de Montréal anthropologist Roland Viau, whose *Femmes de personne* reaffirms the highly unusual position of Haudenosaunee women. The primacy of Sky Woman in the Iroquoian creation myth, the religious celebration of the Three Sisters (the beans, corn, and squash that women cultivated), the frequency of marriages in which brides were older than grooms, and the preference for female infants all attest to women's status. So unusual was the gender balance that Viau singles out Iroquoia as "the human society which, from an anthropological point of view, appears to have come the closest to the definition of a matriarchy."[14] It was *not* a matriarchy, for men as well as women held important ruling positions. There was, Viau believes, a rough *equality* of the sexes. He observes that power was not decided along gender lines at all. It was *elders* of both sexes who held the most authority, which means the society is most accurately seen as a gerontocracy.[15] If this is true, Lafitau did go too far in attributing "all real authority" to women, since male chiefs and elders (who were likely underrepresented in the mission village) played key roles too.[16] In the same vein it seems excessive to claim that clan mothers were *alone* "the arbiters of peace and war." Balance rather than domination seems the fairest approximation of Haudenosaunee gender relations. There was no battle of the sexes, and neither sex "won." In some senses, as we shall see, *everybody* won.

Mother as Empowered Parent

Haudenosaunee daily life affords a view of a nonpatriarchal system in action. In village and longhouse settings mothers were clearly the most powerful actors. Typical Haudenosaunee villages might house as few as a hundred people or as many as two thousand. Couples were usually monogamous, although some polyandry was practiced among the Seneca. Premarital chastity was not expected of either sex. Older women often arranged marriages of their young, to which the latter generally assented. Unsuccessful marriages could be ended relatively easily by either spouse, but apparently social pressure weighed against it. Though there was some variation, new husbands seem generally to have moved into the wife's longhouse, multiple families (typically from twenty-five to sixty people) grouped around the fires, being related through the maternal line. *Mother* was the highest term in a lineage, and names, titles, longhouses, and most of their contents were transmitted through the maternal line. Of particular significance were female rights to the cache of goods or "treasury," which expanded greatly at harvest time when maize and produce of all kinds were crammed into the longhouses along with the dried meat and fish, furs, and wampum belts stored there in casks or pits. Iroquois women, as Judith K. Brown observed, managed food distribution, allowing them to exert considerable control over daily life, including denial of shelter to husbands who did not bring in products of the hunt or otherwise caused offense.[17] The situation must have changed somewhat as living became less communal, as housing types changed from longhouses to the bark cabins and frame houses described by many eighteenth- and nineteenth-century observers.

What were traditional views about children? Male and female children were considered to belong to the mother; if a marriage ended they stayed with her. As adults living in the longhouse they owed obedience to her. Colonial sources reported very tender mother-child relations in which errant children were never struck (though they were sometimes splashed with water). Nurturing is evident in reports of children being trained to carry little bundles of sticks and fetch small vessels of water from the river and in archeological evidence of games and of toy "practice pots," likely made under the tutelage of female kin who were the potters.

Woman as Farmer and Guardian of Land

Women were the chief horticulturalists among the Haudenosaunee, and the maize they grew is estimated to have supplied about sixty-five percent of the diet.[18] The earth's bounty itself was traced to a woman. According to legend, Sky Woman's daughter lay buried just beneath the soil, and tobacco grew from her head, corn from her breasts, squash from her abdomen, beans from her fingers, potatoes from her toes. Women worked in teams under supervision of an older kinswoman, taking children and captives to the fields to help. Seneca adoptee Mary Jemison reported that this self-directed field work was not particularly arduous. Even frail grannies found a niche, sitting on platforms in the fields to scare off crows and animal predators.

There is much support for the tradition that women not only tilled the soil but were its owners or guardians as well. For example, Seneca women asserted to a United States agent in 1791 that "we are the owners of this land, and it is ours. It is we who plant it for our and their use."[19] In the "Constitution of the Five Nations" transcribed by Seneca scholar Arthur Parker in 1910 from documents and wampum belts at the reserve near Brantford, Ontario, provision 44 states that "Women shall be considered the progenitors of the Nation. They shall own the land and the soil."[20] Doctoral research done early in the present millennium by Canadian aboriginal scholar Susan Hill affirms that the concept of women as guardians of the soil is reflected in council records from the Ontario Haudenosaunee during the eighteenth and nineteenth centuries.[21] The contention of Lafitau and certain other observers that lands and harvests belonged to women seems correct.

Clan Mothers in Political Roles

The oldest woman in a maternal lineage, who typically would have been a grandmother, served as clan mother or matron. Alongside the hereditary aspect there was room for merit; a matron might resign because of age or illness in favor of an unusually able kinswoman, and she did not necessarily select her eldest daughter. The choice was important, for the office bestowed the right to choose various kinds of male chiefs as well as to depose or "dehorn" chiefs who ignored a twice-repeated warning that they were thought to be misusing their office.[22] The women in a matrilineage could also convene their own councils, which might then raise an issue with the whole village or with the tribal council, for possible referral to the grand council of all the chiefs of the confederacy. Lewis H. Morgan recorded in 1851 among the Senecas a tripartite governance: clan mothers appointed sachems and decided issues of land possession; warriors hunted and supervised military operations; sachems deliberated on civil issues.[23] This governing structure was illustrated during the 1797 Treaty of Big Tree negotiations when a group of sachems including Sagoyewatha (Red Jacket) opposed a land sale but were overruled by the clan mothers and warriors.

Perhaps aware that traditional ways no longer served them well in a dominant culture that did not regard women as political entities, clan mothers demanded to be recognized by the United States negotiators in several late-eighteenth-century encounters. In 1791 parleys with Colonel Thomas Proctor on the policy to be adopted toward the Wabash and Miami nations to the west, the women made a point of claiming (through their male "woman's speaker") that they were "the principal support of the nation." This was one of several negotiating sessions in which they insisted that their views be heard because they were the owners and planters of the soil. They added that Colonel Proctor must "hear us for we speak of things that concern us and our children." Alluding to a consultation to which the Americans were not privy, they added that "our men shall say more to you; for we have told them." Apparently aware that they needed to be more visible (to an obtuse group that did not realize women were as important as men!), the women put themselves in clear view, sitting next to the sachems when the session recommenced later that day. Red Jacket, the woman's speaker, delivered their decision to join Proctor on his peacemaking mission to the western tribes, observing that "we are left to answer for our women, who are to conclude what ought to be done by both sachems and warriors. So hear what is their conclusion."[24] It seems as though what the women wanted may have been foisted on men who did not like the decision, for Red Jacket concluded his remarks by saying, "Now all that has been done for you has been done by our women, and the rest will be a hard task for us; for the people at the setting sun are bad people this is the words [*sic*] of our women to you, and the sachems and warriors who shall go with you. Therefore, my brother, make your mind easy, for your request is granted."[25]

The clan mothers were also present at the Treaty of Fort Niagara negotiations in 1796,when Red Jacket announced to United States commander James Bruff that the Seneca "have well considered your talk. I therefore beg your attention, and the attention of the warriors and chief women while I speak for the Nation." Another woman's speaker (called Farmer's Brother) later added that "the women wish to be heard. As they sat in council, and the land and the warriors belong to them, they hope the Requests of the warriors about the Road may be attended to. They are much disturbed about the Great Eater [Robert Morris who had acquired huge tracts of New York] devouring their Lands and join in the Request that he might not be permitted to purchase them."[26]

All political powers, male and female, rested on expectations of extensive consultation, allowing free expression of dissent. There was a search for consensus in lieu of majority votes or ultimatums, and a tendency to postpone decisions until general agreement was reached. These flexible arrangements make comparison with modern political systems difficult, and again serve to remind us that distinctions such as "direct" and "indirect" political voice are problematic when *everyone* who wanted a voice could speak up and when enforcement structures were loose or negotiable. Despite these caveats it can be said without question that the voices of mothers and grandmothers were built into the political structures of the Haudenosaunee.

Many observers noted women's political prominence. Marie de l'Incarnation, Ursuline superior at Quebec, a woman of no small clout herself, pointed out the existence of "capitainesses" who "have a deliberative voice at the councils, who reach conclusions as the men do, they even selected the first ambassadors who made peace with the French [in 1653]."[27] To this Lafitau added that women stood up at council meetings and decided whether or not war would be waged. Father Claude Dablon recorded in the late seventeenth century that Mohawk matrons "are greatly respected; they hold council, and the Elders decide no affair of consequence without their opinion."[28] Another key informant, Pierre Millet, served for twenty-two years as a missionary among the Oneida, a group who adopted him and admitted him to their councils. His insider account related the great secrecy that surrounded Councils of Elders, councils in which, the author attested, women and men exercised the same powers.[29] Mid-eighteenth-century French commanders and agents also observed the importance of Iroquois women at councils and in choosing a clan's civil and spiritual leaders. A little later, adopted Mohawk John Norton indicated that at the Grand River settlement women attended the chiefs' council fire and were entitled to speak there.[30] Several ethnographers from Schoolcraft and Morgan onward noted unusual female prerogatives of one form or another. For example, the early-twentieth-century scholar Lucien Carr reported to the Peabody Museum the preeminence of women not only domestically but "also around the council fire her influence was absolutely paramount," while the Men's Grand Council "acted as attorneys for the women rather than independently and of their own volition."[31] In sum, sources differ on the precise degree of female authority, and it certainly would have varied in different times, places, and among different Nations of the Haudenosaunee. However, several widely ranging sources went beyond acknowledging that matrons had power to select and depose peace chiefs to attest that they deliberated in councils of their own, in councils with male chiefs and elders, or in both.

The idea of female councilors is reaffirmed in the two major new monographs on Haudenosaunee women. Mann observes that, despite all the evidence, there have always been people who just could not conceive of women actually determining council decisions, certainly regarding questions relating to war. Notwithstanding the numerous primary sources attesting clan mothers' offices, "academic discussions of the League as a political entity almost exclusively concentrate on the men's Grand Council. The contrapuntal Clan Mothers' councils are studiously ignored, not because they were unimportant to the League but because western scholars are following the prescriptions of male dominance so central to European political history."[32]

Skeptics can find some support for their views in the sources; some colonial witnesses spoke of women being present at various trade and political delegations but staying in the background or being kept there by proprietorial husbands. Mann sees this as a misreading based on the political marginality and confinement of women in the observers' own patriarchal culture. They did not understand that Haudenosaunee etiquette required a woman's council to delegate a male speaker to address men, just as men's councils would delegate a female speaker to address women. Since the European delegates were male, they were always addressed by one of their own sex, sometimes through a formal male woman's speaker, who dressed in a skirt and carried a cornpounder in order to convey the wishes of the women's council. In a neighboring nation, the Lenape (Delaware), this practice was carried on to the extent that men of the group in general were chosen to wear skirts and take on the function of representing the women's council. Mann claims that the Lenape considered this feminization an honor until westerners "enlightened" them that it was not.[33] Further affirming the reality of female leadership, Viau identifies some eleven terms used by seventeenth- and eighteenth-century European observers to indicate Iroquoian head women, terms such as *femme considerable, matrone, captainesse, dame du conseil,* and *femme de qualité.* Writing in the wake of four decades when feminism had a major political impact, scholars are tending to remove the last logjams obscuring our view of what is probably the best-documented nonpatriarchal society originating in past centuries.[34] As the Oneida woman's speaker Agwerondongwas put it during negotiations in 1788, "Brother, our ancestors considered it a great offense to reject the councils of their women, particularly of the female governesses. Who, said our forefathers, bring us into being? Who cultivate our lands, kindle our fires and boil our pots, if not the women? . . . they are the life of the nation."[35]

Participation in War and Diplomacy

In thinking about female powers, it is important to point out a sphere that extended beyond the village clearings. Women who traveled on various missions appear in colonial records. For example, Marie de l'Incarnation at her seventeenth-century convent in Quebec parleyed with a female Seneca chief who arrived in town along with other ambassadors. Dutch New Yorker Harmen van den Bogaert encountered three women, probably Oneida, who journeyed six days to sell salmon and tobacco to the Mohawks. From the 1690s to the 1750s, ledger books of Albany merchants Everett Wendell and Robert Sanders recorded Haudenosaunee women who regularly brought furs along an eight-hundred-kilometer circuit between Montreal and Albany. Also traveling that route several times was a woman of high rank named Susanna who came down from Kahnawake to negotiate release of prisoners with officials at Albany. Young Konwatsi'tsiaenni (Molly

Brant) was said to have accompanied a party of New York Iroquois negotiators traveling to Philadelphia.[36]

Those were not isolated cases. Whatever traditional association there may have been of male initiative in forest activities and female initiative in the clearings, it did not confine even the ordinary kinds of wives and mothers to their villages. Though Iroquois men roamed afar for war, hunting, and trade, women too were regular denizens of the forest, from which they derived much of their livelihood. They foraged for spruce and maple sap, medicinal plants, nuts, all kinds of berries, mushrooms, firewood, and small game. There are numerous reports of their trading, fishing, and hunting trips (including those of "temporary wives" whose work was essential in processing and transporting game). Whole families traveled with diplomatic parties, embodying a Haudenosaunee tactic to strengthen negotiators' positions with a supportive crowd. Women accompanied some war parties as well, serving as provisioners and exhorting the men to bravery. Men of all ages fought harder, Mohawk adoptee John Norton explained, when the women were present. Traveling traders, stereotypically masculine, were frequently female, a fact that is startlingly confirmed by a new study of the Wendell accounts in Albany in which 49.6 percent of aboriginal accounts featured a woman. All this roaming meant that many Haudenosaunee women who spoke in councils did so with firsthand experience of distant forests, foreign peoples, and the gore of battle.[37]

Village goods and services that women provided were another integral part of diplomacy. The League of Five (later Six) Nations relied upon good communications, including trained runners who transmitted information rapidly from village to village within the League. [38] It was essential to refresh and refuel them and hear their messages. After they entered a longhouse marked with the animal emblem of their clan, these runners, and diplomats, traders, and warriors could turn to longhouse matrons to provision them with food, shelter, and dry clothing. The matrons also made the decisions to supply dried corn and moccasins that war parties needed. As dispensers of the stored goods the women in charge in the longhouse exercised some control over the "gifting" that constituted diplomacy with other nations. They had an impact, too, when they forbade younger male relatives to go to war, with chiefs sometimes turning to matrons for help in curbing overeager warriors. Given the genuine sharing of power between the sexes, it is quite possible that women shaped diplomacy—and the historical record—when they strung the wampum belts that recorded various kinds of treaties. Not always an influence for peace, women were known to present wampum strings to warriors outside their kin group as a way of mobilizing them to take to the warpath and capture prisoners who would replace or avenge fallen relatives.

Jan V. Noel

Another political function was to assimilate captive peoples. Haudenosaunee men were often victorious in war, and in the seventeenth century this resulted in villages in which captives sometimes outnumbered newcomers, a potentially dangerous situation. Yet integration of captives was essential, particularly since epidemics reduced the Five Nations population sharply and warfare perennially took a heavy toll. It was women who decided the fate of the numerous captives; the choice of whether to kill them or (more commonly) to keep them as slaves or adoptees was their prerogative. This authority made sense to a community that considered women to be the givers of life. They were also the ones who directed the activities of spared captives as they began living in the longhouses and working in the fields.

This system did not last forever. The early-nineteenth-century religious movement initiated by Seneca prophet Handsome Lake, an important revitalization of Haudenosaunee culture at a time of demoralization, tended to realign traditional practices with some of the gender values of the surrounding patriarchal society. Anthony F. C. Wallace discussed Handsome Lake's violent attacks on (primarily female) "witches," his condemnation of divorce and abortion, his assailing "old women's tendency to breed mischief " by exerting control over their married offspring, his support of male agrarianism and leadership as head of family. They are ripe for investigation as mechanisms for constraining traditional female spheres of authority—an investigation one hopes will be informed by insights from practitioners of Handsome Lake's longhouse religion, which has many contemporary followers. On other fronts there were perennial efforts by governmental agents and Christian missionaries to alter nonpatriarchal practices, although some aspects of older, more egalitarian ways did persist.[39] While the extent to which those ways survived after 1800 remains unknown, we can conclude that records from the mid–seventeenth to the beginning of the nineteenth century indicate the profound empowerment of women's voices in the nation.

Community without Patriarchy

Along with the economic and political roles women held, unusual social practices complete the picture of empowerment. The fact that brides were so often older than grooms is an indication of women's high status. So is the fact that brides in one Haudenosaunee nation, the Seneca, sometimes took multiple husbands (polyandry). Such rare practices affirm Viau's contention that "Iroquoian societies were strongly feminine. Their regime of maternal rights indicates as clearly as can be that in their social formations, authority did not necessarily belong to men."[40] Men certainly occupied esteemed positions as chiefs, councilors, warriors, and hunters; but these were not held up as being more important than the positions women occupied. Not all was rosy here: both sexes shared also in activities that were clearly *un*delightful, such as instigation of warfare and torture of prisoners. But refreshingly different is the way relations between the sexes did not seem to have been founded on exploitation or dependence, on either sex commanding the other. Once one accepts that Haudenosaunee society was not patriarchal, one can begin to contemplate alternative forms of human relations. One opens up to unfamiliar kinds of bonds between children and uncles, mothers and daughters, and twinned pairs that do not rest on hierarchy or rivalry. There are forms of generosity that do not necessarily follow European conventions or constraints. One catches a glimpse of resentment-free respect by males of female authority, indeed of *mutual* respect and a culture based on sharing. It necessarily sounds utopian to minds trained in European paradigms. Yet even so contemptuous an observer as Henry Dearborn, federal agent in 1838 sent to arrange western removal of the Seneca from their valuable Buffalo Creek lands, was quite struck by both the independence of the women and the great respect between the sexes (as well as their fondness for children). The women he described as "ardent, faithful, kind and indefatigable in their exertions to please. They are in no fear of their husbands and feel and act on a perfect equality with them, advise them in all their conduct in the mightiest matters and have immense influence, for they may leave them when they choose and when not treated kindly invariably do so. This induces the husbands to treat their wives well."

Dearborn added that as a result of longstanding traditions of men absent for war and hunting, the women planted, harvested, made the clothes, and prepared the food: "These duties are not arbitrarily imposed and exacted, but are considered as belonging to the females as not only indispensable but proper in all respects, and they therefore cheerfully perform them. The descent is through the females and the children belong to the mother. In fact the wife is more useful and important to the husband than he is to her. She lives with him from love. For she can obtain her own means of support better than he can. I have never seen an unkind look or word between the females, or between them and the men."[41]

Mann noted the importance of the female elder-younger male dyad in making the system work: "Among the Iroquois, half-grown men were subject to their grandparents, male and female elders who had the wisdom and experience to lift their eyes beyond self-aggrandizement to the welfare of the whole community. Grandmother was high on the list of public officials to whom youth was required to defer."[42] This latter point is not fantasy; a scholarly biography of eighteenth-century Mohawk loyalist Konwatsi'tsiaenni (Molly Brant), for example, reveals that she was "head of a society of Six Nations matrons which was particularly influential among the young warriors,"[43] and British and American officials on three different occasions attested that she was able to direct the wartime conduct of such men. Such political power had spiritual underpinnings: young men learned about Sky Woman (not Adam) as the first human and gazed up and saw Grandmother Moon where neighboring settlers saw the Man in the Moon. Iroquois youths heeded shamans and healers who could be either female or male. They wore masks to impersonate Husk Face Women and attended ceremonies organized around female activities such as berry harvests or female deities such as the Three Sisters.

What kind of conduct did "Grandmother" decree? Some scholars, influenced by late-twentieth-century ecological awareness, have shown an ability to appreciate the ways in which nonaboriginal societies could be less grasping and more in harmony with nature in a manner that surprised newcomers. Placing valuable trade goods in graves to accompany the dead to the spirit world (where it was thought such novelties were scarce) balanced spiritual concerns with more immediate material needs of the living. Denys Delage in his *Bitter Feast: Amerindians and Europeans in Eastern North America* argued that Iroquoians lived in greater harmony (in terms of human relations *and* the environment) than Europeans did. Delage quoted missionaries who struck by the fact that "a whole village must be without corn, before any individual can be obliged to endure privation. They divide the produce of their fishery equally with all who come." The clerics added that "it is wonderful how well they agree among themselves [no one displaying] an imperious or dictatorial manner. If so many families were together in our France, there would be nothing but disputes, quarrels and revilings."[44] Delage also stressed the ability of Amerindian societies to sustain ecological balance for thousands of years. Europeans arrived and all too quickly reaped the harvest, soon depleting the fertile soil and virgin timber, the teeming fish and game. While one wishes to avoid the myth of the "Ecological Indian" and acknowledge that conservation and bounty bore some relation to small populations on extensive lands, it remains true that the Haudenosaunee were a First Nations group whose unusual affluence was attested by their physical stature.[45] This good fortune owed much to two contributions primarily from the hands of women: an unusually high-yield agriculture and a redistribution system that left no one hungry. The code of hospitality was so clear on the latter that a hungry person, after announcing the intention, was entitled to take food from another person's field. (This code was in place at a time when such theft could result in a death sentence under English Common Law). Delage's work helps build a case for Iroquoian efficacy in providing and distributing nourishment.

What can we surmise from these recent studies? The monographs on Haudenosaunee women published at the dawn of the twenty-first century by Viau and Mann strengthen the case that they were indeed, as Lafitau and other observers had recorded, the authorities over the longhouses, children, marriages, and slaves. They did indeed control lands, fields, and harvests. While we still strive to understand the precise powers of clan mothers at various points in time, many observers noted occasions on which they spoke up on matters of state, with several of the observers classifying clan mothers' counsel as either equaling or outweighing that of men, either on some specific occasion or in general. Whatever scholars contribute to the question in future, it is undeniable that significant numbers of seventeenth- and eighteenth-century Iroquoian women exercised a range of economic, political, and property rights that were unmatched in Europe, and indeed in any known society of that day. Scholars such as Delage help us appreciate that a certain ecological balance accompanied the unusual gender balance. This was perhaps not an inevitable correlate—but it offers food for thought.

Conclusion

We have seen that recent aboriginal and nonaboriginal scholarship affirms old but contested notions about Haudenosaunee clan mothers. Indeed post-1960 movements advancing feminist, First Nations, and ecological viewpoints permit a view of Iroquoian women that is surely closer to the truth than views that could not imagine women anywhere but in the shadow of males, tied by their apron strings to the clearings. What Viau called a "strongly feminine" culture shines through in the fact that both mother *and* father were considered to be pregnant and needing to take special precautions when a child was expected and in the way that new chiefs were exhorted to rule on behalf of children running, creeping, in cradleboards, and unborn. As children were highly regarded, so were those who brought them into the world. Among the Haudenosaunee we have seen that, first of all, clan mothers did hold a very unusual degree of authority; second, they oversaw practices that were both egalitarian and ecologically sustainable. Even before the Europeans arrived, this was no utopia, but the accomplishments were impressive. Men apparently formed intense and loyal friendships among themselves, and women intensely loved their children.[46] Festivals, preparation of fields, harvesting of fish and crops, and fall hunting brought men and women together for happily remembered events that doubtless included courting. Putting all these elements together, one perceives an equitable gender system that was quite successful in producing and distributing the necessities of life.

The various offices that many Haudenosaunee women exercised allow us to appreciate the full potential of a nonpatriarchal society. Here public policy encompassed the concept of nurturing, revolved around responsibilities rather than rights and around political direction by both male and female elders. Matrilineal and matrilocal customs, control of longhouses and children, and guardianship of land and agricultural production buttressed female authority in the villages. A growing body of contemporary scholarship affirms longstanding claims that both female and male elders shaped the public and political life of their people. Placed in the hands of those responsible for daily nurturing, the distribution of essential resources of food, shelter, and clothing was accomplished in a relatively equitable manner, which led to a strong and vigorous populace. Out beyond the villages, clan mothers and many a more ordinary mother, too, traveled extensively. Respected grandmothers served as elders, council members, religious figures, and diplomats, just as men did. Here was a sharing of authority between the sexes that nonaboriginal societies still struggle to achieve, four centuries after certain unorthodox arrangements were reported in the villages of Iroquoia.

Notes

1. For an indication of the range of opinion, one can consult the collection of essays edited by W. G. Spittal, *Iroquois Women: An Anthology* (Ohsweken, Ont.: Iroqrafts, 1990).

2. Barbara Alice Mann, *Iroquoian Women: The Gantowisas* (New York: Peter Lang, 2000); Roland Viau, *Femmes de personne: Sexes, genres et pouvoirs en Iroquoisie ancienne.* (Montréal: Boréal, 2000).

3. Nancy Shoemaker, "The Rise or Fall of Iroquois Women," *Journal of Women's History* 2, no. 3 (1991): 39–57.

4. Cattaraugus Reservation, Committee of Women to President Zachary Taylor, April 12, 1849. Correspondence (Incoming), Office of Indian Affairs (reel 587), cited in Shoemaker, 43.

5. Shoemaker, "The Rise or Fall of Iroquois Women," 40.

6. The paper was delivered at that time to the Conference on Women during the Era of the American Revolution at George Washington University. It was published in the 1984 collection *Extending the Rafters: Interdisciplinary Approaches to Iroquoian Studies,* ed. Michael K. Foster, Jack Campisi, and Marianne Mithun (Albany: State University of New York Press, 1984); in Spittals's 1990 *Iroquois Women: An Anthology;* and in a number of other venues.

7. Elisabeth Tooker, "Women in Iroquois Society," in Spittal, *Iroquois Women,* 203.

8. Ibid.

9. Joseph-Francois Lafitau, *Moeurs des sauvages Amériquains comparées aux moeurs des premiers temps* (Paris: Saugrain, 1724); Pierre F. X. Charlevoix, *Journal d'un voyage fait par ordre du roi dans l'Amérique septentrionale* (Paris: Berthiaume, 1761); Lewis H. Morgan, *League of the Haudenosaunee* (Rochester, N.Y.: Sage, 1851); Daniel K. Richter, *The Ordeal of the Longhouse* (Chapel Hill: University of North Carolina Press, 1992), and *Facing East from Indian Country* (Cambridge: Harvard University Press, 2001); Viau, *Femmes de personne.*

10. Notable was their exemption from French law despite living within the colony. See Jan Grabowski, "French Colonial Justice and Indians in Montreal, 1670–1760," *Ethnohistory* 43, no. 3 (1996): 405.

11. Lafitau, *Moeurs des sauvages Amériquains,* vol. 1, 66–67.

12. Mann, *Iroquoian Women.*

13. *Gynocracy* is a term also employed by mid-nineteenth-century scholar Lewis H. Morgan, rather surprisingly in view of the somewhat lesser (and inconsistent) evaluation Morgan made of the status of Haudenosaunee women.

14. Viau, *Femmes de personne*, 108, deems ancient Iroquoia "la société humaine qui, du point de vue de l'anthropologie, paraitra avoir été la plus proche de la définition du matiarchat." This position makes his parody of Judith K. Brown and other feminist writers, 52–53, some of whom make lesser claims for feminine power than he does, gratuitous.

15. Viau, 243, notes a gerontocracy. He also considers male and female roles "relatively egalitarian despite a rigid division of tasks." Viau believes female powers expanded in the period after 1650 and remained strong until about 1850, a view shared by some other scholars including Cara Richards (whose essay is included in the Spittal collection). Some of the newer archeological evidence suggests a growth in matrilocality over time (see William Engelbrecht, *Iroquoia: The Development of a Native World* [Syracuse: University of Syracuse Press, 2003], 85–86). One theory is that men's deaths and absences in the context of colonial trade and warfare left village governance increasingly in the hands of women. However, the argument rests largely on negative evidence, the fact that the few early-seventeenth-century accounts we possess have little to say about female powers. Those sources have the additional shortcoming that they usually deal with the related Wendat (Hurons), not with the Haudenosaunee (Five Nations) among whom women's powers were most striking. Regardless of whether female authority remained constant or expanded somewhat after contact, what ones sees in the seventeenth- and eighteenth-century records is clearly an astonishing departure from familiar patriarchal practices. Long-established precontact oral and religious traditions that placed women on at least a par with men in creation and other stories and in the ceremonial cycle suggest that their high status was not a sudden or drastic innovation after 1600.

16. The French regularly recruited these men for war parties; many of the men there also joined long trading expeditions.

17. The Reverend Ashur Wright, cited by Lewis H. Morgan (see Spittal, 18). Adopted Mohawk John Norton's eighteenth-century account also supports this idea, recounted in Charles Johnston, *The Valley of the Six Nations* (Toronto: University of Toronto Press, 1965), 30. Judith K. Brown's influential article "Economic Organization and the Position of Women among the Iroquois" appeared in *Ethnohistory* 17, no. 3–4 (1970): 151–67.

18. Denys Delage, *Bitter Feast: Amerindians and Europeans in Eastern North America* (Vancouver: University of British Columbia Press, 1993), 50. On nutrition see also Richter, *Facing East from Indian Country*, 55–56.

19. Lucien Carr, "On the Social and Political Position of Women among the Huron-Iroquois Tribes," in Spittal, *Iroquois Women*, 19.

20. Arthur C. Parker *"The Constitution of the Five Nations, or The Iroquois Book of the Great Law,"* in *Parker on the Iroquois,* ed. William Fenton (Syracuse: Syracuse University Press, 1968), 42.

21. Susan Hill, "The Clay We Are Made Of: An Examination of Haudenosaunee Land Tenure on the Grand River Territory" (Ph.D. diss., Trent University [Peterborough, Ont.], 2005. Chapter four discusses women.

22. A key function of a chief was to make decisions regarding war, peace, and intertribal agreements. J. N. B. Hewitt, reporting in 1932 to the Smithsonian Institution, distinguished between tribal and federal chiefs; Morgan and some others refer to sachems and their assistants. A matron would consult with the other women in the clan and submit her choice to the council, which generally accepted it.

Hewitt also refers to one or more *ohwachira* (people tracing descent from a common mother). Mothers and adult females of the *ohwachira* gave their consent to actions the *ohwachira* took, but the group's male warriors might be consulted too. It had about forty-nine male members and forty-nine female ones. Hewitt (who provides extensive and specific detail but little documentation) insists on female primacy in the political structure. He also speaks of the decision making powers of female "federal trustees" and male "federal chieftains." The most convenient place to access a variety of useful writers on the subject of political powers is the Spittal anthology *Iroquois Women,* which republishes important studies by William M. Beauchamp, Carr, Hewitt, Ann Eastlack Shafer, and Brown.

23. Morgan, *League of the Haudenosaunee,*90.

24. American State Papers, Indian Affairs 1:159–60; cited in *The Collected Speeches of Sagoyewatha, or Red Jacket,* ed. Granville Ganer (Syracuse: Syracuse University Press, 2006), 19–21.

25. In the end Proctor and his Seneca delegation did not reach the western tribes because the British commander at Fort Niagara denied passage to the colonel.

26. From the O'Reilly Collection, New York Historical Society, vol. 15, items 39–41; cited in Garner, *The Collected Speeches of Sagoyewatha,* 78–79.

27. One version of Marie de l'Incarnation's statement appears in Joyce Marshall, ed., *Word from New France: Selected Letters of Marie de l'Incarnation* (Toronto: Oxford University Press, 1967), 216–17. Was one of these women perhaps the Onondaga woman Teoton-harason, reputed to be noble, wealthy, and highly esteemed (Spittal, *Iroquois Women,* 43), who went with her people's ambassadors to Quebec with some of her slaves?

28. Reuben Gold Thwaites, ed., *The Jesuit Relations and Allied Documents: Travels and Explorations of the Jesuit Missionaries in New France, 1610–1791,* 73 vols (Cleveland: Burrows Brothers, 1898), 43: 292, cited in Viau, *Femmes de personne,* 93. Subsequent references to this edition of *The Jesuit Relations* will use the abbreviation *JR.*

29. Viau, *Femmes de personne,* 93–94, attributes this key text with its revelations about women councilors to Father Millet, whose life is outlined in Daniel St-Arnaud, *Pierre Millet en Iroquoisie au XVIIe siècle: Le sachem portrait la soutane* (Sillery, Quebec City: Septentrion, 1998).

30. New York State Library mss.11350–51, cited in Charles Murray Johnston, *The Valley of the Six Nations* (Toronto: University of Toronto Press, 1965), 28–29.

31. Lucien Carr, "On the Social and Political Position of Women," 13, 30. Parker's *Constitution of the Five Nations* also alludes to equal female and male rights in clan council; see Fenton, *Parker on the Iroquois,* 55.

32. Mann, *Iroquoian Women,* 117. She does note exceptions such as Paul Wallace, Nancy Bonvillain, Renée Jacobs, and Roger Keesing; see 121–24. One of Mann's examples of the obscuring of female actions is New France governor Jacques-Rene de Brisay de Denonville's humiliating defeat in 1690. Although French Canadian sources speak of this as a defeat at the hands of "the Iroquois," Mann cites Haudenosaunee commemoration of this as a French defeat by a great female chief, the *Jigonsaseh,* a topic that warrants fuller investigation.

33. The same line of thinking might lead to reassessing that when Iroquoians called Europeans "women," this was not the insult that European ears heard but a more neutral remark about assuming a role usually assigned to members of the other sex. On the Lenape

see Margaret M.Caffrey, "Complementary Power: Men and Women of the Lenni Lenape," *American Indian Quarterly* 24 (2000): 44–63.

34. While there is much interesting speculation about societies such as that of ancient Crete where goddess-based religion seemed to flourish, the lack of written records from these archaic cultures contrasts with the rich ethnographic data provided by the well-educated Jesuit missionaries from the seventeenth century onward; there are also written accounts of varying value by explorers, military, civil, and ecclesiastic officials, and various travelers, traders, and colonists, joined eventually by dedicated ethnographers who might be amateur or professional, European or Haudenosaunee.

35. W. M. Beauchamp, "Iroquois Women," *Journal of American Folk-Lore* 13, no. 49 (1900): 87.

35. Joyce Marshall, *Word from New France,* 216–17, 222–23; Charles Gehring and William Starna, *A Journey into Mohawk and Oneida Country, 1634–1635: The Journal of Harmen Meyndertsz van den Bogaert* (Syracuse: Syracuse University Press, 1988), 6; Kees-Jan Waterman, ed. and trans., *"To Do Justice to Him and Myself": Evert Wendell's Account Book for the Fur Trade with Indians in Albany, New York, 1695–1726* (Philadelphia: American Philosophical Society, 2008); Library and Archives of Canada (LAC), Robert Sanders Letterbook; on Susanna see Gretchen Green, "Gender and the Longhouse: Iroquois Women in a Changing Culture" in *Women and Freedom in Early America,* ed. Larry D. Eldridge (New York: New York University Press, 1997), 12. Wife of a leader named Thanyuchta, Susanna made frequent trips to Albany from the Haudenosaunee village at Sault St. Louis Kahnawake and parleyed New York commissioners about release of English captives held by her people. See also the primary account of Susanna appearing in Edmund B. O'Callaghan and Berthod Fernow, eds., *Documents Relative to the Colonial History of the State of New York,* 15 vols. (Albany: Weed and Parsons, 1853–1887), 6: 795. "Konwatsi'tsiaenni (Molly Brant)," *Dictionary of Canadian Biography* (Toronto: University of Toronto Press, 1979), 4: 416–19.

36. As Richter noted, the "same women who cultivated the fields also collected wild plants from far-flung locations"; and treaty councils "typically . . . attracted dozens if not hundreds of men, women and children" (*Facing East from Indian Country,* 57, 139). For a long list of forest tasks of women see Viau, *Femmes de personne,* 174–77. For the impact of women on war parties see Norton's description in New York State Library mss. 13350–51, "Iroquoian War Tactics," cited in Johnston, *Valley of the Six Nations,* 33. On the percentage of trade accounts featuring female participants, see Waterman, *Wendell's Account Book,* 48.

37. Morgan, *League of the Haudenosaunee,* claimed a system based on runners could transmit information one hundred miles per day.

38. Traces of older, matrilineal practices during the reserve period are discussed in Shoemaker, "Rise or Fall," 39. For gendered aspects of Handsome Lake's message, see Anthony F. C. Wallace, *The Death and Rebirth of the Seneca* (New York: Knopf, 1970), esp. 281–86, 310–13. Wallace supports the idea that an earlier "'matriarchal' character of certain of their economic, kinship and political institutions was drastically diminished" and asserts that "these changes were codified by the prophet Handsome Lake" (Wallace, 28). Haudenosaunee women today, along with other aboriginal and nonaboriginal writers, reflect on past transformations and present situations in collections such as Barbara Alice Mann, ed., *Daughters of Mother Earth: The Wisdom of Native American Women* (Westport, Conn.:

Praeger, 2006), and Rebecca Kugel and Lucy Eldersveld Murphy, eds., *Native Women's History in Eastern North America: A Guide to Research and Writing* (Lincoln: University of Nebraska Press, 2007).

39. Viau, *Femmes de personne,* 243.

40. "Henry A. S. Dearborn Journals" (1838–1839), *Publications of the Buffalo Historical Society* 7 (1904), 111–114.

41. Mann, *Iroquoian Women,* 231. Certain flaws weaken Mann's enlightening text, such as a mistranslation of women's having "beaucoup d'autorité" as women's having a "surfeit of authority."

42. "Konwatsi'tsiaenni," *Dictionary of Canadian Biography,* 4: 416–19 .

43. Delage, *Bitter Feast,* 67 (Father Le Jeune on the Huron) and *JR* 43:271–3 (Father Rageneau on the Iroquois).

44. For the initial critical review of the concept of the "Ecological Indian" and the vigorous discussion it generated see Shepard Krech III, *The Ecological Indian* (New York: Norton, 1999), and Michael Harkin and David Rich Lewis, *Native Americans and the Environment: Perspectives on the Ecological Indian* (Lincoln: University of Nebraska Press, 2007).

45. See Spittal, *Iroquois Women* 121, n. 38 of the editor's supplemental notes, for a discussion of these relationships among men. See also Wallace, *Death and Rebirth,* 78, on the deep bond that could form between two warriors on an expedition.

Who Was Salvadora de los Santos Ramirez, Otomi Indian?

~ DOROTHY TANCK DE ESTRADA

In August of the year 1762 a woman died in the city of Querétaro in New Spain, that is, in what we often call Colonial Mexico. She was one of thousands who perished in the epidemic of smallpox that swept through the country that year.[1]

Her name was Salvadora de los Santos Ramirez, and she was sixty-one years old.[2] There were several things about her that might have captured the attention of her contemporaries. First, she died at an advanced age in an era when such longevity was uncommon.[3] Second, Salvadora de los Santos knew how to read and write. This was unusual because she was an Otomi Indian, judged by many, including the Aztecs who were the most numerous Indian group in central Mexico, to be the most backward and uncouth people in the region.[4] The Aztecs used the term *Otomi* to signify someone lazy and clumsy. Priests and other Indian groups considered their language extremely difficult; in fact, the first catechism in Otomi was not published until 1759, a century or more after religious texts existed in the other principal Indian languages of New Spain.[5]

More important was the fact that many people in Querétaro considered Salvadora de los Santos Ramirez a holy, even saintly Indian. One of the prominent Jesuit priests of the city, Father Antonio de Paredes, agreed with this opinion enough to write the story of Salvadora's life and publish it at the end of 1762, only four months after her demise. The format for the eighty-page biography chosen by Father Paredes was that of a genre popular in the eighteenth century, the edifying letter.

The Genre of the Edifying Letter

The *carta edificante,* or edifying letter, was a type of publication written mainly by Jesuits, but also at times by clerics of other religious orders, with the purpose of describing a recently deceased person who was thought to have been exceptionally holy. The eight-volume bibliographical study of the printing press in New Spain compiled by José Toribio Medina mentions this type of literature. It first appeared in 1632, and these publications virtually ended in 1767 when the king of Spain expelled the Jesuits from all of the empire, including New Spain. After 1767 very few edifying letters were published. Among them were two about Salvadora de los Santos (1784 and 1791). At times, instead of entitling the work "Edifying Letter," the authors called the biography "Life" or "Exemplary Life" or just "Letter." In most cases it was about a member of the Company of Jesus but sometimes concerned a nun, brother, friar, or diocesan priest. However, the book about Salvadora de los Santos was an exception. It was the only full-length biography of an Indian written and published in all of the Americas during the colonial period.[6]

The Jesuits often printed these edifying letters on their own press, located in the College of San Ildefonso in Mexico City. Most of these editions did not include the legally required preliminary approvals by ecclesiastical and civil censors or simply mentioned that they had "licenses" without giving any details. The last page of these works contained the "Author's Protest," in which he pointed out that he based the life described in the text on creditable witnesses but that these witnesses could be fallible so that the judgment of the virtues and miracles of a person was left to the Holy Mother Church as ordered in pontifical decrees.[7]

Information about the number of copies of each book printed from 1539 to 1821 in New Spain is almost impossible to find, since documentation concerning the printing presses has not yet been uncovered in the archives. However, it is certain that the first, 1762 edition of the edifying letter about Salvadora de los Santos sold quickly, since the book was immediately reprinted in 1763 and duly noted as a "reprint." The historian of Querétaro, Joseph Maria Zelaa, stated in 1802, when describing the life of Salvadora de los Santos, that "Father Paredes wrote about her surprising and saintly life in an edifying letter, published in 1762 and reprinted the following year in order to satisfy the interest of many people who desired to have a copy."[8] Fortunately, in the case of the 1784 and 1791 editions of the biography of Salvadora de los Santos, the accounts of the two Indian sections of Mexico City that financed the publications reveal that one thousand books were probably printed in each of the two editions.[9] For New Spain this was a very large number; no other edifying letter achieved four editions in the colonial period.

Daily Life and Extraordinary Happenings

Paredes's biography of Salvadora de los Santos follows a chronological development, beginning with her birth in the northern mining district of Zacatecas, the move of her family to a town near the city of Querétaro, and her work as a shepherdess for her father. Seventy people appear in the story, nineteen of whom are identified by name. The author describes ordinary events in Salvadora's life, most related to her great virtue, and also includes fourteen extraordinary happenings that some thought were miraculous. In total approximately fifty episodes are presented in the book.

In this period death by sickness or accident was common, and one such occurrence almost ended Salvadora's existence. While she was a child watching sheep in the countryside, the scourge of rabies appeared and caused the wild animals of the region to leave the woods. One rabid coyote attacked Salvadora "ripping her clothes but without its teeth hurting her body or even the poisonous spit from its mouth touching her skin." Because of this good fortune Paredes commented that without a doubt the hand of God had protected the young girl.[10]

Even at the time of her birth her family was in contact with both Indian and Spanish families. Her godparents were a Spanish couple living nearby. Later on, when she was a young woman, a Spanish friend asked her to be the godmother of her baby. The woman's mother, however, opposed the idea because "it would lower the status of her grandson if he were baptized by an Indian." Thus the woman and her mother decided not to notify Salvadora when the child was born and chose a Spanish godmother, "but the Lord foiled their plans with a special circumstance." Even though the baby was born early, Salvadora, although not informed of the birth, suddenly arrived at the home and in fact participated as the godmother in the child's baptism.[11]

After moving to the region near Querétaro, Salvadora's father had enough land to sustain his family of ten children (Salvadora being the last) and a herd of sheep that provided wool for their clothing. As a young woman, "she ardently wished to learn how to read," since she thought that books would show her with certainty the way to heaven. Father Paredes described how she taught herself to read and write, not giving this extraordinary achievement much notice: "[She] directed all her efforts toward learning, but not having a teacher to guide her, gained knowledge of the letters by asking whomever could help her. Afterward, with great work and dedication she joined the letters together, until she was able to understand the words and read books. She also proceeded in the same way to form letters, imitating what she observed in manuscripts."[12]

Besides farming, Salvadora's father worked as a guide and companion to traders and businessmen in their travels. At times his children accompanied him to Querétaro and stayed in the house of his employer, Don Juan de Dios Estrada. One Christmas Salvadora joined Estrada's family as they visited the Nativity crib scenes displayed in homes, churches, and convents around the city. One beautiful arrangement was in front of a small house, the abode of a group of lay women, known as *beatas,* who were following the religious life without being nuns or living in a convent. Inspired by the beauty of the Nativity scene and especially by the shepherds near the crib, Salvadora requested that she be able to join the group of women and help them by doing the chores and seeking donations.[13]

Thus began the part of her life that most interested the author Antonio de Paredes. For twenty-six years until her death, Salvadora served the *beatas,* washing clothes, weaving cloth, carrying water, cleaning, and especially traveling in the city and surrounding farms to collect funds and donations of grain or food for her companions. The people considered her an expert in herbal medicine and especially consoling in her treatment of the sick; she calmed them by placing her hands on their bodies and praying the Magnificat in Latin "with barbarous pronunciation," as noted by Paredes.[14]

Additionally, Salvadora had a gift with animals, "such as that of our first parents during the few days they lived in paradise." Often while she was weaving in the yard, in a kneeling position with her loom tied to an orange tree and around her waist, the songbirds she kept in a cage came out the open hatch door "and going down the loom and along the cloth, climbed onto her head, then to her shoulder and from there to her back."[15]

One of the events that astounded her neighbors concerned a song bird, the famous Mexican tzenzontle. A wealthy benefactress, having to travel from the city for a few days, left her tzenzontle, "the love and delight of her life," in the care of the sisters. But they were careless while opening the cage to feed it and the bird escaped. Enjoying its newfound freedom, it flew high into the trees and crossed over to the orchard of the next house. All the women ran, calling and trying to get the bird back, praying to their favorite saint and begging their neighbor, "a goodly Indian," to help them. The Indian did all he could, but the bird did not want to be caught, perching in the very top of a tree. After three hours Salvadora arrived from her travels around the city "and chattering in a high voice to the fugitive tzenzontle exclaimed 'Disobedient little bird, what are you up to? Come back to your little cage.' Upon hearing her speak, the bird returned to its cage." The event frightened Salvadora's Indian assistant, and he ran to tell the *beatas* who asked him how Salvadora had done it. He responded by "shrugging his shoulders, arching his eyebrows and crossing his arms, all filled with confusion and stuttering in half words, only could blurt out: 'Here Madre Salvadora unable to go any further.'" So Salvadora explained that the bird had returned because of its love for food, but "the word got out about the happening in all of the city and no one doubted in recurring in their troubles to the help of the saintly Indian."[16]

Other narrations concerned Salvadora's ability to read the thoughts of others, to console them in their tribulations, or to counsel them when they were lying. On one occasion she predicted the death of a baby. Many claimed that she could help find lost or stolen articles. Once some valuable candlesticks disappeared; they belonged to the wife of Captain José Velázquez de Lorea, captain of the feared rural police (the *Acordada*). The woman sought the aid of the soldiers, of the saints, and of Salvadora, for she was "very fearful of the great harangue she would receive from her husband." As was her custom, Salvadora said she would ask the *beatas* to pray for the cause since she never assumed the role of directly interceding with the Lord. After eight days a friar returned the stolen items that had been left anonymously at his home. The lady went to the *beaterio* to announce the intercession of Salvadora and spread the same news in the city.[17]

Salvadora often traveled outside Querétaro to pick up donations from hacienda owners and Indian farmers. Once a group of teenagers gathered on a street corner were trying to saddle and ride a wild horse. They finally got the saddle on, but no one dared to mount the animal. When Salvadora passed by they challenged her: "Salvadora, here's this horse for you so you can go and beg for alms. Are you brave enough to ride it?" Salvadora responded in her usual manner: "With the grace of God, why not?" The owners responded, "Well, here it is for you until noon." Salvadora put her foot in the stirrup, sat upon the saddle and rode away, being sure to return the animal on time, "with a great improvement in the horse's behavior, testified by people worthy of good faith and of distinction in the city. These special happenings, which upon being spread about, made her famous in Querétaro, not only among the common people but also among the wealthy of the city."[18]

In two instances Father Paredes reported sinister occurrences. Once Salvadora was on the road to the city of Salamanca in order to collect alms when suddenly a cowboy appeared at her side, "as evil looking as he was uninhibited," and with words and actions he invited her to sin. Salvadora, fleeing from danger, said to the treacherous man: "Get away from me. Look, I have in my defense the staff of Señor Saint Joseph." The cowboy tried to come near, and Salvadora, taking out her spindle, which she carried with her, stuck him with it so hard that he jumped back from her. Paredes commented: "Because at that instant he disappeared from sight, one can say with good reason, that the being was the spirit of darkness, which in the figure of the cowboy came to see if he could break her vow of chastity."[19]

In a similar vein, in relation to Salvadora's great patience, Paredes tells the story of how Salvadora, when traveling to the town of Apaseo, met a hermit who spent a good part of the trip insulting her: she was a vagabond, a trickster, someone who wanted everyone to consider her a saint; that she, like all women, should stay at home and not go adventuring on the road. Moreover, he wondered if she had a license for soliciting donations. Despite these harsh words, the author noted that "Salvadora, in imitation of the Divine Savior, was deaf to the insults and never opened her mouth to defend herself." At this point the hermit went his own way but strayed into a swamp, covering his foot with mud. He demanded that Salvadora "the fake *beata*," help him as Christ had done with his apostles, and so she washed his foot. The hermit, however, made fun of her, called her a hypocrite and, after threatening her, he was gone. Father Paredes interpreted the event in the following way: "The never-before-seen attire of the man and his insistence on provoking Salvadora to anger give grounds to say that the hermit was not a human person but the devil who wanted to try her patience but could not, because grace was working in Salvadora."[20]

Hagiography about Indians

In the sixteenth century, after the Spanish conquest, friars and Indians began gathering facts on the lives of saintly natives. By the eighteenth century a few narratives had been published: for example, about Juan Diego and the Virgin of Guadalupe and of the child martyrs of Tlaxcala (comparing them to the two fourth-century children, Justo and Pastor, killed by Diocletian in Spain).[21]

Interest in holy Indians increased because of the desire of various native, ecclesiastical, and governmental leaders to establish convents for Indian women in New Spain. To counteract the negative opinions concerning the ability of the natives to adhere to the vow of chastity as required in monastic life, those in favor of a new convent pointed to examples of pious Indian virgins whose lives were recorded in manuscripts and in printed form as part of larger works.[22] The most important published biography was that of Catherine Tekakwitha, an Iroquois Indian who lived in French Canada. Originally written in French by a Jesuit, Pierre Colonec, and published in Paris in 1717, the biography was translated into Spanish by another Jesuit living in Mexico City, Juan de Urtassum, and published in Mexico City in 1724,[23] precisely when ecclesiastical and civil authorities were debating the feasibility of founding a convent for Indian noble women. In the volume Urtassum described the hardships, sickness, and devotional life of Catherine, who, as a convert to Catholicism, suffered for her faith among the hostile members of the pagan Indian society and found refuge in the new Christian community formed in Canada. Included in the book with Catherine's biography, the Mexican priest Juan Ignacio de Castorena y Ursua offered a defense of the Mexican Indian noblewomen who would enter the projected convent of Corpus Christi, showing that they had all the qualities needed to be nuns and even exceeded many Spanish women in their abnegation and ability in the Latin language. He also referred to the pre-Hispanic maidens who cared for the sacred rites of the Aztec religion and lived as virgins in a sheltered environment, comparing them to the vestal virgins of Ancient Rome. What tipped the debate in favor of the establishment of an Indian convent was the viceroy's donation of forty thousand pesos for constructing the building and chapel. The convent of Corpus Christi, following the Franciscan rules of Saint Clare, opened in 1724.[24]

By the time Paredes wrote his edifying letter in 1762, however, it was no longer necessary to present a labored defense of the virtues of Indian women, since two convents had already been opened for them, Corpus Christi and one established in 1737 for noble Tarascan women in Valladolid (now called Morelia). Instead the focus of the book was different, narrating the daily experiences, extraordinary virtues, and probable instances of divine intercession concerning a woman well known to the inhabitants of Querétaro, in order that her life be imitated.

The pious content of the book is of a hagiographic nature. As Antonio Rubial has pointed out, two types of hagiography existed in New Spain.[25] Some works published from 1680 to 1730 specifically aimed at promoting the cause of the beatification of nuns, hermits, and bishops. Others, especially the edifying letters of the Jesuits, were designed to inform readers about exceptionally holy persons so as to promote them as models of virtue. These biographies and others in the form of funeral sermons were not part of the four-step ecclesiastical process for beatification or canonization ordered by the pope in 1640. Moreover, for the ecclesiastical process to begin, ten years had to pass after the death of the subject.

The biography of Salvadora is of the second type, somewhat similar to the first, but not following its baroque language, sentiments, and interpretations. By the middle of the eighteenth century when Paredes published, the style of writing and the tone of the biographies were more rational and less emotional, avoiding explicit affirmations and descriptions of supernatural visions, diabolical presences, and sexual temptations.

Paredes presented the life and times of Salvadora and the society of Querétaro as if he were en external observer. Only in the last pages did he indicate indirectly that he was present at Salvadora's deathbed. But in fact Paredes probably knew Salvadora well and certainly had contact with the *beatas*. Born in 1691 in San Juan de los Llanos, Puebla, he lived in Querétaro as a professor of theology in the Jesuit college from 1725 to 1743, returning there in 1751 for one or two years as rector of the college and probably again in 1762.[26] The Jesuit documents describe him in the following manner: "Of good intellect, judgment and literature; of normal prudence; having some experience; of a melancholy complexion; of talent for writing and priestly ministries."[27] Nevertheless in his narrative the priest did not mention that he had an intimate knowledge of the Indian woman.

When he wrote about the ceremony in which the archbishop gave his authorization for the *beaterio,* Paredes did not inform the reader that he himself was present and in fact delivered the sermon. Then he was appointed as the confessor of the *beatas*. He gave weekly talks to the sisters and prepared the statutes for the organization of their religious life according to the rule of Saint Teresa of Avila.

Probably Paredes served as the confessor not only to the sisters but also to Salvadora from 1740 until 1743 when he left for Mexico City and Puebla.[28]

Paredes's View of Salvdora de los Santos

As the biography unfolds, it is obvious that Father Paredes liked and admired Salvadora. Perhaps she was one of the few women that the priest accepted. With regard to the *beatas,* he was ambivalent. At times he referred to them as angels and as the hidden spiritual treasure of the city. But it seems that he gave more weight to negative ideas. They were demanding and inconsiderate of Salvadora, hypochondriacs who rarely appreciated her services and sometimes insulted and made fun of her. The Jesuit also rejected the wealthy women of Querétaro, for in the last judgment the voice of the archangel would sound "to condemn many Spanish women considered noble and knowledgeable, with more aids, lights and means, but filled with worldly pleasures [who] did not want to follow the road to heaven, when a poor, rustic, and scorned Indian, obtained in this world great progress which we piously believe will have won her much glory."

Page by page Salvadora's timid and solitary personality blossoms to reveal a charitable, competent woman who overcame difficult circumstances in the outside world while the sisters, on account of the cloister rules, stayed within the *beaterio;* thus the *beatas* were unable to reveal themselves as interesting or likable persons. The Otomi Indian emerges as a virtuous individual who is well aware that her life, as Saint Paul writes, was a "race" in which one must strive for holiness, combat evil, and sacrifice oneself for others. As Asunción Lavrin has pointed out, what is distinctive about Salvadora de los Santos is that an Indian woman was considered a model of piety for the elite of Querétaro, "certainly new in the discourse of spirituality."[29]

True to hagiographic form, the Jesuit commented that it was only owing to God's grace that Salvadora was able to overcome her rustic background (which he repeatedly mentions) and achieve holiness. He also gave credit to Salvadora herself for developing abilities that enabled her to serve the sisters for twenty-six years. (He repeats the cipher of twenty-six years at various times, obviously impressed by this.) Although he could not rid himself of the notion that Salvadora, being an Otomi, was from a barbarous nation, almost all of his text shows her as an able, hard-working and even smart individual who interacted with all social classes and ethnic groups. Paredes observed: "Although simple, Salvadora was not stupid. She could speak with intelligence when considered necessary: thus if the point of Divine Providence came under discussion, she fervently talked about the Lord in such a way that by her reasoning she surpassed her interrogator: for in a few words she said a lot."[30]

According to Paredes, the greatest virtue of Salvadora de los Santos, even above chastity, poverty, and humility, was her extraordinary patience, her ability to put up with the harsh treatment of the women she was serving:

> The sisters, although virtuous people, as women had their temperaments, some tedious, others violent, others harsh, and if Salvadora was not able to please them in what they ordered her to do, the response was scolding, nicknames and nasty remarks. Confronted with this, the patient Indian didn't let it bother her, continuing to try to serve them in whatever way possible. Nothing in my opinion proved the virtue of Salvadora as much as this constant mortification during twenty-six years. Although it had come from only one person that she was serving, to have tolerated it for such a long time would be much admired: but being many, now it is seen, that in serving them she refined her patience to be invincible to the blows which they inflicted on her as with so many hammers.[31]

Part of the poor treatment toward Salvadora was probably due her being an Indian. Most of the day she was outside the *beaterio,* but when she was there at midday she did not eat with the sisters but rather in the kitchen, sitting on the floor. Nor did she sleep in the rooms with the others, having built her own hut in the patio. If she had been a Spaniard, probably she would have been a formal member and not a *donada,* that is, one who donates her services in a convent. She did, however, participate with the *beatas* in daily Mass and Communion and in the specified hours of prayer and singing. This could have been because of a changing attitude of the church, which was becoming more inclusive since the two convents for Indian noblewomen had proven that the natives were capable of observing the strict religious life.

On three occasions Paredes observed that the Indians in the market, a benefactress, and the city itself considered Salvadora a "saintly Indian." Twice the author himself directly affirmed that she was a "saintly Indian."[32] When the author referred to Salvadora's taming of the wild horse, he used the phrase "could be called a miracle," and when Salvadora revived a dead chicken the observers spread the news as a "miraculous" event. In general the author was careful not to affirm divine intervention or approval of Salvadora's life, but his admiration of her virtue is constant and he was impressed by the fact that she predicted the exact hour and day of her death.[33]

The Indians' View of Salvadora

The Indians of New Spain knew Salvadora de los Santos at two different points in time: those from Querétaro were in personal contact with her from 1736 to

1762 when she was living in the city and those Indian authorities from Mexico City knew her indirectly through Paredes's biography from 1763 to 1821.

Not only in the market but also among the general Indian population, Salvadora was known for the help she could give to those in need, whether it be to apply homemade medicines to the sick, to comfort pregnant women, to recover a lost chicken, or to assist somehow in obtaining a good sale of vegetables. She also helped to cure sores and wounds with ointments, but the Indians who came for her assistance "confided more in the hand of the anointer than in the medicine." Often the sick waited for her outside the *beaterio* and upon recovering they often returned to thank her. Therefore she had a large following among the natives who never refused to do her bidding: [34] "On the feast days of the *beaterio* the street was filled with drums, clarinets, chirimias [flutes] and trumpets that the Indians brought from the barrios. They came to play their instruments without any pay and only because Salvadora had invited them."[35] The natives called her Mother Salvadora, remembering how she had coaxed the tzenzontle into its cage or treated the sick with "motherly love." This tendency continued among the Indians of Mexico City since in their financial accounts they mentioned expenditures for the book about "Mother Salvadora."

The Aztec Indian governmental authorities in Mexico City had a somewhat different view of Salvadora from that of the Otomi Indians of Querétaro. They had never met Salvadora and knew her only through her biography. For the Indians of Mexico Salvadora emerged as an outstanding woman, an example for other natives and for all of society. It can be assumed that they were less interested in her as a holy person than as a leader.

This view is reflected in the modifications to the book's title for the editions of 1784 and 1791. First of all, they suppressed the word *donada,* that is, "donated," perhaps feeling that this term put Salvadora in a subservient position, as a helper to the *beatas.* They also left out the geographic description "of the beaterio of the Carmelites of the City of Querétaro." Hence in the title Salvadora emerged as a person for the whole country and not specific to Querétaro. In addition the title included only one of the three outstanding characteristics of the Otomi woman, her "exemplary life," and left out what Paredes had included in the first two editions: her "solid virtues and holy death." The changes might have resulted from the desire to make the title shorter and to focus more directly on her life rather than on her holiness and her death.

What is clear, however, is that for the Indians of Mexico City Salvadora was a role model for native schoolchildren. They emphasized her honored position among the urban and rural populations and declared that she was a person whom the students could follow while maintaining their own ethnic identity. Indeed in

1784 the Indian governors added the following prologue to the Paredes biography: "The reprint of this Edifying Letter has the recommendable objective of providing the schools and migas [girls' schools] where our children are educated with a type of reading primer in which, while teaching them to read, they learn at the same time to imitate Christian virtues with the sweet, powerful and natural attractiveness of seeing them practiced by a person of their same lineage."[36]

For thirty-seven years the native children who studied in the schools financed by the Indian municipal authorities in the Valley of Mexico came to know Salvadora de los Santos as the heroine of an interesting story.[37] As they read about her life, they probably were entertained by her familiarity with animals, scared by her adventures on the road, impressed by her charitable works, and pleased by her honored place as one of the most outstanding and interesting members of a multiracial society.

The *Beatas'* View of Salvadora

The women who lived in Querétaro's *beaterio* were not wealthy. This lack of means meant they could not pay the dowry needed to join a convent, so they gathered together as members of the Third Order of Carmelites, an organization of laywomen who did not take solemn vows but rather simple vows of poverty, chastity, and obedience.[38]

The author mentioned only a few instances concerning the treatment of the sisters toward Salvadora, almost all showing a lack of consideration, "injustices," "offenses" and "scorn."[39] The doorkeeper scolded her for coming in late from her rounds. The cook at times forgot to give Salvadora her second course. The sisters complained that the water wheel squeaked as Salvadora brought up the buckets, so that she had to pull the buckets up by hand in order not to make noise.[40]

Almost no signs of gratitude are reported, nor of companionship with the sisters. But perhaps there was some friendship and care, since the author mentions a custom that indicates a certain closeness and esteem among the sisters: when Salvadora was greeted with an embrace by one of the *beatas,* the bronze crucifix she wore around her neck, cut into her skin, another corporal punishment that she inflicted upon herself. And the sisters expressed their admiration for Salvadora when she presented theatrical plays and songs in the *beaterio* at Christmas time. Laughingly they enjoyed the poems and dances that she prepared, amazed that "an Otomi Indian could present such a combination of words, actions and sentiments."[41]

But, all in all, during the years she served in the *beaterio,* not a kind word of appreciation by the sisters was recorded in the biography. Probably the women had assumed the attitudes of the wealthy nuns in other convents who often had a number of lay women as servants. Thus they took Salvadora for granted, when in fact only she was sustaining the eighteen women.

Even as Salvadora took ill at the end of her life, the superior reprimanded her for lying down on the floor of the choir room in such an irreverent position. This time Salvadora did not obey by standing up but rather asked permission to stay there since it would be the last time she participated in the ceremony.

It was just in the last hours of her life that Salvadora found herself "amidst the tears and sighs of the sisters who surrounded her bed, feeling the loss of the one to whom they owed in great part the survival of the beaterio" for they "felt like orphans with the absence of the one who had been their mother." But apparently they never expressed these emotions to Salvadora when she was alive. The *beatas* finally "glorified at having had her as their companion and sister, giving example to them and to outsiders."[42]

Querétaro's View of Salvadora

In contrast to the lack of appreciation on the part of the sisters toward Salvadora, the city of Querétaro showed her many signs of acceptance and affection, although such was not always the case at the beginning. When Salvadora began serving the sisters by searching for donations in the streets, market, homes, and haciendas, her figure attracted attention and sometimes disparagement as she passed by dressed in a type of homemade Carmelite habit. This reaction was not so much because she was an Indian but because she was a *beata*: "The common-ers whistled at her as to a simpleton, some saying she was a hypocrite, others using mocking words and others calling her a deceiving *beata,* deluded and full of cer-emonial attitudes."[43] But as time passed her virtue became well known, and the people admired her kind, humble manner, as well as her intercession and prayers on their behalf.

> Outside the urban center, she visited haciendas and traveled to distant cities, such as Salvatierra, Valladolid [now Morelia], and Apaseo, some 125 miles away. She made trips to farms and markets, gathering wheat and corn; some called her the "grain-carrying ant." As time passed the inhabitants of Querétaro recognized her wherever she went. Salvadora was tall in stature, hefty for work and of notorious virtue. She walked with a grave pace, her eyes cast downward, and with great modesty. She always had her hands occupied—either with a rosary or with some type of weaving. She spoke lit-tle, and only when asked a question. Her attire was more than lowly; it was ludicrous because she wore a small cape of sackcloth, a covering for her head of coarse canvas, and hanging from her shoulders a big white sombrero like those used by the Carmelite priests, while under her arm a basket in which

she gathered her donations. The figure was strange and it could not help but provoke laughter to see an Indian who with a serious countenance was dressed in such a habit which seemed fit for a masquerade.[44]

At first she was an object of scorn, but as she became known, the scorn turned into veneration. Paredes observed that "even the youngsters, who on any occasion make fun of someone seen on the street who looks strange, always went up to greet her kindly." The neighbors living near the *beaterio,* "witnessing her prudence and simplicity, grew to love her." They helped her grind corn and carry water. For instance the boys living on the same street first fetched water for Salvadora and then carried some to their homes.[45] The commoners and the Indians were not the only ones who esteemed her; "the most illustrious inhabitants of the city [also] granted her recognition and courtesy spreading her fame in Querétaro." With great detail and, at times, giving names and locations, events described in the biography revealed how Salvadora helped the wealthy, as when she revived a dead baby chicken; when she interceded to recover lost candlesticks; when she read the thoughts of a troubled matron; when she convinced a wayward songbird to return to its cage; when she knew that a housewife was hiding the truth; when she recovered from a mysterious traveler some valuable objects that had been stolen from a priest.[46] Paredes concluded: "Adding the testimony of this cleric to those others here recorded, there is no doubt that Salvadora's fame could have given her abundant reason to be proud; but neither the honors nor the applause penetrated her heart."[47]

Salvadora's View of Herself

In her early years as a shepherd Salvadora led a solitary life in the countryside. She loved being alone so she could pray, spin coarse wool into yarn, and be in contact with animals and birds. Yet she also showed traits of sociability, enjoying trips into the city of Querétaro and friendship with the daughters of her father's employer. In her activities as a provider of food and funds for the *beatas,* Salvadora overcame her tendency to silence and solitude (and perhaps her natural timidity) whenever contact with others would be of benefit to the sisters. In fact she was quite astute in planning the time, place, and manner of soliciting donations from wealthy merchants and landowners.[48]

On eleven occasions Paredes presented scenes in which he directly quoted Salvadora's conversations revealing her intelligence, courage, and a sense of humor.[49] She also had her own type of religious devotions. Of course Mass and Communion were central, but she chose additional devotions: praying the rosary while traveling to collect alms, singing hymns from the *Aljaba Apostólico* (*Apostolic Quiver*) while staying at wayside inns, and the reciting of the Magnificat in Latin while attending patients.[50] Perhaps her choice of the Magnificat had to do with her perception of the unsettling, revolutionary content of the prayer:

> My soul doth magnify the Lord,
> and my spirit hath rejoiced in God my Saviour.
> For he hath regarded the lowliness of his handmaiden.
> . . . .
> He hath scattered the proud in the imagination of their hearts.
>
> He hath put down the mighty from their seat
> and hath exalted the humble and meek.
> He hath filled the hungry with good things.
> And the rich he hath sent away empty.

As is characteristic of hagiographic texts, Paredes pointed out that Salvadora was conscious of the fact that her life was a constant combat: to serve the *beatas*, to endure personal hardships, to reach out to help others, to spread the faith, and to strive for eternal life.[51]

When she had a high fever and was sick for several days, Salvadora, surrounded by the *beatas* and several priests, showed a determined personality. For example, when she asked the chaplain to sing a hymn to the Virgin Mary, "he, thinking she was affected by fever, pretended not to hear her; Salvadora started to sing herself and he was obliged to sing along." Paredes reported that "on the tenth day of her illness, Salvadora told everyone not to worry since she would not die immediately but two days later and at three in the morning."[52]

Even in her last hours she was acutely aware of her life's work and of the efforts she had made to fulfill her duties. "She raised her eyes to God and said with a clear voice 'Oh Lord, I did what I could: from now on you will have to care of your spouses.'" She assumed her responsibility as the only link of the cloistered sisters with the outside world. And, as she had predicted, on Tuesday morning, August 25, 1762, she died at 3:00 A.M.[53]

Gender and Sexuality in Eighteenth-century Querétaro

The biography by Paredes sheds light on aspects of gender and sexuality in a specific part of eighteenth-century New Spain. It is important to remember that the setting of Querétaro presents social and ethnic situations that were not typical of the other nineteen cities in the country.[54] These aspects must be taken into account in assessing the role of an Indian woman in a place that was originally founded as a native town. In 1530 a group of Indian nobles of the region allied with the Spaniards in order to defeat the rest of the indigenous warriors. They were rewarded with appointments to head the local government of the new settlement and dominated economic and political life for a century.

By the middle of the next century an influx of Spaniards settled in Querétaro, becoming prosperous merchants and hacienda owners. The population of Indians and non-Indians also grew rapidly. Through large donations to the king, those of Spanish descent ("criollos") were in 1656 able to obtain for Querétaro the status of a city and permission to form a Spanish municipal government council, although the city was still a place where the Indians, who were numerous, some with prosperous economic positions, continued to conserve their local government. In fact, at the time Salvadora lived there Querétaro was larger than New York City.[55] Of the 31,500 inhabitants, 48 percent were Otomi Indinas, 10 percent were persons of African descent, and 42 percent mestizos and persons of Spanish descent.[56] This multiethnic mix with a high percentage of Indians was not typical of most of the other Spanish cities where the number of indigenous persons was generally small because the great majority of the natives lived in towns throughout the country. Thus by the eighteenth century the Indians of Querétaro enjoyed diminished political power but continued to govern in their own Indian municipal council (called the republic), collecting the tribute and administering justice for the Indian population, while the Spanish municipal council ("ayuntamiento") governed the other inhabitants.[57]

In this setting Salvadora held a high position since she was of a noble Indian family. Paredes noted this fact directly by saying that her parents were nobles, and indirectly, since he preceded the names of her father and mother with the titles of *Don* and *Doña* but for her Spanish godparents used their names without such titles. Thus by her very ancestry Salvadora was a special person in Querétaro. Hers was one of 197 cacique families in the city, a large number in comparison with the rest of the country.[58] Every year the inhabitants witnessed the annual elections in Querétaro in which noble Indian electors voted for the governor, judges, and aldermen who formed the municipal council.[59] The natives living in the city intermingled with Spaniards, mestizos, and black people. There were never any restrictions concerning the residence of the Indians. The census of 1791 showed Indian homes, some as costly and as fine as those of Spaniards, located in all parts of the city.[60] In fact, next door to the *beaterio* the owner of an orchard was a "goodly Indian." Salvadora and her sisters often stayed in the home of her father's employer, a wealthy businessman of Spanish descent.

Salvadora enjoyed high status among the Indians because of her nobility. They considered her a holy person and a revered friend. Salvadora did not cut off her contacts with the natives, often visiting them in the marketplace where she purchased products for the sisters and gathered donations in kind from the merchants. As Paredes noted: "Since she was an Indian, the venders looked on her with love, celebrating that one of their own was said to be a saint." They offered fruit, cheese, cream, tomatoes, squash, and maize to her, sometimes with such generosity that Salvadora had to make three trips to bring all the donations to the *beaterio.*[61]

In at least three areas Salvadora acted in a manner distinct from the social norms for women in that period. She learned to read and write when some parents worried that if their daughters knew how to write they would exchange letters with their suitors. Even in 1815 a teacher in Mexico City found that manner of thinking in vogue. He informed the municipal council: "Some parents do not allow their daughters to learn to read or write with the stubborn excuse that thereby the girls cannot be seduced by love letters."[62]

As Paredes noted, Salvador walked with her eyes downcast, a sign of modesty. Pre-Hispanic rules also required such demeanor as well as that girls stay within the family. Spanish norms insisted that a woman's place was in the home, caring for her husband and children. This insistence was shared in the early nineteenth century by José Joaquín Fernández de Lizardi, author of a novel about two diametrically different cousins. In contrast to many of his liberal social and political opinions, Lizardi wrote that because women were physically weaker than men, they should be protected. Moreover, this protection included avoiding social gatherings outside the home and going out only to Mass. He advised parents not to send their daughters to the dame schools ("amigas"), but rather to educate them at home, for they could learn bad habits by being with other children.[63]

However, Salvador, having the specific task of sustaining the *beatas,* was free from this generalized role for women. Society allowed her to be out on the streets and highways, presenting, of course, a reserved manner. That she knew how to ride a horse and gladly jumped into the saddle on a wild steed might have surprised the reader of Paredes's biography. Apparently, however, this was not an extremely unusual occurrence. As a noble Indian she was permitted to ride. In the case described by Paredes in the biography, the saddle was likely not a sidesaddle, which would be the type used by women at that time. In the end the important point was that the Indian woman immediately tamed the horse rather than that she knew how to ride.

Because she was a *donada* it is unusual that Salvadora did not have as her confessor the Carmelite priest who was the chaplain of the *beaterio.* Instead, in 1746 she began confessing with the Franciscan priest Juan Domingo de Arricivita and continued to do so for sixteen years until her death.[64] Perhaps this change of confessor was a result of her independent spirit or to the fact that Arricivita probably understood the Otomi language, since he was the director of the Missionary College of the Holy Cross, the most numerous religious group in the city.

Besides emphasis on demure conduct and womanly tasks in the home, in eighteenth-century Querétaro three cultural inheritances influenced the role of women in society: the norms of the pre-Hispanic Otomi Indian culture, the

Moorish tradition present during eight centuries of domination in Spain, and the Spanish Catholic culture. All required that women conserve their virginity until marriage. With regard to sexuality outside of marriage, the Catholic religion considered adultery and impure desires to be violations of the sixth and ninth commandments.[65] Thus chastity, a virtue to be strived for by both men and women, meant purity in body and mind. Since religion permeated all aspects of the society of New Spain, it reinforced the role women inherited from their ancestors concerning sexual purity.

Although chastity and sexual restraint were expected of both men and women, in reality they were essentially feminine requirements that males could violate without loss of family or personal honor. Promiscuity and illegitimate births existed among all ethnic groups, although at higher rates in the cities and much lower among the Indians in rural areas. In the countryside, guided by a combination of indigenous community norms and Catholic religious practices, marriage was practically universal and illegitimate births almost nonexistent.[66] With regard to an urban setting, statistics for a Mexico City parish in 1777 show that illegitimate births occurred at a higher percentage among black people and mulattoes (24 percent), than among Spaniards and mestizos (20 percent), and Indians (17 percent).[67] Given the fact that Indians formed a much larger part of the population of Quertéaro (48 percent) than of Mexico City (12 percent), a survey of illegitimate births would probably show a lower percentage in Querétaro than in the capital city.

Given the social and religious norms, Salvadora became even more prestigious by taking the vow of chastity in January of 1737. Because of this "she could not marry [for] she had dedicated the treasure of her virginity to tender Jesus, recognizing him from that moment on as her husband."[68] She, like the other Spanish women in the religious community, took simple vows that could be modified in contrast to formal vows taken by nuns in a convent, which were obligatory for life. Although a bit less prestigious than cloistered nuns, the *beatas* were a group of eighteen women who were well respected and honored by all the inhabitants since their *beaterio* was officially authorized by the archbishop in 1740. Because Salvadora could travel outside the walls of the *beaterio*, the population knew that she was not on the same level as the cloistered *beatas* were, but because she had taken a vow and was living as a member of the *beaterio*, she eventually was respected by all.

At the beginning people made fun of her or even insulted her as a "fake" *beata*. This treatment could be attributed to her position as an Indian, although it seems that other non-Indian women also were rebuffed by the inhabitants when they presented themselves as *beatas*. A true *beata* had to prove herself to a suspicious population who liked to insult and belittle those who might be fooling them.

It seems that at this time in Querétaro, and perhaps in other cities, a good number of women presented themselves in this manner, some holy and helpful but others of dubious conduct. Such a position was perhaps sought out since it enabled single women to have more freedom, be admired, and obtain donations and some economic advantages. It could represent an alternative to the restrictions on movement in a closed family atmosphere experienced by single women of the upper and middle classes. Paredes indicated that there was a plague of such women in Querétaro and other cities, "women who are always using mysterious words praying the rosary in their hands, visiting the sick, staying in church venerated as saints receiving alms and the first place in public gatherings."[69] The apparent freedom of these women indicates the ineffective control of the church over their activities.

The manner in which Paredes treats the subject of chastity in the biography indicates the changing attitudes of mid-eighteenth-century Querétaro. The opinion that Indian women were not capable of observing the vow of chastity had been discarded because of the continued existence of two convents for Indian nuns. On the one hand, Paredes stresses that Salvadora really had little trouble in maintaining her chastity, for she was of an innocent nature and by living as a shepherdess in the countryside was able to devote her time to weaving, prayer, and watching the sheep, far from temptation. The author further reflects that in her numerous activities of collecting donations, imposing corporal penances upon herself, caring for the *beatas,* and devoting hours to constant prayer, Salvadora remained free from temptations to her chastity. Because of her vow the native men did not flirt with her, respecting that she was a "holy woman."

Unlike some seventeenth-century hagiographic works, Paredes's biography did not overemphasize Salvadora's virginity. In fact, Paredes mentions Salvadora's purity and innocence briefly four times in the biography[70] and spends at least eight pages describing different aspects of her patience and humility.[71] Curiously, he was obviously very impressed by her ability to weave cloth, decorate textiles with beautiful flowers, and mend clothes for the poor, referring to these talents at various times.[72]

The Life of Salvadora Compared with Other Biographies

Although Antonio de Paredes is named as the author of the edifying letter, probably he was not the only author and perhaps not the principal one. Since the biography includes episodes and conversations that occurred when Paredes was not in Querétaro (1743–50; 1752–61), the information about Salvadora during those years could have come from her confessor, Friar Arricivita, who lived in the convent of Santa Cruz, located on a hill in the eastern part of the city.[73] Possibly he kept notes on her spiritual development and took an interest in making them known to others upon her death. Certainly it would have been easier for the Jesuit Paredes to publish the biography, since the order had its own printing press in Mexico City.

In order to contextualize the style and content of the biography of Salvadora de los Santos, the book by Paredes can be examined in relation to similar works of the period. From 1752 to 1765 five funeral sermons presented the lives of pious women.[74] Two concerned lay women and three memorialized nuns. In the sermons four of the orators described the life of the subject by means of metaphors and comparisons: the Michoacan bee, the mystical marvelous stone, the builder of three houses, and the mirror of water and light. Most of the biographies related a few incidents in the early life of the subjects that were somehow related to holiness, divine protection, and future virtue. Likewise, at death the subject was surrounded by others drawn to her side by the completion of a holy and dedicated existence. One of the nuns had been married before entering the convent, but the sermons made almost no mention of her family nor did they give details about the husbands and children of the married laywomen. Only of interest was her life within the convent. The virtues mentioned with regard to the nuns were humility, obedience, acceptance of sickness, and fasting, while the laywomen were praised for helping the poor, prayer, and serving as good examples. Only in one of the biographies, that of the laywoman from Michoacan, did the orator present conversations of the lady with her confessor (who is not named) and reproduced direct quotes by the subject. Never did the authors say that any of these women were saintly nor did they report that others considered the subjects to be holy. For the laywomen the adjectives employed were *"virtuous* and *venerable* and the noun used was *heroine.* The authors considered the nuns to be "wise," "prudent," and "patient."

However, quite different from the funeral sermons were the three edifying letters published by Jesuits in 1758, 1763, and 1764. These authors obviously had personal knowledge of the subjects and verified facts about them from their close associates. Their main objective was to publicize the holy life of Jesuits and not to create oratorical gems, as seemed to have been the case of the funeral sermons. In addition to the biography of Salvadora de los Santos, the only other edifying letter written by Antonio de Paredes narrated the life of the Jesuit Francisco Xavier Sochiaga.[75] Similar to the title of Salvdora's biography, the title of this work referred to the "solid virtues and holy death" of Sochiaga but substituted the expression "religious posts" for the "exemplary life" of Salvadora. Paredes presented Sochiaga's life in chronological order, noting that he was born in Querétaro, a region of "fertile soil" and "eternal spring," and as a student in Mexico, five Jesuits, whose names were stated, influenced the young man. Posts in parishes in Puebla, in colleges in Guatemala, and in difficult missionary activities in

Nicaragua were followed by his return to Mexico where he was the favorite orator of the viceroy. A professor in several Jesuit institutions, he died in the college in Puebla, where Paredes knew him personally. The biography includes conversations between Sochiaga and others and mentions several religious authorities, but only referred to some aspects of daily life in Central America without giving such information about the rest of Sochiaga's life in Mexico. Most attention was given to the subject's funeral, at which everyone wanted to obtain relics from his garb and personal belongings because of his fame as a "great Jesuit" and "meritorious man." At no time did Paredes describe the physical aspect of the subject, call him a "saintly" person, or present scenes of his life, as he did in the biography of Salvadora de los Santos.

The edifying letter written by Bartholomé Braun about the missionary activities of the German Jesuit Francisco Glandorf in the rugged mountains of Chihuahua was somewhat similar to the biography of Salvadora. Braun described various extraordinary incidents in the subject's life, reproducing Galndorf's conversations and statements by him. The author recorded the opinions of at least eleven clerics of different religious orders concerning the dedication and efficacy of the "apostolic life, virtues and holy death" of the Jesuit. The author described two extraordinary happenings: the great rapidity with which Glandorf traveled by foot in the rugged terrain, covering ground in three hours that by horse required a whole day; and the one-sentence description of heaven made at her own funeral by an Indian woman, after which she reclined in her coffin. The biography mentioned the opinion of others concerning Glandorf as "the apostle of the Tarahumara Indians," "such a saintly man," "such a saintly missionary," and "the holy apostle." In fact, at his death many took relics of the Jesuit and some wished to collect funds to promote his canonization. Braun on one occasion wrote that Glandorf was one among "saintly men." This edifying letter contained testimonies concerning the subject similar to those that would be used in a process for beatification. These therefore were more formal and less spontaneous compared to the descriptions of daily activities presented in the text of Paredes about Salvadora de los Santos Ramirez.

The third biography published by a Jesuit in this period treated the life of Francisco Javier Lascano, university professor and theologian. Its title did not include the term *edifying* and stated only that it was a "Letter about the life and death" of Lascano written by the rector of a Jesuit college, Salvador de la Gándara. At Lascano's demise many people close to the Jesuits, as well as civil authorities and the general public, acclaimed him as a "saint" and a "saintly man." A native of Puebla, Lascano lived in the same period as Salvadora de los Santos, 1702 to 1763. When he was young, he preferred prayer to playing with his companions. As a professor Lascano gave funds to students and poor children. When he died so many people came to his funeral that the doors had to be closed; the people yearned for relics of the Jesuit, "raising their voices to call him a saint or truly virtuous." His portrait was painted and hung in the chapel of the college. After presenting facts of Lascano's life, the author proceeded to relate his virtues: counsel to the afflicted, assistance to the victims of the smallpox epidemic, purity and humility. Although Gándara never stated directly that Lascano was "saintly," he did note that it was a well-founded opinion that he was a "saintly man." The author praised him as a wise Jesuit, serving many with his writings, virtue, and Christian charity, although the biography hardly mentioned his academic life. Cautiously the author stated that the authorities in Rome were the ones to verify the prophecies that Lascano had apparently made, although he did mention two of them: that a nun would become the abbess of her congregation and that a healthy child would soon die. This long account of 130 pages was somewhat disorganized in the presentation of Lascano's life and less readable than that of Glandorf and the two edifying letters of Paredes about Salvadora de los Santos and Father Sochiaga.

These letters and sermons reflected the situation at mid–eighteenth century, when the creoles (Spaniards born in New Spain) were eager to obtain the canonization of an American saint.[76] Only Saint Rose of Lima, Peru, had been so designated by the pope, and the inhabitants of Mexico desired that one of their own should be so honored, especially since many Spaniards were being canonized in the same period. A Mexican saint would prove the excellence of the kingdom and put it on an equal footing with the mother country. But the authors writing about deceased persons who were deemed to have led a holy life were careful in their use of the terms *saint* and *saintly*, since pontifical decrees greatly limited the proliferation of the term in religious writings. Thus the fact that Paredes referred to Salvador as a "saintly Indian" but did not state that Father Sochiaga was a "saintly man," and that the other authors, with the exception of Braun in reference to the missionary Glandorf, also refrained from directly appropriating the term for their own use, indicates that the Otomi Indian and the Jesuit Glandorf were considered in a special manner by their contemporaries and by the authors of their biographies.

The inclusion of realistically presented scenes in the biographies of Glandorf and Salvadora, as well as the reproduction of conversations, transforms at times these hagiographic biographies into works bordering on the historical. For example, in the Paredes book Salvadora's excursions into the market, her contacts with wealthy women, travels on the road by horseback, work in the *beaterio,* and musical presentations contain descriptions of everyday life in New Spain and provide a glimpse of Salvadora as a real person and not only as a model of virtue.

A portrait of Salvadora was probably painted soon after her death[77] and the following epitaph written at its base:

Dorothy Tanck de Estrada

SISTER SALVADORA DE LOS SANTOS, OTOMI INDIAN, DONATED TO THE BEATERIO
OF THE CARMELITAS OF QUERETARO: WHOM SHE SERVED FOR TWENTY-SIX
YEARS, SOLICITING DAY BY DAY DONATIONS FOR THEIR SUSTENANCE. SHE WAS
TRULY HUMBLE OF HEART, PURE BOTH IN BODY AND SOUL, AND A HOME
OF DIVINE LOVE. SHE DIED THE DEATH OF THE JUST, SINGING DIVINE PRAISES,
ON AUGUST 25, 1762 AT 61 YEARS OF AGE.
REST IN PEACE. AMEN.[78]

Epilogue

Six years after the death of Salvadora de los Santos, the *beatas* obtained the arch-bishop's permission to establish a boarding school for girls. This was necessary as a means of income, since they no longer had the help of Salvadora for their maintenance. Later in 1791 they were permitted to convert their establishment into a convent of Carmelite nuns and continue with educating approximately one hundred Spanish and Indian girls in a free primary school, supported in part by the municipal council of Querétaro.[79]

During the nineteenth century the boarding and day schools continued until the Reform Laws of the 1850s closed the convent. The building was converted into small apartments that were sold, and by the end of the twentieth century it was in poor condition. In the year 2000 the structure was completely renovated and converted into a boutique hotel. In the courtyard behind the hotel stands a big tree where one can imagine Salvadora weaving her cloth and chatting happily with the songbirds.

Notes

1. Antonio de Paredes, *Carta edificante en que el P. Antonio de Paredes refiere la exemplar vida, sólidas virtudes, y santa muerte de la hermana Salvadora de los Santos, india otomí, donada del beaterio de las carmelitas de la ciudad de Querétaro* (1762; reprint, Colegio de San Ildefonso, 1763), 69. The archbishop of Mexico considered the epidemic to be one of the three worst suffered in New Spain and described it as a combination of smallpox and "matlazáhuatl" (Archivo General de la Nación, *Epidemias,* vol. 13, exp. 2, 1762). Dionisio Martínez Pacheco, *México afligido. Carta métrica . sobre la epidemia de las viruelas acaecidas en este año de 1761* (México: Imprenta de D. Christobal y D. Felipe de Zúñiga, 1762).

2. Paredes writes that Salvadora's father was Joseph Ramirez (pp. 3, 15), while a manuscript about the history of the *beaterio* gives her father's name as Jose Ramos. See Josefina Muriel, "Notas para el estudio de la educación de la mujer durante el virreinato. El Real Colegio de San José de Gracia en la ciudad de Querétaro," *Estudios de Historia Novohispana* 5 (1976): 103.

3. The German scientist Alexander von Humboldt had been impressed in 1803 by the low mortality rate in New Spain, which was less than that of any country in Europe that he had studied and only above the mortality rate of the United States. Alexander de Humboldt, *Ensayo político sobre el Reino de la Nueva España* (México: Editorial Porrúa, 1966), 40–42.

4. Pablo Escalante, "Sentarse, guardar la compostura y llorar entre los antiguos nahuas (el cuerpo y el proceso de civilización)," *Familia y vida privada en la historia de Iberoamérica,* Pilar Gonzalbo Aizpuru and Cecilia Rabell Romero, coordinators, (México: El Colegio de México / Universidad Nacional Autónoma de México, 1996), 445. Paredes, *Carta Edificante,* 2.

5. Pablo Escalante Gonzalbo, "La ciudad, la gente y las costumbres," in *Historia de la vida cotidiana en México,* vol. 1, ed. Pilar Gonzalbo Aizpuru (México: Fondo de Cultura Económica, 2005), 200. Francisco de Miranda, S.J., *Catecismo breve en lengua otomí* (México: Imprenta de la Biblioteca Mexicana, 1759). In José Toribio Miranda, *La imprenta en México (1539–1821),* facsimile of the 1909 edition, vol. 5 (México: Universidad Nacional Autónoma de México), 371.

6. There are two other biographies of Indians published before 1850, but the first was published in Spain and the second was written by a French priest and originally published in France and later translated into Spanish and published in Mexico. Bernardo Sartolo, S.J., *Vida admirable y muerte prodigiosa de Nicolás Ayllón y con renombre más glorioso Nicolás de Dios, natural de Chiclayo en las Indias del Perú* (Madrid: Imprenta de Juan García Infanzón, 1684); Juan Urtassum, S.J., *La gracia triunfante en la vida de Catharina Tegakovita India Iroquesa, parte traducida de francés en español de lo que escribe el P. Francisco Colonoc, parte sacada de los authores de primera nota y authoridad como se verá en sus citas por el P. Juan Urtassum, profeso de la Compañía de Jesús* (México: Joseph Bernardo de Hogal en la Puente de Espíritu Santo, 1724). For information on the biography of Nicolás Ayallon, see Jaime Cuadriello, *Las glorias de la República de Tlaxcala o la conciencia como imagen sublime* (México: Universidad Nacional Autónoma de México, Instituto de Investigaciones Estéticas, 2004), 248–61.

In various books published in the English colonies and later in the independent nation of the United States, until the middle of the nineteenth century there are only brief mentions of the Indian Pocahontas but no complete biography. See Edward J. Gallagher, "Bibliography of works on Pocahontas," http://digital.lib.lehigh.edu/trial/pocahontas/bib.php.

7. "Protesta del autor: Aunque lo contenido en esta Vida, consta por testimonios de Personas verídicas, mas como estos son falibles, protesto, que no es mi ánimo darles más crédito, que el que se debe a la fee humana, dejando la calificación de la Persona, virtudes, y milagros, al juicio de nuestra Madre la Santa Iglesia, conforme a los Decretos Pontificios, que assí lo mandan" (Paredes, *Carta edificante,* 80). Martha Ellen Whittaker, "Jesuit Printing in Bourbon Mexico: The Press of the Colegio de San Ildefonso, 1748–1767" (Ph.D. diss., University of California, Berkeley, 1998).

8. Joseph María Zalaá e Hidalgo, *Glorias de Querétaro* (Querétaro: Gobierno del Estado, 1958), 61. All translations from Spanish to English are mine. So far I have not been able to find this first edition of 1762. The second edition, consulted for this article, is located in the National Library of Chile. This 1763 edition is extremely rare (in three libraries), as are those of 1784 (in four libraries) and 1791 (in three libraries), according to worldcat.com. The scarcity is not because of the small print runs but because the editions were bought by contemporaries of Salvadora or distributed over the years in the Indian schools.

9. Archivo General de la Nación, *Parcialidades,* vol. 2, exp. 29, 1805. Dorothy Tanck de Estrada, *La educación ilustrada, 1786–1836: Educación primaria en la ciudad de México,* 6th ed. (México: El Colegio de México, 2005), 187.

10. Paredes, *Carta edificante,* 7. Archivo Histórico del Distrito Federal, *Policía y matanza de perros,* vol. 3662, exp. 1, "Concerning the plague of rabies in Mexico City, April 23, 1709."

11. Paredes, *Carta edificante,* 11.

12. Ibid., 14.

13. Ibid., 15–17.

14. Ibid., 37.

15. Ibid., 19–20.

16. Ibid., 56–58.

17. Ibid., 23, 59–61.

18. Ibid., 26.

19. Ibid., 41.

20. Ibid., 49.

21. Fray Juan Bautista, *La vida y muerte de tres niños de Tlaxcala* (México: Imprenta de Diego López 1601); Miguel Sánchez, *Imagen de la Virgen María Madre de Dios de Guadalupe* (México: Viuda de Bernardo Calderón, 1648).

22. Josefina Muriel, *Las indias caciques de Corpus Christi* (México: Universidad Nacional Autónoma de México, 2001).

23. Juan Urtassum, *La gracia triunfante en la vida de Catharina Tegakovita, India Iroquesa,* translated from the French (México: Joseph Bernardo de Hogal, 1724); Allan Greer, "Iroquois Virgen: The Storey of Catherine Tekakwitha in New France and New Spain," in *Colonial Saints. Discovering the Holy in the Americas, 1500–1800,* ed. Allan Greer (New York: Routledge, 2003), 235–50; Nancy Shoemaker, "Kateri Tekawitha's Tortuous Path to Sainthood," in *Negotiators of Change. Historical Perspectives on Native American Women,* ed. Nancy Shoemaker (New York: Routledge, 1995), 48–71.

24. Asunción Lavrin, *Brides of Christ: Conventual Life in Colonial Mexico* (Stanford: Stanford University Press, 2008), 248, 255–66.

25. Antonio Rubial García, "Los santos milagreros y malogrados de la Nueva España," in *Manifestaciones religiosas en el mundo colonial americano. Espiritualidad barroca colonial. Santos y demonios en América,* vol. 1, ed. Clara García Ayluardo and Manuel Ramos Medina (México: Universidad Iberoamericana, 1993), 71–105. Rubial notes that the hagiographic biographies, full of anecdotes, can be considered the antecedent of the trend in magical realism found in contemporary Latin American literature and suggests that this trend has emerged from the substrata of the myth and magic of colonial society.

26. Paredes died in 1767, the twenty-ninth of thirty-four Jesuits who succumbed during the expulsion from New Spain. Francisco Zambrano and José Gutiérrez Casillas, *Diccionario Bio-bibliográfico de la Compañía de Jesús en México,* vol. 16 (México: Editorial Tradición, 1977), 337.

27. Ibid.

28. Muriel, "Notas para la historia," 100.

29. Asunción Lavrin, *Brides of Christ,* 239.

30. Paredes, *Carta edificante,* 63.

31. Ibid., 44–45.

32. Ibid., 24, 55, 59, 40, 30, 33.

33. Ibid., 26, 54, 75.

34. Ibid., 25, 38.

35. Ibid., 39. The Otomies continued to use these instruments from pre-Hispanic to modern times. Vicente T. Mendoza, *Música indígena otomí. Investigación en el valle del Mezquital, Hidalgo, en 1936* (México: Universidad Nacional Autónoma de México, 1963), 117.

36. "Tiene el objeto recomendable de proveer las Escuelas y Migas donde nuestros hijos son educados, de una especie de Cartilla, en que enseñándose a leer, aprendan al mismo tiempo de imitar las virtudes cristianas, con el dulce, poderoso y natural atractivo de verlas practicadas por una persona de su misma calidad." Antonio de Paredes, *Carta edificante en que el P. Antonio de Paredes de la extinguida Compañía de Jesús refiere la vida exemplar de la Hermana Salvadora de los Santos, india Otomí, que reimprimen las parcialidades de S. Juan y de Santiago de la Capital de México, y la dedican al Exmo. Señor Don. Matías de Gálvez* (México: La Imprenta Nueva Madrileña de los Herederos del Lic. D. Joseph de Jáuregui, en la Calle de San Bernardo, 1784), prologue and 112 pp. I thank the Getty Research Institute of Los Angeles, California, for the grant enabling me to consult the 1784 edition of the *Carta edificante.*

37. The schools were located in two sections of Mexico City, Tlatelolco and Tenochtitlan, and in the towns of Chapultepec, Churubusco, Culhuacan, Ixtacalco, Iztapalapa, Magdalena de las Salinas, Mexicaltzingo, Mixhiuca, Nativitas, Nextipac, Xocotitlan y Zacatlamanco. In the lists of schoolbooks requested by the schools in Ixtacalco in 1821, just before Mexico won independence, were two dozen "Books of Salvadora." Archivo General de la Nación, *Indiferente virreinal,* box 5401, exp. 16, Parcialidades, folios 1–26, April 1821.

38. In eighteenth-century Quertéaro, besides the Carmelite *beaterio* there was another *beaterio,* Santa Rosa de Viterbo, of the Third Order of Franciscans, founded in 1698. There were also two convents, Santa Clara (1607) and the convent of Capuchinas (1718). Mina Ramírez Montes, "Monacato femenino en Querétaro. Un esbozo de vida cotidiana," in *Creencias y prácticas religiosas en Querétaro, siglos XVI–XIX,* ed. Juan Ricardo Jiménez Gómez (Querétaro: Plaza y Valdés Editores, 2004), 155–56.

39. Paredes, *Carta edificante,* 47.

40. Ibid., 44–47.

41. Ibid., 63.

42. Ibid., 77.

43. Ibid., 47.

44. Ibid., 17, 23.

45. Ibid., 23, 52.

46. Ibid., 53–62.

47. Ibid., 62.

48. Ibid., 60.

49. Salvadora is quoted directly on pp. 10, 24, 26, 32, 33, 41, 55, 56, 57–58, 74, 75.

50. Ibid., pp. 28, 33. Joseph Diez, *Aljaba apostólica de penetrantes flechas para rendir la fortaleza del duro pecador en varias canciones y saetas, que acostumbran cantar en sus misiones los RR PP misioneros apostólicos de nro. S.P.S. Francisco* (México: Imprenta real del superior gobierno de los herederos de la viuda de Miguel Rivera Calderón, 1731). Another version of this type of songbook is Joseph Joachin de Ortega y San Antonio, *Nueva aljaba apostólica con*

varias canciones y saetas para el ejercicio de las misiones con los ofrecimientos de una sacra Corona y Rosario de nuestra Señora (México: Imprenta de la Bibliotheca Mexicana, 1757). Probably Salvadora used the 1731 book.

51. Paredes, *Carta edificante,* 66.

52. Ibid., 74–75.

53. Ibid., 76.

54. In 1800 there were 20 Spanish cities, approximately 35 to 50 Spanish villas, and 4,468 Indian towns in the kingdom of New Spain. Dorothy Tanck de Estrada, *Atlas ilustrado de los pueblos de indios. Nueva España, 1800* (México: El Colegio de México, El Colegio Mexiquense, Comisión Nacional para el Desarrollo de los Pueblos Indígenas, Fomento Cultural Banamex, 2005), 267–68.

55. The population of New York in 1776 was about twenty thousand. David McCullough, *1776* (New York: Simon and Schuster Paperbacks, 2005), 122.

56. Joseph Antonio de Villaseñor y Sánchez, *Theatro americano. Descripción general de los reynos y provincias de la Nueva España,* facsimile of the 1746 edition, vol. 1 (México: Talleres de Editora Nacional, 1951), 92–93.

57. An excellent history from the Indian point of view of this dual government of Querétaro is Juan Ricardo Jiménez Gómez, *La república de indios en Querétaro, 1550–1820* (Querétaro: Instituto de Estudios Constitucionales, 2006).

58. Juana Patricia Pérez Munguía, "Negros y castas de Querétaro, 1726–1804. La disputa por el espacio social compartido con naturales y españoles," seminar paper, El Colegio de México, September 2009, 116, 119, 123.

59. Tanck de Estrada, *Pueblos de indios,* 36. Jiménez Gómez, *La república de indios,* 84–100.

60. John C. Super, *La vida en Querétaro durante la Colonia, 1531–1810* (México: Fondo de Cultura Económica, 1983), 183–84.

61. Paredes, *Carta edificante,* 24–25.

62. Archivo Histórico del Distrito Federal, *Instrucción pública en general,* vol. 2477, exp. 330, julio de 1815, f. 12.

63. José Joaquín Fernández de Lizardi, *La Quijotita y su prima* (México: Editorial Porrúa, 1967), 50–60.

64. Paredes, *Carta edificante,* 70.

65. Asunción Lavrin, "La sexualidad y las normas de la moral sexual," in *Historia de la vida cotidiana en México,* vol. 2, ed. Pilar Gonzalbo Aizpuru (México: Fondo de Cultura Económica, 2005), 494.

66. Pilar Gonzalbo Aizpuru, "Familia y convivencia en la ciudad de México a fines del siglo XVIII," in *Familias iberoamericanas. Historia, identidad y conflictos,* ed. Pilar Gonzalbo Aizpuru (México: El Colegio de México, 2001), 168.

67. Ibid., 174.

68. Paredes, *Carta edificante,* 18.

69. Ibid., 51.

70. Ibid., 13, 14, 40–41, 43.

71. Ibid., 44, 45–52, 62, 64.

72. Ibid., 8, 18, 46, 64.

73. At the end of the eighteenth century Arricivita published the history of the mission-ary work of the friars of the Santa Cruz Convent of the Propagation of the Faith. In that work I have not found any mention of Salvadora de los Santos, which is not surprising since the subject of the book was the Franciscan missionaries. Arricivita is mentioned by name as Salvadora's confessor and he was present at her deathbed. Paredes, *Carta edificante,* 70, 76.

74. I thank Yovana Celaya her assistance in the analysis of these biographies and the works by Jesuit authors. Joseph Antonio Eugenio Ponce de León, *La abeja michoacana, la venerable señora doña Josepha Antonia de N. Señora de la Salud. Breve noticia de su vida* (México: Imprenta del Nuevo Rezado de doña María de Rivera, 1752), 147 pp.; Juan Joseph de Eguiara y Eguren, *La mujer edificativa. Panegírico fúnebre. M. R. madre Agustina Nicolasa María, abadesa* (México: Imprenta de la Bibliotheca Mexicana, 1755), 17 pp.; Miguel Rodríguez de Santo Tomás, *Memorial ajustado de la vida y virtudes de la M. R. M. Sor Antonia del señor S. Joaquín* (México: Imprenta de los herederos de doña María Ribera, 1760), 17 pp.; Joseph Ignacio de Cabrera, *Gloriosa exaltación de la mística piedra maravilla. Sermón fúnebre de Sor María Petra Trinidad religiosa laica del convento del señor san Joseph de Gracia y pobres capuchinas de la ciudad de santiago de Querétaro* (México: Imprenta de la Biblioteca Mexicana, 1762), 35 pp.; Joachín de San Antonio Ortega, *Parentación lúgubre en el cabo de año del espejo de aguas y luces de dona María de Lleva y Bayas, esposa y consorte que fue del muy ilustrísimo señor don Joseph de Escandón . conde de Sierra Gorda* (México: Imprenta de el Real y más Antiguo de San Ildefonso de México, 1764), 30 pp.

75. Antonio de Paredes, *Carta edificante en que el P. Antonio de Paredes de la Compañía de Jesús, rector del colegio del espíritu santo da noticia a su provincia mexicana de las sólidas vir-tudes, religiosos empleos y santa muerte del P Francisco Xavier Sochiaga, profeso de la misma com-pañía* (N.p., 1758), 59 pp.

76. Rubial, "Los santos milagreros y malogrados de la Nueva España," 76–77, 89. Dorothy Tanck de Estrada, "Enseñanza religiosa y patriótica. Historia de la primera histori-eta en México, 1802" in *Iberoamérica,* ed. Pilar Gonzalbo Aizpuru (México: El Colegio de México, 1999), 99–113.

77. The last sentence of the biography reports that a portrait of Salvadora was painted: "Dióse pronta providencia para que copiada en un lienzo, se pusiesen en el locutorio con esta inscripción, que suple por el honorífico epitaphio, que debiera gravársele en su sepulcro." However, later historians of the eighteenth and nineteenth century did not mention the exis-tence of any portrait of her, so possibly it was never painted, or, if made, was lost or rests now in a private collection. Paredes, *Carta edificante,* 79.

78. Ibid.

79. Muriel, "Notas para la historia," 100. Archivo General de la Nación, *Archivo Histórico de Hacienda,* bundle 1013–1, December 22, 1809. Pilar Foz y Foz, *La revolución pedagógica en Nueva España (1754–1820)* (Madrid: Artes Gráficas Clavileño, 1981), 365–67.

Hannah Freeman

Gendered Sovereignty in Penn's Peaceable Kingdom

⏤ Dawn G. Marsh

On July 28, 1797, Hannah Freeman, a tall, lean woman bent over with the burdens of age and illness, gave an account of her life to Moses Marshall.[1] Marshall
was Chester County's newly appointed representative for the region's first poorhouse, still in the planning stages. Marshall presumably set the tone for this interview with an emphasis placed on where Hannah lived, how she made her living,
and the corresponding dates. The overt reason for the interview was to establish
which township in Chester County would be recorded as the township of her residence and thereby qualify her as an inmate of the poorhouse. Hannah's story did
not follow the chronological order Marshall needed, because he started the tran-
scription in ink, stopped, turned it over and took several paragraphs of notes in
pencil. He then reorganized her story into the linear narrative he needed to present to the Commissioners of the Poor. There were other motives equally important to Marshall and Hannah's Quaker neighbors. Hannah was a living reminder
that the Lenape did not completely abandon their lands in southeastern Pennsylvania. As long as she lived, she remained an obstacle to their nearly complete
claim to lands in southeastern Pennsylvania.[2]

Hannah Freeman's account reveals the complex nature of the Indian-European
colonial encounter and the critical importance of gender in understanding those
relationships. Hannah enters history's stage through the pen of Moses Marshall, a
colonial authority, and through the subsequent recollections of Chester County's
residents. For Moses Marshall and Hannah's Quaker benefactors, she deserved
their sympathy and charity because she was an old woman with no one to take
care of her. Her persistent claims to the lands along the Brandywine River were
perceived as a minor problem because as an Indian woman she posed no serious
legal challenge. Her "autobiography" is the culmination of her personal memories
shaped by the demands of circumstance and the needs of Moses Marshall, who
sought to legitimate Hannah's status as an indigent resident of Chester County.

The complicated relationship between Hannah and her Anglo-European
neighbors and how it was shaped convey some understanding of the nature of

both gender and Indian-white relations in eighteenth-century Pennsylvania. Hannah and her matrilineal family initiated and applied a series of strategies all designed for one purpose: to reside successfully on their traditional homelands. Hannah Freeman, her aunts, mother, and grandmother exercised autonomy and authority along the Brandywine River despite the vast changes taking place around them as a result of colonial expansion and local residents repeated efforts to remove them.[3] Hannah's Quaker neighbors never challenged her rights to those lands and quietly learned to accept the resolve of these Lenape women. Moses Marshall and Hannah's Quaker neighbors took legal steps to condemn Hannah Freeman to spend her final years in the county poorhouse. Their decision to remove Hannah forcibly from her home revealed their vulnerability to the persistent land claims made by one Lenape woman.

Hannah Freeman's day-to-day life in southeastern Pennsylvania mirrored the experience of her seventeenth-century ancestors. Her life was also a life of negotiations, strategies, and diplomacy. Her goal was simple: she wanted to remain a resident of the Brandywine River Valley, maintain her autonomy, and enjoy the success of her labors, providing for her extended family and herself. She understood that the land on which she was born and the land on which she would die belonged to the Lenape. She also understood that the English settlers far outnumbered the remaining Indian presence in the area, but she was willing to share the Brandywine lands with the settlers who dispossessed her people. The Lenape understood peaceful coexistence and Hannah's choices reflected that worldview. Hannah Freeman also understood her legacy, and it included a philosophy of shared sovereignty. She shared that sovereignty in the Brandywine River Valley with the Quaker colonists who followed William Penn's ambitious plans for a different kind of colony best understood as the "peaceable kingdom." Hannah Freeman had something for which the local Quakers were willing to negotiate and trade: a legitimate claim to the lands along the Brandywine River. Her presence on the river was a living reminder to the local "landowners" that Penn's colony had been neither benevolent nor peaceful for the Lenape. Whether motivated by legal concerns or collective guilt, the local settlers willingly negotiated with Hannah and her family. In exchange for her medical knowledge, crafts, and labor, Hannah and her family successfully maintained their sovereign rights in the region despite the century-long exodus of most Indians west, across the Appalachian Mountains.

In 1797 Hannah recalled the names of twenty-four employers, acquaintances, and relatives, named eleven distinct locations of residence and employment, and referred to five different occupations in her account. The erratic phrasing suggests a series of promptings on Marshall's part rather than an uninterrupted narrative by Hannah. Marshall rewrote the text to manipulate it into a temporal framework that was more suitable for the purpose at hand. He was obliged to demonstrate that Hannah lived a productive life and thus deserved the benevolence of the local county administrators. "Examinations" like the one for Hannah Freeman were rare and required only if there was some question or dispute over the applicant's claim for support.[4] The commissioners were faced with unique circumstances because Hannah's mode of living did not fit into the typical Anglo-European pattern and because there continued to be a question of land title. Hannah Freeman lived all of her life along the Brandywine according to a Lenape way of life.

The agenda driving the examination was born out of their relationship as colonized and colonizer. As colonizer, and representative of a Quaker community that claimed to operate from a high moral ground regarding its "former" Indian residents, Marshall, like Hannah's other Quaker neighbors, was motivated by his sense of paternalism and benevolence—his desire to present her case so that Hannah would be helped.[5] Marshall assumed that Chester County authorities would find the details on the locations of Hannah's lifelong residences and her recent work record as the most compelling evidence for her support. There can be little doubt that Hannah Freeman said more than Moses Marshall recorded if we consider the recollection process we all experience when remembering the past. He probably decided to leave out much of Hannah's personal history because he thought it unnecessary for her case. Marshall was familiar with much of her story because he had many ties to Hannah Freeman. The burial grounds for Hannah's family and other members of the Brandywine Lenape were located on land deeded to Abraham Marshall, Moses' great uncle. Hannah's own cabin was situated on a tract of land claimed by Moses Marshall's uncle, Humphrey Marshall. All of these properties were part of a 1729 treaty dispute in which the provincial government decided in favor of the Brandywine band of Lenape. Also residing on these contested lands were three Quakers who were among those who signed an informal contract to provide for Hannah's care prior to the completion of the Chester County poorhouse. This intimate network of benefactors recorded only those details they believed were pertinent to expediting the institutionalization of the elderly woman they wanted to believe was the "last of her kind."

Hannah's responses to Marshall's inquiries can be read as a story of independence and self-reliance. The extent to which Hannah understood the ramifications of her deposition and how that shaped what memories she was willing or able to share remains a mystery. As an event in Hannah's life, it was probably without precedent. We have no clue about how the event took place. Perhaps Hannah went with one of her male sponsors to an official site for her deposition or, more likely, Moses Marshall interviewed Hannah at the home of one of those same benefactors. The interview, whether it proceeded as a series of questions or as a request that she tell her own story, must have evoked some curiosity and doubt on her part. Hannah grew up with the Brandywine Lenape oral tradition, which held that a family history was a living thing of great value.[6] She also understood the value of the written word in the colonizer's community; she knew she was "going on the record." In creating this narrative Hannah's memories, as well as accurate and inaccurate interpretations of those memories, are imbued with power and authority. Hannah's recollections reflected what she valued and what her people valued: place and kinship. Marshall's construction of her memories into text reflected what European colonists valued: property and labor. In Hannah Freeman's "Examination" two stories collide based on two ways of knowing that are epistemologically distinct and the resultant story may reveal ways in which those two discourses corroborate, contradict, and create the details of Hannah's life. The "Examination" as a composite of oral history and autobiography has little meaning or value standing alone. When considered with the political, economic, cultural, and social contexts in which Hannah lived, however, the autobiography offers a rare view into a Lenape woman's life that would otherwise be dismissed as trivial and without validity.

Early Life

Hannah Freeman was born in a cabin on the property of William Webb in March 1730 or 1731. Her family's cabin was situated along a small tributary to the Brandywine River known as Bennett's Run.[7] This fertile stretch of land was protected by dense forests and was the location of numerous springs. It was undoubtedly an ideal location for her family's cabin. Local residents remembered the area as the "big woods" because of its isolated and pristine nature.[8] William Webb, like many local settlers, made no efforts to force Hannah's family off of this land, even though he, like most of his Anglo-European neighbors, claimed the property as his own. Webb had both the means and connection to take action against the Indians living on his land. He was a well-respected assemblyman, judge, businessman, and slave owner. But Webb, like many other local landowners, tolerated the presence of the scattered settlements throughout the region. As the beginning of a decade that witnessed the mass diaspora of the Lenape out of southeastern Pennsylvania, 1730 is a particularly significant year. However, if we take into account all the references to the Indian presence in Chester County after their exodus, it appears that many chose not to leave but continued to live in southeastern Pennsylvania. Local records are rife with recollections of Indian settlements of five or six houses, usually located near springs and along streams.[9] Many settlements had orchards and gardens suggesting a well-established way of life that tolerated the presence and land claims of the white people who surrounded and outnumbered them after the 1730s. There is no record of any one landowner in the decades following Hannah's birth making any attempt to remove these scattered settlements. No legal actions were filed or land cases disputed in the local courts. Everyone kept these negotiations off the record.

Little is known about Hannah's childhood or youth. Her immediate family consisted of her grandmother Jane, maternal aunts Betty and Nanny, her father, and her mother Sarah.[10] During her early years the family spent the winter months in their cabin on Bennett's Run, and in the spring they spent much of their time a bit further north up the Brandywine River, past the forks, to plant their gardens and tend orchards. Hannah recalled that her two brothers, both younger than she, were also born at the winter cabin.[11] Along with tending the gardens and orchards, her family fished in the local streams. Local residents recalled that before the streams were all dammed for farming, the Indians used to make nets out of grapevine and easily caught an abundance of fish.[12] They also harvested turtles from the streams, a Lenape favorite that Hannah continued to enjoy into her old age, much to the distaste of the local residents. Hannah's family appears not to have suffered from a lack of resources in these earliest years of her life. This would not last. Perhaps they temporarily benefited when most of their people left the region, leaving an excess of resources that were thinly spread over the earlier larger settlements.

While we do not know many details about Hannah's early years, it is important to expand on what we do know. Her immediate family, and the family that would remain her closest circle all of her life, was woman-centered. During her lifetime the political and economic structure of Lenape society along the Brandywine collapsed as a result of the diaspora of her people, and she, along with other Indians who stayed behind, found ways to survive this isolation. They were surrounded by colonial political, economic, and cultural influences that altered their way of life. Hannah is important because she remained true to her Lenape identity and was extremely successful in resisting total acculturation. But we also know that she, along with the other women in her family, altered the organization of family descent and participated in the larger market economy and in the arrangement of power relationships.[13]

Lenape women in the seventeenth and eighteenth centuries were horticulturalists. They were in charge of their community's food production, distribution, and exchange.[14] If we consider the landowners in Algonquian culture as the people in the society who were responsible for the land use, then Lenape women such as Hannah, Sarah, Jane and Nanny were in a position equivalent to the Quaker men who "tolerated" their presence.[15] Again, it is important not to apply any strict gender division in women's relationship to the administration of their responsibilities. The division of labor in Lenape society was complementary, with most major tasks being shared. A more significant division of labor can be seen in the seasonal organization of tasks. Men were away for long periods of time, mostly in the winter and spring. These male-centered responsibilities coincided with political and trade activities that were increasingly dominated by the demands of overwhelming colonial settlement. Women stayed wedded to the land, organizing the labor and production of food throughout the year. Their responsibilities kept them close to their villages and settlements, varied by seasonal gathering of resources and as traders. This pattern, while changing in the details, remained fairly consistent on a larger scale for generations. Grandmother Jane as a young bride in the seventeenth century probably managed cornfields and orchards just as Hannah did in the eighteenth century. Her aunts, mother, and grandmother traveled the local pathways of the region while trading baskets, mats, and other goods, just as Hannah continued to do in Chester County throughout her life.

The rapidly changing demographics of southeastern Pennsylvania in the decades before Hannah's birth played a critical role in the path Hannah's family chose after her birth. The major exodus of many indigenous peoples out of the region resulted directly from the invasive flood of colonial settlers who answered Williams Penn's call. There is no doubt that European colonization resulted in devastating consequences for indigenous communities throughout the Americas.[16] In Pennsylvania, however, the demographic impact of contact and colonization is often overshadowed by the benevolent design of Penn's colonial policies. When viewed through the same lens as other colonial settlements in North America, the Indian residents of his peaceable kingdom were ravaged by the same genocidal forces experienced in other, better-studied regions of the Americas.[17] In addition the settlement of Pennsylvania after Penn's takeover proceeded at a pace unprecedented in the English North American colonies. By 1690 more than 8,800 colonists immigrated to the Delaware Valley. By the first decade of the eighteenth century the European population jumped to 28,000, and by 1730, the time of Hannah's birth, the population was 49,000. The ready availability of inexpensive and extremely productive land fed this rapid growth throughout Hannah's life. By 1760 the Lenape homeland was exploding with a foreign population of more than 175,000 inhabitants.[18] For the first peoples of southeastern Pennsylvania, their ancestral home was no longer a good place to live; hunting and gathering sites were destroyed or cultivated, their traditional planting sites were fenced off, and access to trade was impinged. They were also concerned about what these changes meant for their souls. Like many people, the Lenape sought spiritual explanations for the loss and calamity they were experiencing, and many believed *kwulakan,* the loss of balance and harmony, might lead to worse conditions if they did not leave.[19]

In 1730 Hannah was born into a radically different *Lenapehoking* than either her mother or her grandmother, and the impact of the changes were immediate.

Hannah's father left his family sometime during Hannah's childhood. She remembered that he departed around the time that widespread colonial settlement prevented them from planting corn in their regular summer locations near Newlin.[20] Not all of Chester County's new settlers accommodated their Indian neighbors as easily as William Webb.

The identity of Hannah's father and his motivations for leaving remain unclear. Hannah connected two events together: their inability to grow corn in her family's traditional garden plots and her father's departure to Shamokin. There are many reasons why Hannah's father might have left, and his failure to return may or may not have been intentional. It is possible that Hannah's father left to find another way to support his family. Perhaps he sought temporary labor, a strategy Hannah and other members of her family were destined to adopt. Two obvious possibilities are that her father was killed or he may have abandoned his family. Perhaps it was a deliberate choice and Hannah's father left as the result of an agreed-upon divorce, ending his relationship with Hannah's mother and her kin in a fashion that all parties recognized.[21] Whether the result of divorce or abandonment, her father's departure would not have the same repercussions in Lenape society as it would have among European colonists. Since Hannah's family and a large part of their economy was woman-centered, the loss of the father did not dissolve the ties that bound her family together. "Family" was constructed in a way that allowed a group of kin, such as Hannah's enclave, largely composed of women and children, to survive. Conversely women and children without a male provider were the most vulnerable members of the European colonial society. Hannah's maternally centered family remained strong and continued to thrive in the midst of colonial expansion and domination.

After her father left, Hannah's family changed their seasonal strategies. The inhospitable changes in Newlin Township led her family to seek an alternative location for their spring and summer gardens. They maintained the cabin in Bennett's Run, but established a new second home near Centre on the Brandywine River just below the present boundary between Pennsylvania and Delaware. Hannah and her family's choice to move south proved to be beneficial to this woman-centered enclave, but it was counter to the general migration patterns of other Lenape during this period. Most Lenape leaving the Brandywine River Valley were then relocated to sites along the Susquehanna River and further north and east.

Between 1735 and 1763 Hannah acquired the knowledge and skills she would employ throughout her life.[22] She knew where to find local botanical sources for medicine and food. She learned the art and skill of basket making, a trade on which she would rely for support most of her life. She learned when and how to plant corn and other crops, along with methods of storage and preparation. The knowledge she gained from her grandmother, mother, and aunts represented generations of expertise and information, traditions and rituals that Lenape women successfully employed. Maternal networks, represented by Hannah's close circle, continued to play a central role in the cultural success of the Lenape in Pennsylvania for a very long time, perhaps even into the present day. This woman-centered network was not unlike the cultural strategies the Lenape employed in Pennsylvania throughout the colonial period. Acting as a cultural net and moving around and through the European populations that eventually overwhelmed them, these tactics continued to serve the Lenape people, those who left and those who stayed, for a very long time.

Hannah lived in a world that was eventually dominated by a foreign culture. Perhaps the greatest strength Hannah and her maternal kin had was their ability to participate selectively in and take advantage of local economic opportunities presented by their English Quaker neighbors.[23] Along with Hannah's indigenous skills, she learned how to spin yarn and weave cloth. While the Lenape were proficient in using local vegetation to produce baskets, mats, and other woven objects, using European tools to spin flax into yarn and yarn into cloth were new skills she acquired from the Quaker families for whom she worked.[24] Hannah and her indigenous maternal network found common ground with their English sisters while learning these new skills. Not unlike the way they were in Lenape traditional culture, life and work for Anglo-American women in the Brandywine Valley was seasonally structured. For those Quaker women who lived on farms, planting and dairying dominated the spring season. Harvest, which demanded the most intense work schedule, began in July with haying followed by flax pulling in August and September. Concurrent with these tasks and through the fall came the harvesting of the remaining crops such as potatoes and apples and their preparation and preservation. Flax processing dominated winter's work that included spinning, weaving, carding, and dyeing. Correspondingly, for Hannah's kin, this was a time of year, during long winter days and nights, when she and her kin produced the baskets, besoms, and mats they would sell to their Quaker neighbors throughout the rest of the year.[25]

Women's work and roles in Lenape communities were also built around seasonal demands. Lenape women structured their lives on subsistence patterns that included agriculture, gathering, and hunting. According to Hannah's testimony and the plans made for her by her Quaker benefactors later in her life, Hannah's lifelong mobility reflected a traditional Lenape pattern.[26] Winter and summer residences made use of the availability of fields for planting, streams for fishing and access to environmental resources including materials for basket making and medicine. Along with the agricultural responsibilities, Lenape women maintained the household and raised children, with husbands and fathers limited to the periphery of family life. Within the traditional Lenape family structure women exercised a great deal of authority and autonomy in the management of their time and their tasks.[27]

Early studies of the changing status and roles of Indian women during the colonial period often conclude that Indian women lost status and autonomy when indigenous cultures came in contact with European cultures. These conclusions are based on studies of the effects of assimilation policies instituted by governments and churches.[28] The focus of these assimilation policies was on the transformation of the Indian family into the Anglo-American family model. The status and authority of Native American women declined because the expectations of native women's roles were defined by parameters set for Anglo-American women. Transforming woman-centered extended families into patriarchal, nuclear units disrupted gender roles and devalued Indian women's economic, social, and political roles in their communities. There is no doubt that colonization transformed the social, economic, and cultural patterns of Native American societies. But assuming a loss of autonomy and authority overlooks the strategies that Indian women employed to resist, modify, and adapt their roles in the newly forming and constantly changing multiethnic communities in which they found themselves. It is not just a story of loss but also one of resilience and transformation.[29] In southeastern Pennsylvania a number of factors worked to shape Hannah's future and in some ways were responsible for protecting her status and autonomy in Chester County. Comparing Hannah's social, economic, and cultural roles as a Lenape woman with those of an Anglo-American woman sheds light on those factors.

The "last of her kind"

The source of Hannah Freeman's autonomy and authority rested in her ethnic identity as the "last of her kind." The Anglo-American community accommodated Hannah's residential and work patterns because they recognized them as eccentric and transient. Their expectations were defined by parameters set by generations of experience living and working in a region with a significant Indian population. This familiarity with *Indian* ways led most local Brandywine residents to accept Hannah's behavior as peculiar to her Lenape heritage. The patterns of subsistence employed by Hannah were readily accommodated because she was protected by her ethnic identity. The local community was willing to tolerate Hannah's continued residence on their lands largely according to her schedule and her choices because of the uniqueness of her status. More important, this shield of invisibility may have allowed many other Indians to hide in plain sight of their colonial neighbors as long as their numbers or their presence was not perceived as a threat. The continued presence of Indian families residing on their historic homelands throughout the eighteenth century is supported by the testimonies of local Quaker residents. All maintained autonomy and cooperation from their neighbors.

If Hannah had been a non-Indian, landless woman, her options would have been severely curtailed. An indigent Anglo-American woman without a family to support her fell under the domain of the overseers of the poor, a position to which Hannah succumbed only in the last few years of her life. Another factor that helped protect Hannah's autonomy and authority in the region was the status of women within the largely Quaker community. Although Chester County had a diverse ethnic composition, Quaker culture provided the leadership and community network that dominated the region. The Quaker culture in turn gave rural Quaker women privilege and independence that was unique in American colonial culture, a status that was increasing during this period. Hannah recalled that she sewed for the wives of Sam Levis and William Webb, indicating that these Quaker women were in charge of employing, paying, and managing their outside help, which may have included other women besides Hannah.[30] The independence and precedent set by these largely self-directed farm women must have influenced community expectations for the roles women could fill. Further, the women who sold their skills and labor in exchange for wages and goods appeared to manage those transactions independently. Hannah, like other women in the Brandywine Valley, performed a variety of tasks in exchange for wages, room and board, and commodities.

Understanding how rural Anglo-American women of Chester County lived and worked is as important as understanding how traditional Lenape women lived in evaluating Hannah Freeman's role in the Brandywine Valley community. As the larger Lenape community receded from the Brandywine Valley, Hannah and her extended family were forced to combine old and new strategies for economic survival if they were going to live successfully in the Quaker-dominated community without completely abandoning their Lenape traditions. Quite early in Hannah's life she and her female kin must have understood that their survival depended on adapting their skills and the commodities they produced to the needs of the Anglo-American community around them, not unlike generations of Lenape before them. Basket making, a traditional Lenape craft that was largely the domain of Lenape women, became the mainstay of a commodity that could be sold for cash or exchanged for other goods. The resources were readily available and the demand for these goods increased with the growing numbers of colonists. One anonymous writer recollected that "the Indians carried on a considerable trade with baskets from the first settling of the country by white people," and another recalled that "Indian women in considerable numbers" gathered together in encampments for months at a time to "engage in their common employment of basket making."[31] The traditional basket-making gatherings lasted months at a time and probably coincided with the time when men were away from the settlements hunting. Hannah Freeman probably acquired her basket-making skills at such gatherings during her early years. The basket-making sessions offer a powerful example of how this cultural net reemerged and provided far-flung and isolated Lenape communities an opportunity to share knowledge and skills with younger generations, as well as an income for their support.

Most of the recollections about Hannah Freeman by Chester County residents include at least one reference to her basket trade. Little is known about Lenape basket-making practices during this period or the role that basket making played in the survival tactics of Indian women south of New England. A substantial body of scholarship suggests that basket making in New England is evidence of one way that Indians eked out a living in a society where they were actively oppressed and marginalized.[32] According to numerous accounts, Hannah produced a variety of baskets to trade or sell throughout her life. Martha Lamborn told her granddaughter that Hannah would come to their farm "as she did many other places throughout that section" and stay for some time making baskets.[33] She apparently favored particular areas for the splints and materials required by her craft. There is no evidence that anyone in Chester County objected to her freely making use of the resources on their land. In fact some families, such as the Lamborns, were accustomed to providing her with board while she gathered and produced baskets on their properties. When Hannah had finished making use of the materials on the family farm, Martha Lamborn recalled that Hannah "would make her charge which she understood how to do." Without question or gaining any permission from the colonial property owners, Hannah gathered the materials that were readily available from the lands that were traditionally sources for Lenape women's basket making. Ever a shrewd entrepreneur, Hannah would in turn sell the baskets to families such as the Lamborns for money or other goods. From the Lamborns' perspective they would "cheerfully pay her" because they believed it was charity. From her perspective Hannah owed the Lamborn's nothing for these resources.

As frequently as stories of Hannah's basket trade appear in the recollections of Chester County residents, so too do repeated stories of Hannah's persistent refusal to accept charity. This story serves two purposes. First, it is evidence of Hannah's unrelenting refusal to be economically dependent on her colonial neighbors as well as her unfailing claim to the lands that her family and kin never relinquished. Second, the account reveals the racist assumptions of the white storytellers. Hannah Freeman's story, thus far, is a construction produced by a regional population who wanted to see her life as evidence that she was the "last of her kind." Their charitable and kind acts, which they perceived as a benevolent tolerance of an old Indian woman's eccentricities, support the widely accepted but erroneous paradigm of William Penn's exceptional and peaceful relations with Indians. Chester County's sympathetic and skewed interpretations of Hannah's basket trade are indicative of their failure to understand fully the implications of the actions taken by Hannah and other Indians in the region. When considered from Hannah's perspective, her decisions reveal a different understanding of Pennsylvania's colonial policies and practices.

One of the most critical events Hannah recalled was her family's forced exile to New Jersey as a response to the massacre of the Conestoga Indians by the Paxton Boys in 1763.[34] Her family moved to New Jersey at "the time the Indians were killed at Lancaster" in response to the Paxton Boys' attack.[35] The violence erupted in Lancaster in December 1763 when a group of Scots-Irish vigilantes descended upon Conestoga Manor, a reservation not unlike the Brandywine lands, with the intention of killing all of its Indian inhabitants. The Conestoga were "peaceful" Indians according to the Assembly in Philadelphia and were under provincial protection when the atrocities occurred. The massacre ended with six dead, the majority of Conestoga being away from their homes that day selling baskets and brooms. When word reached the scattered families they sought protection in the town of Lancaster where the remaining fourteen were confined in the workhouse as a "safety" measure. The Paxton Boys, as the murderers were called, subdued the local authorities and proceeded to murder the fourteen innocent indigenous residents of Conestoga who were trapped in the jail.

The response of Hannah's family to the Paxton Boys event marked a turning point in Hannah's life. This event signaled a forced exile away from the Brandywine River Valley, the collapse of her closest family network, and Hannah's entry into wage labor. The violence itself must have been terrifying for Indians living in Pennsylvania and sent shock waves throughout their far-flung communities. The violence inflicted by the local residents of Paxton and Lancaster against the Conestoga families was an extension of the increased hostilities and anti-Indian sentiment resulting from the French and Indian War and Pontiac's rebellion. Despite the fact that these wars took place far from Chester County, the sentiment of Indian hating was pervasive. The murders of Indian families who were guaranteed protection by the late William Penn signaled to all Indians in the vicinity that no one was safe from these attacks. For Hannah this incident undoubtedly represented a frightening turn of events. If she and her family assumed that Pennsylvania, and more particularly, the Brandywine River Valley, provided a safe haven for Indians, this incident and its aftermath surely shattered that illusion. This memory, recalled in her old age, must have reignited the fear and vulnerability she felt, surrounded by and at the mercy of the Euro-American community. In 1797 she was in no position to make ringing denouncements about the event, and neither Hannah, nor Moses Marshall elaborated on the episode. Most scholars considered the Paxton massacre an aberration in the "peaceable kingdom," an abrupt halt to years of tranquility proclaimed by many of Penn's historians.[36] If the incident was exceptional and if Hannah's family and other Indians were living in a "peaceable kingdom," then why was their response so drastic? Could this incident have so severely undermined their faith in Penn's legacy of benevolence that they saw no option except to abandon their homes, their resources, and all things familiar to an exile in New Jersey? Or was Penn's legacy of a benevolent Indian policy an idea that existed only in the minds of white Pennsylvanians?

The Paxton massacre and the hasty and drastic response of Hannah's family also suggest that, as the colonial population increased, so too did the interactions with the Indians. Tensions between these groups escalated as a result of the local needs and demands of both groups. More Indians sought alternative ways of supporting themselves and their families and turned to the new settlers for work. The settlers, in turn, relied on trade goods and labor from the Indians to support their growing needs. Indian laborers were found on farms, in mines, and in the towns. Their visibility increased at a time when rumors fueled the greatest fears of the already paranoid settlers. Rather than seeing it as an anomalous event, Hannah and her family considered the Paxton massacre the final straw. It forced them into a seven-year exile. The event introduced Hannah and her family to violence on a new scale that once and for all destroyed the veneer of harmonious relations in Pennsylvania.[37] Indians no longer felt safe in Pennsylvania. Even Hannah's redoubtable kin group was forced to flee.

Hannah, the Woman

Hannah Freeman and her family left New Jersey and returned to Pennsylvania when she was approximately forty years old. What induced them to return or what sign suggested that the Brandywine River Valley was once again a safe home is unclear. At some time, before her exile in New Jersey or while she was there, Hannah acquired a family of her own. When she returned to the county after 1770 she was living "with her aunt Nanny [and] her husband & Son."[38] Many Chester County residents recalled Hannah's husband Andrew and her two sons. Some of those recollections were quite detailed. In a newspaper article published twenty-two years after Hannah's death, the author recalled Chester County's Indian past and reported that "there was a boy named Isaac belonging to the family of Indians residing in Kennett remarkably smart and active, who mostly carried his bows and arrows with him, the neighboring boys would put up pennies for him to shoot at, if he struck the penny it was his, but if he mist it he gave one."[39] The same author also claimed that about 1775 a family of Indians lived near Kennett and that the family then consisted of husband Andrew, Sarah (Hannah's mother), and Hannah's Aunt Nanny. Mary Ash, who was born in 1765, recalled spending time with Indians near her father's farm. She remembered that Nanny and Betty had a cabin near Hannah. Ash also recalled they "made baskets and the women tried to learn me to talk Indian" without success. One final note from this record states that Hannah's husband Andrew died in 1780 and was buried in Middleton. Other Chester County elders recalled that Andrew was buried near Kennett, closer to Hannah's birthplace. No other records offer the faintest evidence about Hannah's marriage or her sons.

In the years after their return from exile in New Jersey, Hannah's family suffered several losses. Her Grandmother Jane died "at Schuylkill" followed by her Aunt Betty who died "at Middleton."[40] Later that same year, in October 1770, Hannah's mother died at Centre on the Chandler farm in Delaware. Chester County residents later recalled that Hannah's mother died in Centre and her relatives carried her fourteen miles north to be buried in a traditional Lenape cemetery near Northbrook, a site where Hannah also wished to be interred.[41] This funeral procession is significant for two reasons. It strongly suggests that the act of taking her mother's body back to their lands along the Brandywine, in Newlin Township, signified the family's continued claims to those lands. It also marks the return of Hannah specifically to Newlin Township, after her exile in New Jersey. This time Humphrey Marshall, a well-known Quaker botanist, offered no resistance to her family taking up residence on his lands, which were also the site of a her mother's interment. Humphrey Marshall, Moses Marshall's uncle, was once referred to as Hannah's protector.[42] His concern for her claims and her access to the land and its resources ran deep. In his will he ordered his benefactors not to alter or dam any streambeds on his property until there were no longer any Indians living there.[43]

Hannah's most detailed years as a laborer began after her return to Chester County in the 1770s. With the lands along the Brandywine once again the foci of her seasonal movement, her visibility in the surrounding communities increased. Hannah and her neighbors remembered her work as a seamstress, basket maker, broom maker, servant, and healer. Hannah remembered working for at least eight different families, all within fifteen miles of her Brandywine Valley home. During this time Hannah first recalled receiving wages for her work. She received wages from "Black" Thomas, "White" Thomas, and Jonathan Chandler.[44] Hannah worked for room and board or for goods and services when she did not receive wages. During one three-year period at Black Thomas Chandler's, Hannah received "good sheets" (yardage of fabric) in exchange for her employment as a seamstress for the family. The "Examination" is problematic because it enumerates her employment during a very short span of her life. It is not difficult to suppose that these work patterns emerged much earlier and continued until she was physically incapable of maintaining the autonomous and independent life to which she was accustomed. Nevertheless, Hannah's employment history reveals a combination of traditional Lenape women's roles with those of eighteenth-century rural Anglo-American women.

Hannah also earned wages as a healer. The earliest newspaper reminiscence of Hannah Freeman reported that J. Parker of Kennett went to Hannah's home to seek her assistance for his sick children. According to this account Hannah provided a prescription for his children and charged him five shillings for the service.[45] Traditional Lenape culture had two classifications for those with the ability to use the healing properties of plants: those who "know medicine well" and those "who use medicine for magical purposes."[46] Parker's visit to Hannah suggests she practiced the former. In traditional Lenape culture those "who know medicine well" were usually women who had obtained this knowledge from their female kin. The knowledge was based on a gift bestowed by a vision and enhanced by a guardian spirit who served as a lifetime adviser. Hannah most likely learned her medical arts from her mother or her maternal grandmother after displaying a gift or propensity for understanding the healing properties of the botanical medicine cabinet around her. Practicing and maintaining her medical skills, as well as cultivating the botanical resources necessary, suggests a lifelong commitment on Hannah's part. Hannah's work as a healer also suggests that she carried a great deal of accumulated knowledge and history for her people. Her botanical knowledge and her understanding of the rituals, prayers, and practices that encompassed an indigenous medical practitioner's toolkit also suggests that Hannah and her maternal group were highly esteemed and powerful members of the Brandywine Lenape community, perhaps for generations. Her skills as a medical practitioner for her people and for the local Quaker community cannot be separated from the greater Lenape ideology and belief in magic and ritual. The effectiveness of her botanical skills rested in her continued belief in the power of her Lenape spirituality and religious practices. Only the spirit world gave the plants and roots she collected the power to heal. She was only a transmitter of these curative properties, not the originator.[47] Hannah and her Quaker neighbors lived in very different spiritual worlds. There is no record that Hannah embraced any Christian missionary efforts, nor is there any indication that her Quaker neighbors and benefactors tried to convert her.

Hannah Remembered

Hannah spent a lifetime living and working among the Anglo-American residents of the Brandywine Valley. The peculiarities they attributed to her "Indianness" were willingly accommodated. There are several peculiarities that Chester County residents collectively remember about Hannah. The most significant of these was her continued occupation and use of land and resources that colonists believed to be their rightful property but that they duly recognized to be hers. Unlike the landless Anglo-American colonists who were required to pay for land use as tenants or as bound laborers, Hannah and her family were never objects of such demands.[48] Not only did they accept her seasonal relocations to cabins on their properties; they also accommodated her family's absences from those lands even though the family was gone for as long as seven years.

The most salient peculiarities remembered about Hannah Freeman, attributed to her Lenape identity, were the quality of her character and the lasting impression she made on those who remembered her. While the recollections are peppered with condescending remarks about how she lived, more often the local residents' memories describe a woman who truly considered herself "queen of the whole neighborhood."[49] How she looked to local residents was important in establishing and maintaining her separateness in the community, but it was her personality that accounted for the most enduring and important recollections. Hannah had a superior countenance described as "wild and fierce" and showed a great veneration for the land. Some described her as the "pride of her race" and noted that she displayed a "calm faith in her own superiority." Hannah Freeman was a woman cautiously regarded and respected as the mistress of her own affairs, "shrewd in her answers and remarks."

Hannah Freeman's character, her identity as a Lenape woman, and her authority over the lands where she lived and worked were recognized and acknowledged by her Quaker neighbors. The steps they took to legitimize her right to institutionalized care in her old age according to their laws and customs had the dual purpose of acknowledging and legitimizing her claims to the lands along the Brandywine River. For her Quaker neighbors her death ended any Indian claim or presence in Penn's "peaceable kingdom," but it also acknowledged Hannah Freeman's sovereign authority in southeastern Pennsylvania until her recorded death in 1802. The legal document reinforced her status as "the last of her kind" and removed any question of other Lenape claims to the land left in dispute for so long. It is clear that the local residents accommodated the Lenape lifestyle much more than Hannah accommodated theirs. The community was never able to restrict her movements on the lands she claimed as her own. They acknowledged that Hannah's "Indianess" established for her a unique status in their community that they protected, accommodated, and sustained to the end of her life. Even in these last years of her life they recognized Hannah's authority, autonomy, and sovereign rights that included open access to the land along the Brandywine and unrestricted occupation of the dwellings on those lands. The relationship Hannah shared with her Quaker neighbors was replicated throughout the region.

Quaker recollections of Indian families and cabins and more than one "last of her kind" stories are testimony to the continued presence of others such as Hannah Freeman and her kin. Whether moved by guilt, sympathy, or a desire to clear once and for all the titles of the lands along the Brandywine River, Hannah's Quaker neighbors found their actions shaped by her presence in their townships until the very last days of her life. Only then did the local community abandon Hannah Freeman and place her in an institution that was established to replace family with formal, community support for the poor.

Hannah Freeman was delivered to the Chester County Poorhouse on the first day of admittance, November 12, 1800. "Indian Hannah," the second entry on the page, is listed as sixty-nine years old and a resident of Newlin Township. The record fails to state how she was delivered to the almshouse. She was left in the care of strangers appointed by the county officials and by all appearances her neighbors washed their hands of any obligation they had toward their longtime neighbor. It is difficult to imagine what mental or physical condition Hannah was in when the community she had lived and worked in all of her life abandoned her to the new caretakers. No official poorhouse records suggest that she caused any problems for the caretakers or that she demanded any special attention or care. The effects of abandonment, unfamiliarity, and the inability to journey freely through her lands probably led to the rapid deterioration of her physical and mental health. Hannah Freeman did not thrive under the care of the poorhouse staff. She died on March 20, 1802, less than two years after her admittance to the Chester County Poorhouse.[50] With Hannah Freeman's death, the Chester County residents reassured themselves that the last Indian in Chester County was gone, and any threat or discomfort that Hannah Freeman had even remotely represented vanished as quickly as the poorhouse doors closed behind her. Hannah Freeman was a living reminder to the colonists that the lands they lived on were never completely abandoned by the Lenape, and Hannah's defiant presence and her claims of sovereignty were daily reminders of the region's Indian past.

Notes

1. Moses Marshall, "Examination of Hannah Freeman," July 28, 1797, Albert Cook Myers Papers, Chester County Historical Society, West Chester, Pa.

2. Donald H. Kent, ed., *Pennsylvania and Delaware Treaties, 1629–1737,* vol. 1, *Early American Documents: Treaties and Laws, 1607–1789* (Washington D.C.: University Publications of America, 1979).

3. At the core of the body of evidence available are three documents: "The Examination of Indian Hannah alias Hannah Freeman," her autobiography transcribed by Moses Marshall; "Kindness Extended," a contract for Hannah Freeman's care authored by Joseph Barnard; and the Minutes of the Directors of the Poor. "The Examination of Indian

Hannah Freeman" dated July 27, 1797, was described in its first publication in 1990 as the earliest Native American autobiography yet known to scholars.

4. According to Laurie Rofini, director of Chester County Archives and Records, Chester County had no official demand or procedure for the deposition Hannah Freeman gave.

5. On the impact of colonial processes on Native American women, see Devon Abbott Mihesuah, *Indigenous American Women: Decolonization, Empowerment, Activism* (Lincoln: University of Nebraska Press, 2003); Diane Rothenberg, "The Mother of the Nation: Seneca Resistance to Quaker Intervention," in *Women and Colonization: Anthropological Perspectives,* ed. Mona Etienne and Eleanor Leacock (New York: Praeger, 1980), 63–83. On Quaker relations with Indians, see Robert F. Berkhofer, *Salvation and the Savage: An Analysis of Protestant Missions and American Indian Response 1778–1862* (Lexington: University of Kentucky Press, 1965); Jane T. Merritt, "Cultural Encounters along a Gender Frontier: Mahican, Delaware, and German Women in Eighteenth-Century Pennsylvania," *Pennsylvania History* 67, no. 4 (2000), 502–31.

6. The Lenape valued their history and were able to recite these histories through the use of a marked staff that was a mnemonic device for the storyteller.

7. Albert Cook Myers Papers, Indian File, Chester County Historical Society, West Chester, Pa.

8. "Indian Hannah," July 9, 1885, and "Reminiscences for the Register," February 26, 1839, Indian File, Chester County Historical Society, West Chester, Pa.

9. "For the Record," 1824, and "Untitled Article," *Poulson Advertiser,* 1885, Albert Cook Myers Papers, Chester County Historical Society, West Chester, Pa.

10. The only names on record for Hannah's family are their first names. Various records in Chester County that acknowledge an Indian identity rarely list a surname. The more frequent acknowledgment of an indigenous identity is the application of "Indian" before a first name, such as Indian Hannah, Indian Pete, and so on. The surname Freeman is acquired from her husband Andrew.

11. Marshall, "Examination of Hannah Freeman."

12. "For the Record," 1824, Chester County Historical Society, West Chester, Pa.

13. Jean M. O'Brien, "Divorced from the Land," in *After King Philip's War: Presence and Persistence in Indian New England,* ed. Colin G. Calloway (Hanover: University Press of New England, 1997), 145–46.

14. Ives Goddard, "Delaware," in *Northeast,* ed. Bruce G. Trigger, vol. 15 of *Handbook of North American Indians* (Washington D.C.: Smithsonian Institution, 1978), 244; Regula Trenkwalder Schèonenberger, *Lenape Women, Matriliny, and the Colonial Encounter: Resistance and Erosion of Power (C. 1600–1876): An Excursus in Feminist Anthropology,* European University Studies (Bern and New York: P. Lang, 1991), 141–44.

15. Anthony F. C. Wallace, "Woman, Land and Society: Three Aspects of Aboriginal Delaware Life," *Pennsylvania Archaeologist* (1947): 2, Trenkwalder Schèonenberger, *Lenape Women.*

16. Alfred W. Crosby, *The Columbian Exchange: Biological and Cultural Consequences of 1492* (Westport, Conn.: Praeger, 1972); Alfred W. Crosby, "Virgin Soil Epidemics as a Factor in the Aboriginal Depopulation of America," *William and Mary Quarterly* 33 (1976):

289–99; William M. Denevan, ed., *The Native Populations of the Americas in 1492* (Madison: University of Wisconsin Press, 1976); Henry F. Dobyns and William R. Swagerty, *Their Number Became Thinned: Native American Population Dynamics in Eastern North America.* (Knoxville: University of Tennessee Press, 1983); Wilbur R. Jacobs, "The Tip of an Iceberg: Pre-Columbian Indian Demography and Some Implications for Revisions," *William and Mary Quarterly* (1974): 123–32; Dean M. Snow and Kim Lanphear, "European Contact and Indian Depopulation in the Northeast: The Timing of the First Epidemics," *Ethnohistory* 35 (1988): 15–33.

17. Thomas J. Sugrue, "The Peopling and Depeopling of Early Pennsylvania: Indians and Colonists, 1680–1720," *Pennsylvania Magazine of History and Biography* 116, no. 1 (1992): 5–7.

18. James Lemon, *The Best Poor Man's Country: A Geographical Study of Early Southeastern Pennsylvania* (Baltimore: John Hopkins University Press, 1972), 51–57; Barry Levy, *Quakers and the American Family; British Settlement in the Delaware Valley* (New York: Oxford University Press, 1988), 126–37; Sugrue, "The Peopling and Depeopling of Early Pennsylvania," 27.

19. Jay Miller, "Kwulakan: The Delaware Side of the Movement West," *Pennsylvania Archaeologist* 45, no. 4 (1975): 45–46.

20. Marshall, "Examination of Hannah Freeman."

21. In general see S. Grumet, "Sunksquaws, Shamans, and Tradeswomen: Middle Atlantic Coastal Algonkian Women during the 17th and 18th Centuries," in *Women and Colonization: Anthropological Perspectives,* ed. Mona Etienne and Eleanor Leacock (New York: Praeger, 1980); Rothenberg, "The Mother of the Nation"; Trenkwalder Schèonenberger, *Lenape Women.*

22. The year 1763 marks another critical turning point in Hannah's life that is discussed below.

23. On the social and economic development of Chester County, see Eugene Ball, "The Process of Settlement in 18th Century Chester County, Pennsylvania: A Social and Economic History" (Ph.D. diss., University of Pennsylvania, 1973); Jeanne Boydston, *Home and Work: Housework, Wages, and the Ideology of Labor in the Early Republic* (Oxford: Oxford University Press, 1990); John William Florin, *The Advance of Frontier Settlement in Pennsylvania, 1638–1850: A Geographic Interpretation,* Papers in Geography, no. 14. (University Park: Deptartment of Geography, Pennsylvania State University, 1977); Adrienne D. Hood, *The Weaver's Craft: Cloth, Commerce and Industry in Early Pennsylvania* (Philadelphia: University of Pennsylvania Press, 2003); Joseph E. Illick, *Colonial Pennsylvania: A History* (New York: Charles Scribner's Sons, 1976); Joan M. Jensen, *Loosening the Bonds: Mid-Atlantic Farm Women, 1750–1850* (New Haven: Yale University Press, 1986); Joseph J. Kelley, *Pennsylvania, the Colonial Years, 1681–1776* (Garden City, N.Y.: Doubleday, 1980); Lemon, *The Best Poor Man's Country;* Jack D. Marietta, "The Distribution of Wealth in Eighteenth-Century America: Nine Chester County Tax Lists, 1693–1799," *Pennsylvania History* 62, no. 4 (1995): 532–45; Mary M. Schweitzer, *Custom and Contract: Household, Government, and the Economy in Colonial Pennsylvania* (New York: Columbia University Press, 1987); Lucy Simler, "The 'Best Poorman's Country' in 1783: The Population Structure of Rural Society in Late-Eighteenth-Century Southeastern Pennsylvania," *Proceedings of the American Philosophical Society* 133 (1989): 234–61; Lucy Simler and Paul

G. E. Clemens, "Rural Labor and Farm Households in Chester County, Pennsylvania, 1750–1820," in *Work and Labor in Early America,* ed. Stephen Innes (Chapel Hill: University of North Carolina Press, 1988), 106–43; Frederick B. Tolles, *Meeting House and Counting House: The Quaker Merchants of Colonial Philadelphia 1682–1763* (New York: Norton, 1948).

24. On Quaker women and textiles see Adrienne D. Hood, "The Material World of Cloth: Production and Use in Eighteenth Century Rural Pennsylvania," *William and Mary Quarterly* 53 (1996): 43–66; Hood, *The Weaver's Craft;* Adrienne D. Hood, "The Gender Division of Labor in the Production of Textiles in Eighteenth Century, Rural Pennsylvania (Rethinking the New England Model)," *Journal of Social History* 27 (1994): 537–61; O'Brien, "Divorced from the Land"; Simler and Clemens, "Rural Labor and Farm Households in Chester County,"; Laurel Thatcher Ulrich, *The Age of Homespun: Objects and Stories in the Creation of an American Myth,* (New York: Alfred A. Knopf, 2001); Laurel Thatcher Ulrich, "Sheep in the Parlor, Wheels in the Common: Pastoralism and Poverty in Eighteenth Century Boston," in *Inequality in Early America,* ed. Carla Gardina Pestana and Sharon V. Salinger (Hanover: University Press of New England, 1999); Laurel Thatcher Ulrich, "Wheels, Looms, and the Gender Division of Labor in Eighteenth-Century New England," *William and Mary Quarterly* 55, no. 1 (1998): 3–38.

25. Ann Taylor recalled that Hannah came to their house in winter to spin flax and wool all day with the other Quaker women and spent the long winter evenings making baskets near the fire. Albert Cook Myers Collection, Indian File, Chester County Historical Society, West Chester, Pa.

26. Joseph Barnard, "A Kindness Extended," 1798, Albert Cook Myers Papers, Indian File, Chester County Historical Society, West Chester, Pa.

27. Trenkwalder Schèonenberger, *Lenape Women,* 147–86.

28. In general see Marla N. Powers, *Oglala Women: Myth, Ritual, and Reality* (Chicago: University of Chicago Press, 1986).

29. For other examples see Duncan Hirsch, "Indian, Metis, and Euro-American Women on Multiple Frontiers," in *Friends and Enemies in Penn's Woods: Indians, Colonists and the Racial Construction of Pennsylvania,* ed. William A. Pencak and Daniel K. Richter (University Park: Pennsylvania State University, 2004); O'Brien, "Divorced from the Land"; Theda Perdue, ed., *Sifters: Native American Women's Lives* (New York: Oxford University Press, 2001); Nancy Shoemaker, ed., *Negotiators of Change: Historical Perspectives on Native American Women* (New York: Routledge, 1993).

30. Marshall, "Examination of Hannah Freeman."

31. Untitled article, *Poulson's Advertiser,* January 31, 1824, Newspaper File, Correspondence from P. Chandler regarding recollections of his grandmother Mary Lamborn; Correspondence to Albert Cook Myers from Emma Taylor, Albert Cook Myers Collection, Chester County Historical Society, West Chester, Pa.

32. Ann McMullin and Russell G. Handsman, eds., *A Key into the Language of Woodsplint Baskets* (Washington, Conn.: American Indian Archaeological Institute, 1987); Ulrich, *The Age of Homespun.*

33. Correspondence from P. Chandler regarding recollections of his grandmother Mary Lamborn; Indian File, Albert Cook Myers Collection, Chester County Historical Society, West Chester, Pa.

34. Krista Camenzind, "Violence, Race, and the Paxton Boys," in *Friends and Enemies in Penn's Woods,* ed. Pencak and Richter, 201, 220; James E. Crowley, "The Paxton Disturbance and Ideas of Order in Pennsylvania Politics," *Pennsylvania History* 37, no. 4 (1970): 317–39; Brooke Hindle, "The March of the Paxton Boys," *William and Mary Quarterly* 3, no. 4 (1946): 462–86; Wilbur R. Jacobs, *The Paxton Riots and the Frontier Theory* (Chicago: Rand McNally, 1967); James Kirby Martin, "The Return of the Paxton Boys and the Historical State of the Pennsylvania Frontier," *Pennsylvania History* 38, no. 2 (1971): 117–33; Alden T. Vaughan, "Frontier Banditti and the Indians: The Paxton Boys' Legacy, 1763–1775," *Pennsylvania History* 51, no. 1 (1984): 1–29.

35. Marshall, "Examination of Hannah Freeman."

36. Jane T. Merritt, "The Long Peace in Pennsylvania," *History Compass,* Wiley Online Library, Vol. 2, no. 1, 2004, available at http://onlinelibrary.wiley.com/doi/10.1111/j.1478 –0542.2004.00106.x/full.

37. See Sharon Block, *Rape and Sexual Power in Early America* (Chapel Hill: University of North Carolina Press, 2006).

38. Marshall, "Examination of Hannah Freeman."

39. Miscellaneous Notes, Indian File, Albert Cook Myers Collection, Chester County Historical Society, West Chester, Pa.

40. Ibid.

41. Correspondence from Edith Pennock to Albert Cook Myers, 1903, Indian File, Albert Cook Myers Collection, Chester County Historical Society, West Chester, Pa. Edith Pennock recalled the burial of Hannah's mother as a remarkable event that ended at an Indian cemetery on Humphrey Marshall's land in Newlin township.

42. Miscellaneous Notes, Indian File, Albert Cook Myers Collection, Chester County Historical Society, West Chester, Pa.

43. Ibid.

44. The names Black Thomas and White Thomas did not signify racial descriptions. The terms were used to identify closely related individuals with the same name living in the same community.

45. Indian File, Albert Cook Myers Collection, Chester County Historical Society, West Chester, Pa.

46. Gladys Tantaquidgeon, *Folk Medicine of the Delaware and Related Algonkian Indians* (Harrisburg: Pennsylvania Historical and Museum Commission, 1972); Gladys Tanta-quidgeon, *A Study of Delaware Indian Medicine Practice and Folk Beliefs* (New York: AMS Press, 1980).

47. See Paula Gunn Allen, *The Sacred Hoop: Recovering the Feminine in American Indian Traditions* (Boston: Beacon Press, 1992); Tantaquidgeon, *A Study of Delaware Indian Medicine Practice and Folk Beliefs;* Trenkwalder Schèonenberger, *Lenape Women.*

48. Lucy Simler, "Tenancy in Colonial Pennsylvania: The Case of Chester County," *William and Mary Quarterly* 43, no. 4 (1986): 542–69.

49. Indian File, Albert Cook Myers Papers, Chester County Historical Society.

50. "Minutes of the Directors of the Poor," Poorhouse Record of Admissions, 1798–1805, Chester County Archives and Records, West Chester, Pa.

Women, Labor, and Power in the Nineteenth-Century Choctaw Nation

Fay A. Yarbrough

Over the course of the nineteenth century, the people of the Choctaw Nation experienced tremendous change in almost every facet of their lives. Whereas traditional practices and understandings of clan obligation and responsibility had once governed the behavior of Choctaw men and women, the nineteenth century marked a transition to writing down laws to govern behavior and punish criminality in the nation. The American federal government then forcibly removed many Choctaws from their homeland in the southeastern United States to the Indian Territory in the center of the country. Choctaw Indians also adopted African slavery, participated in the Civil War as allies of the Confederacy, and strained against federal demands during Reconstruction just as their Southern brethren did.

In response to these changes the Choctaws adjusted their understandings of gender relations and women's roles in families and society. Because of their roles as agriculturalists, landowners, and producers of future members of the nation, Choctaw women retained some of their traditional authority in Choctaw society. And at the same time that Choctaw society was struggling to accommodate and resist the notions of gender that Americans attempted to force upon them, they also began to construct their own ideas about race. So while in some ways Choctaw women's power diminished, they still remained important actors whose marital decisions, in particular, could have dramatic consequences for the nation as evidenced by the careful way that Choctaw legal officials attempted to police Choctaw women's marriages to outsiders.[1]

This essay explores shifting ideas about gender and race in the Choctaw Nation by considering Choctaw regulation of marriage law. First, the essay outlines some of the basic social organization of traditional Choctaw society. For Choctaws clans were a central component of identity that shaped family and marriage structure. Within these Choctaw families labor was gendered with men and women performing different, complementary tasks for the household. Next, Choctaws moved to formalize practices through written laws and began to shift away from traditional labor arrangements and to intervene in women's marital choices. Marriage law in particular demonstrated Choctaw women's changed position in society. Legislators circumscribed Choctaw women's property rights and limited women's marital options, giving careful consideration to race. This emphasis on and definition of race through marriage laws in the Choctaw Nation is the final subject of this essay. Again, these dramatic changes in Choctaw thinking about race and gender occurred while the nation was besieged by American threats to Choctaw territorial claims and national sovereignty.

Clan, Family, and Marriage

Choctaw Indians determined clan membership, traditionally a key part of Choctaw identity, matrilineally; that is, children became members of their mother's, not their father's, clan.[2] Thus, within a household a mother and her children were kin while the husband was "a guest rather than a relative," according to scholar Patricia Galloway.[3] Elizabeth Kemp Mead may have been referencing the practice of assigning clan membership matrilineally when she remarked, "In old time the Choctaw children took the mother's housename instead of taking the father's name."[4] Given the traditional lack of the use of surnames among the Choctaw, this description of how one traditionally received a "housename" may have served as a kind of shorthand for clan membership or a nineteenth-century interpretation of what clan membership meant.[5] Matrilineal kinship arrangements also meant that the family sought the advice of the oldest maternal uncle or oldest maternal male relative in important decisions regarding children. The maternal family took responsibility for raising children who lost their mother through death. And the woman's children, not her husband, inherited her property. A Choctaw man's siblings or other members of his clan took possession of his property if he died: "His children, being looked on as members of another *ogla*, since they belonged to their mother's family, were not considered as entitled to any of this property."[6]

Clan membership had been so vital as a form of social organization because of the traditional practice of blood revenge among the Choctaw Indians: "*Iksa* [clan] members were obligated to aid each other and to obtain blood revenge for the killing of one of their members." It was the "right, but also the imperative duty of the nearest relative on the male side of the slain, to kill the slayer wherever and whenever a favorable opportunity was presented."[7] If the guilty party fled, which was an unusual occurrence, a male relative might volunteer or be chosen as a substitute whose death would fulfill the debt. The victim's family would never choose a female relative of the perpetrator to serve as a substitute, though a female relative could choose to volunteer.[8] Once the debt was paid there was no further retribution. In other words the perpetrator's, or substitute's, clan did not feel obliged to avenge his or her death. Michelene E. Pesantubbee argues that the term *blood revenge* is a mischaracterization of the practice. Clan members were not obliged to kill the murderer of a kinsperson but to "restore balance to their world" or to "seek restitution for a life."[9] Thus a Choctaw family or clan could seek the death of the person responsible for the death of their kinsperson or adopt the responsible party into the family's clan. In rare instances the family might accept some form of payment as restitution.[10] The recognition by all Choctaws, as well as other native peoples, of the clan obligations in the event of a member's death served to curb warfare and personal violence.[11] When Choctaws chose to go to war with another group that shared a similar perspective about clan obligations, they recognized that not only warriors were put in jeopardy. Any Choctaw could be the target of retribution. This practice may, in part, explain the Choctaws' avoidance of offensive wars.[12] Similarly one would tread carefully in daily personal exchanges because a misstep could obligate kinsmen in complicated ways.

While children joined the clans of their mothers, both Choctaw men and women were responsible for the care and nurture of children, the difference being that Choctaw men were not always the primary decision makers regarding their own biological children but instead played an important role in the lives of their nieces and nephews. A situation in which it remains ambiguous if and how responsibility was shared regards the practice of infanticide. According to historian Richard White, "infanticide was widespread in the nation, but it was a practice about which little is known. Which children the Choctaws killed and why remains unclear."[13] And who made the decisions about which children were targeted is also unclear. Was the child's maternal uncle part of the decision-making process, as one would expect given the operation of matrilineal clans, or was the decision left to the child's parents? H. B. Cushman quoted Choctaw chief Aboha Kullo Humma of the Okla Hunnali who claimed that "the Choctaw women sometimes killed their infants, when they did not want to provide for them," which suggests that Choctaw women in particular practiced infanticide.[14] Given the concept of blood vengeance, the death of one member of a Choctaw clan at the hands of another member of the same clan could circumvent the need for external retribution, perhaps lending further weight to the participation of Choctaw women in the practice.

Choctaw households were not only matrilineal, they were also matrilocal: husbands joined their wives' households upon marriage.[15] These two facts, that Choctaws assigned clan membership matrilineally and that Choctaw men joined their wives' households, may explain the ease with which marital unions could be dissolved, though separations seldom occurred.[16] By the nineteenth century, according to Chief Aboha Kullo Humma, separations between Choctaw husbands and wives may have been more common. By 1822 the Choctaws of Six

Towns enacted a law punishing men who ran away with other men's wives with whippings of thirty-nine lashes.[17] Runaway wives received the same punishment. Chief Aboha Kullo Humma did not mention punishments for runaway husbands; perhaps Choctaws found errant wives more threatening because their behavior emasculated Choctaw men. In any case, when a couple separated there were no questions about who would be responsible for raising the children: the wife and her family would maintain any children. The husband remained a member of his own clan and could return to his mother's or some other female relative's household. Such social factors may also explain the traditional Choctaw acceptance of polygamous unions. Polygamy was not widespread among the Choctaws and tended to occur when the plural wives were sisters.[18] Such women may have shared a household anyway and adding one husband rather than two may have lessened labor burdens for the women.[19] By 1849 the General Council outlawed polygamy and penalized those individuals found guilty of polygamy with a fine of ten to twenty-five dollars for each count.[20]

Labor and Gender

Within these matrilocal households, men and women performed different kinds of labor.[21] Choctaw men provided meat for their families through hunting.[22] Men also served as warriors in larger Choctaw society. While men might help with the planting and harvesting of crops, women were primarily responsible for maintaining the crop and might even ridicule men who performed too much agricultural labor.[23] Such men were stepping outside of the prescribed gendered division of labor, and Choctaw women tried to push these men back into their accepted roles through public shame. William Edward Baker, a Cherokee resident of Indian Territory familiar with his Choctaw neighbors, described native labor practices more generally, but his depiction could easily have applied specifically to the Choctaws: "The Indian women did all the work unless they hired it done. The men hunted and fished and sat around eating and drinking sofkey."[24] Knowledge of the traditional division of labor among the Choctaw Indians even filtered down to their slave property. Jefferson L. Cole, a slave owned by a Choctaw family, recalled that Choctaw women had initially farmed while men hunted until "after the white people came in large numbers and brought their customs." Then Indian men also helped with farming.[25] The traditional division of labor and tasks between Choctaw husbands and wives may best be encapsulated by the Choctaw marriage practice in which "the man offers meat and the woman corn to seal the relationship."[26]

Women controlled the home and communally owned farm lands and performed the bulk of agricultural labor. In fact, as H. B. Cushman stated, Choctaw women performed all of the "drudgery work about the house and hunting camp."[27]

Nineteenth-century Indian Territory resident Lucy Case, who described both of her parents as "full-blood" Choctaw Indians, said, "I remember that my mother did most of the work. She always did the breaking of the land."[28] In particular, Choctaw women were responsible for growing corn, a staple of the Choctaw diet.[29] Anna McClendon Smallwood, a Choctaw woman, recalled that "the only crops raised by the Indians of early territory days were small patches of squaw corn, called Tom Fuller corn and later named squaw corn because the squaws, or women, did all the raising of this particular crop."[30] Emmaline Terrell also related that squaw corn was so named because women did all of the work to cultivate it.[31] Women also seemed to be responsible for the making of corn into other food products.[32] Rodolphus Gardner remembered his mother beating corn in a morter [sic]."[33] Many different traditional Choctaw dishes began with pounded corn as their base.[34]

Women's management of corn production was a source of influence in Choctaw society.[35] Corn provided important sustenance for Choctaw families; Richard White extrapolates that corn could have provided roughly two-thirds of the daily caloric intake for Choctaws. Choctaw women, then, provided the bulk of a family's food supply. Corn was also a gift for a daughter's wedding. A feast was generally a part of the marriage ritual, and corn would have figured predominantly in such a meal.[36] Friendly diplomatic negotiations often included an exchange of corn, and corn was at the center of hospitality more generally because many dishes that Choctaws would offer to their guests included corn as an ingredient.[37] Corn also could serve as a form of medicine that "drew on the power of all three worlds to bring health."[38] For warriors, corn sustained expeditions by providing important nutrition when using rifles to shoot game would have alerted enemies of their presence.[39] Finally, corn was an important part of ceremonial life. The appearance of green corn indicated that the end of the Choctaw year was near.[40] The Choctaws also held most of their feasts at this time, including a Green Corn Dance.[41] This celebration of green corn may also have served as an acknowledgement of Choctaw women and the important agricultural work they did in providing corn.[42]

Corn was so important to the Choctaws that they created legends to explain its origins. In one account two unsuccessful hunters found a beautiful woman in a moonlit forest after hearing some strange noises. She was hungry, and the hunters offered her some of their meager roasted black hawk. She accepted the food and then promised to remember their kindness when she returned to her father, "The Great Spirit of the Choctaws." She asked the hunters to meet her at midsummer at the mound on which she was standing. The hunters returned and did not find the woman, but instead a strange plant covered the mound "which yielded an excellent food, which was ever afterwards cultivated by the Choctaws, and named by them Tunchi (corn)."[43] Another story explaining the introduction of corn to the Choctaw people involved a crow dropping corn near a child playing in a yard. In one version of the story the child, an orphan, then named and planted the corn. In another the child's mother knew the grain was corn and planted it.[44] One should note that in two of these corn origin stories, women played an important role in introducing corn to the Choctaw people, either as a fully formed plant, in the case of the mysterious woman, or as a seed for cultivation. The child's mother knew immediately what the grain was and what to do with it. Presumably the mystery woman planted the corn at the mound. These origin stories suggest a rationale for Choctaw women's responsibility for growing corn and for their role as agriculturalists more generally.

White observers appear to have held a wide range of opinions about marriages between native peoples, often based on the division of labor between native husbands and wives. H. B. Cushman's comment that a Choctaw woman "as the wife of the Choctaw warrior and hunter was regarded as the slave of her husband" suggests that some white observers had an extremely negative view of such unions because Choctaw women performed so much labor.[45] Admittedly, Cushman tempers his comment by adding "so likewise may equally be regarded the unfortunate wives of many of the boasted white men of this 19th century"; however, this statement does not suggest that the lot of native women was better than it might appear at first glance but that the lot of many white women was the same. White observers noted the perceived uneven division of labor between Choctaw men and women and sometimes assumed that it indicated the lower status of women in Choctaw society.[46] Similarly, some white women disparaged native unions more generally because of "what they perceived as degrading treatment of native women by their men" as it pertained to labor.[47] In contrast J. E. Northrup, whose family moved to the Indian Territory late in the nineteenth century, remarked: "It seems that the Indians get along better with their wives than most of the white people; they are not getting divorces like the white people do these days."[48] Comments about the infrequency of separation between Choctaw spouses might support Northrup's observation.

Choctaw women also played important roles as captives and slaves. Some native groups captured and adopted individuals, often women and children, in order to replenish population losses sustained through warfare or disease; however, these groups frequently killed male captives because they represented a threat as present or future warriors. As native groups became active in the Indian slave trade with European settlers, they frequently sold into slavery those captives, women and children, that they once had adopted.[49] British and French settlers also seemed to prefer female Indian slaves, most likely because the Europeans saw native women as less hostile and aggressive or more manageable.[50] Native women were also more experienced agriculturalists, and farming was the primary activity, along with household labor, which the settlers deemed women's work, that settlers purchased slaves to perform.[51] Thus, prior to 1750 female Indian slaves outnumbered male Indian slaves.[52] Finally, other native groups may have recognized the importance, both symbolic and actual, of Choctaw women as producers of corn in Choctaw society and targeted them for capture and enslavement because of the upheaval their absence would cause for a Choctaw enemy.

Written Law

During the first third of the nineteenth century, the Choctaws would begin formalizing their practices in written laws, and women's role in Choctaw society would change dramatically. The Choctaw Nation began the century holding territory in the southeastern United States that included part of central Mississippi territory and a small portion of the present-day state of Alabama. After the forced removal of the southeastern tribes to Indian Territory in the 1830s, the Choctaw Nation consisted of the southeastern corner of the present-day state of Oklahoma. By 1838 the nation established a government that bore a strong resemblance to that of the United States.[53] The Choctaw government included four branches that shared power: the legislative, executive, judiciary, and military branches. The General Council, composed of forty annually elected representatives who debated and created legislation, formed the legislative branch. Only male Choctaw citizens could vote in elections or serve as representatives. The executive branch consisted of four district chiefs who were responsible for approving or rejecting legislation, notifying the council about the affairs of his district, and enforcing laws in his district. The supreme and district courts oversaw civil and criminal matters as the judiciary branch. Finally, each district elected a general who served in the military department and commanded the district military force in the event of an invasion or war.[54] The Choctaw Constitution also included a Declaration of Rights along the lines of the American Bill of Rights.[55]

The new Choctaw Constitution did not grant Choctaw women the legal rights to govern that one might expect given women's traditional importance as corn producers. The Choctaw Constitution did not include women in the electorate or permit them to serve as representatives in the General Council.[56] The language of the constitution also assumed that the four district chiefs were male: "Each Chief shall from time to time give the General Council information respecting the affairs of his own district, and recommend to their consideration such measures as he may think expedient."[57] The constitution did not make any clear statement about the sex of judges, but, again, did assume that jurors and light-horse-men (the Choctaw equivalent of law enforcement officers) were males.[58] Finally, the authors of the constitution also referred to the generals in the

Military Department with the male pronoun.[59] Thus, while the constitution did not explicitly bar women from holding offices in the Choctaw government, it did adopt language that reflected the assumption that all elected officials would be men. This linguistic practice was all the more purposeful given the careful way in which the legislators did use gender neutral language in other legislation prohibiting persons of African descent from holding office in the government or in establishing penalties for crimes.[60] It seems, then, that Choctaw lawmakers wanted to avoid any confusion about whether people of African descent could hold office. Further, they recognized that Choctaw women were capable of social deviance and criminal behavior, though not of civic responsibility and governance.

During the larger process of formalizing Choctaw laws, women lost some control over reproduction. Chief Aboha Kulla Humma enacted a law by 1822 to punish women who committed infanticide with whipping. In one case the woman's "husband also received the same punishment for not restraining his wife in the destruction of the child."[61] Perhaps he bore responsibility in part because he was involved in the decision making. The punishment for the crime of infanticide seemed to target the unseemliness of the practice to outsiders: Chief Aboha Kulla Humma stated, "we have made the above laws because we wish to follow the ways of the white people. We hope they will assist us in getting our children educated."[62] The chief thought by conforming to what white people saw as acceptable behavior, he might in turn gain access to education for his people. A dozen years later the Choctaw General Council set the punishment for conviction of committing infanticide at sixty lashes without distinction as to the gender of the perpetrator.[63] Interestingly, while infanticide fell into the category of a "willful murder" because it was not an act of self defense or an accidental death, infanticide did not receive the same punishment as willful murder, that is, death.[64] Thus Choctaws must not have understood infanticide as murder. This distinction lends further credence to the idea that infanticide was an accepted practice in traditional Choctaw society. The council then outlawed an established practice in which Choctaw women had played an important part.

Choctaw authorities also sought to protect women from sexual predators. By October 1836 those convicted of the crime of rape or ravishment received sixty lashes on their bare backs regardless of race. Crimes of attempted rape or ravishment warranted half of this penalty—no more than thirty lashes.[65] Ten years later the Choctaw legislature passed a much harsher law. Authorities increased the punishment for a man convicted of "committing rape or forcibly ravishing a woman or girl" to "one hundred lashes well laid on his bare back." For a second conviction for the same crime, the perpetrator received a death sentence. In the case of attempted rape the court had some latitude in determining the penalty as long as it did not exceed thirty lashes.[66] The escalation of the punishment for the crime

130

of rape prompts speculation that its occurrence was becoming more frequent. At the very least more non-Choctaw men were coming into contact with Choctaw women, which may have triggered fears about sexual contact between them.

Women, Property, and Marriage

As Choctaw authorities enacted legislation that reduced women's decision-making power in national and family life, they also prescribed a different formula for disposing of property within families that deviated from the inheritance patterns provided for by clan relationships: "All property shall, upon the death of the husband, descend to the wife or children of the deceased husband, and in case of the death of the wife, the husband shall inherit the estate."[67] This change suggests larger transformations in Choctaw social organization: the importance of tracing kinship matrilineally may have been giving way to patrilineal kinship connections; clan kinship more generally may have been losing force as the primary means of social organization; and husbands may have been playing a more active role in decision making regarding their own children as opposed to the children of their sisters.[68] These changes in property inheritance patterns may also reflect changes in gendered labor practices. For instance women might have been performing less agricultural labor and had less control over land use. Choctaw men may have been replacing hunting with agriculture as their primary labor responsibility. Certainly in the nineteenth century the Choctaw Indians faced strong pressure to conform their labor and inheritance practices to American patterns, which may explain why two-thirds of the members of the Choctaw General Council approved this law.

In 1848 the General Council offered further clarification on the property rights of married individuals. In a move in keeping with traditional Choctaw practice, the council stipulated that each party in a marriage retained "the right of the property that he or she may bring into the marriage union."[69] Neither party could dispose of the property of his/her spouse without the spouse's consent. Failure to obtain spousal consent could result in a lawsuit. Thus far, the law respected each marriage partner's individual property rights. At the moment of the death of either spouse, however, the law diverged from traditional practice and no longer respected individual property rights: "And be it further enacted, That no will that is made by the husband or wife, conveying property without the consent of the other, shall be valid."[70] In other words a married person retained control over his/her property to do with as s/he wished until s/he died. Then s/he had to obtain the consent of his/her spouse to convey that property, presumably to someone other than the living spouse. The act also recognized the concept of joint property, that a married couple could accumulate property together and both have some claim of possession. Husbands would seem to have greater authority over this joint property, as the property was "subject to the disposal of the husband for the mutual support and benefit of the family."[71] And the earlier 1835 marriage law remained in effect, which resolved pesky questions about the disposal of joint marital property by stipulating that in the case of the death of one of the partners, the surviving spouse inherited this marital joint property, not members of the deceased spouse's clan.

The attempts by Choctaw legislators to protect the property rights of married women may indicate that some outsiders unfamiliar with Choctaw marital practice were marrying Choctaw women. At first blush the traditionally matrilocal and matrilineal households of the Choctaws might make it easier to incorporate male outsiders into society. After all, any children produced in unions between Choctaw women and non-Choctaw men would have kinship ties and clan membership through their mothers, and other Choctaws would view these children as fully Choctaw because of these connections. The male outsider would seamlessly join the household of his Choctaw wife and contribute meat to the family's diet. If the marriage dissolved, he could return to his own "clan" outside the nation. Given the social organization of the Choctaws, members of the Choctaw Nation might have viewed the introduction of male outsiders to the nation as the husbands of Choctaw women with little trepidation. In actuality, however, some Choctaw Indians did respond with alarm at the prospect of Choctaw women marrying non-Choctaw men.

Marriage and Race

Pete W. Cole, a nineteenth-century resident of the Indian Territory, and H. B. Cushman both recounted similar stories about the initial reluctance Choctaws felt to accept marriages between Choctaw women and white men. In both accounts the birth of a child provoked a council meeting. Some council members argued successfully that permitting these marriages would allow white people to "become more numerous" and lead to the loss of the nation's characteristics. Thus the council prohibited "all future marriages between the Choctaws and the White Race," ordered the white husband to leave the nation, and condemned the child to death. The committee appointed to execute the child, however, "felt reluctant" to do so. In the meantime the mother found out about this decision and hid her baby. The committee blamed the Great Spirit for the child's disappearance and decided that if the baby returned, he would be spared. The mother then reappeared with her son and claimed that the Great Spirit had returned him to her. Thus the boy lived, and others considered the child to be under the protection of the Great Spirit. He later became chief of the Choctaw Nation. The council eventually repealed the ban on intermarriage, recalled the father to the tribe, and adopted him as a member.[72] This story, then, also sets the precedent for the practice of adopting the white spouses of Choctaw Indians into the nation.

It is difficult to determine the accuracy of this account of the first marriage between a member of the Choctaw Nation and a white person. For instance a record of a legislative ban on intermarriage between Choctaw Indians and white people does not appear in compilations of laws passed by the General Council. And the decision to execute the child of the union seems surprising: given matrilineal clan membership, the boy should have been seen as fully Choctaw and the member of a clan. Some clan members might have balked at accepting his death sentence when he had committed no crime. The story also takes on mythical proportions because of its explanatory power; the story provides the origins for the introduction of laws regulating marriages between Choctaws and outsiders, the practice of adopting the white spouses of Choctaws into the tribe, and the presence of Choctaws of European ancestry in positions of authority. The tidiness of the explanations necessarily provokes questions about when this "accepted fable" emerged.[73] Did some members of the Choctaw Nation develop the story once marriages between Choctaw Indians and white people, along with the procedures governing them, had become common occurrences and well established? And it is possible that Pete W. Cole read Cushman's account and regurgitated it for the Indian Pioneer History Collection. In any case the story does demonstrate that some parties in the Choctaw Nation viewed marriages between Choctaws and white people with deep suspicion and reservation.

The hostility that some Choctaws felt toward marriages between Choctaws and white people is less surprising if one focuses on the labor that Choctaw women performed rather than on the social organization of matrifocal and matrilineal families. Choctaw women performed important functions in society, so authorities carefully monitored whom they married. In 1836 the General Council passed an act requiring "any white man, who shall hereafter take a Choctaw woman for a wife, will be required to marry her lawfully by a Minister of the Gospel or other authorized person, after procuring license from any of the Judges or District Clerks for that purpose."[74] In effect, white men had to register with national authorities befor_ _hey could marry Choctaw women. And though the act did not state it expli_'_ _y, the implication was that a white man's request for such a license cou'_ _ _.ied. A white man could not access Choctaw citizenship unless he had follow__ these procedures. Moreover, Choctaw legislators recognized that within marriages between white men and women, women ceded control of their property to their husbands. In order to protect Choctaw women's traditional property rights, legislators included this proviso: "That any white man who shall marry a Choctaw woman, the property of the woman so married shall not be subject to the disposal of her husband contrary to her consent."[75] The law demonstrates that Choctaws recognized the value and importance of preserving women's property rights. Finally, this act stated that white men who left their wives without just cause lost their citizenship rights in the Choctaw Nation and would be ordered to pay their wives a sum to be determined by legal officials for breach of marriage.

By 1840 the General Council expanded on the law regulating marriage between Choctaw women and white men.[76] This act retained the license requirement for white men seeking to marry Choctaw women; preserved the property rights of Choctaw wives; and continued to impose a financial penalty and a legal penalty, the loss of Choctaw citizenship, on white men who left their Choctaw wives. Choctaw lawmakers also added a residency requirement of two years for white men to marry in the nation, which suggests a desire to know the quality or character of the applicant for the marriage license. Choctaw authorities wanted to know exactly to whom they were granting citizenship. Last, this act included a steep penalty in the form of a one-hundred-dollar fine for any person who performed a marriage that did not adhere to the requirements of this act. The fine suggests that not everyone was abiding by the license and residency restrictions. Thus lawmakers hoped to circumvent white men who sought to evade the proper legal course for marriage by making collusion expensive.

Just nine years later the General Council addressed another aspect of relationships between white men and Choctaw women when it demanded "that every white man who is living with Indian woman in this Nation without being lawfully married to her, shall be required to marry her lawfully, or be compelled to leave the Nation, and forever stay out of it."[77] Perhaps some couples found the two-year residency requirement for white men onerous and could not wait to establish their households. These couples might also represent an older pattern of traditional Choctaw marriage that did not require governmental sanction to be accepted and respected by community members. The second part of this marriage act suggests that some of these couples were the result of white men being denied licenses to marry Choctaw women: "That no white man who is under a bad character will be allowed to be united to an Indian woman in marriage, in the Nation, under any circumstances whatever."[78] The language is clear; Choctaw authorities wanted to prevent white men of questionable character from accessing Choctaw citizenship specifically and to push those men out of the Nation more generally.

The most complicated iteration of marriage laws governing unions between white men and Choctaw women came in 1875.[79] The General Council continued to require that a white man, who could be a citizen of the United States or some other foreign government, obtain a marriage license from a Choctaw circuit clerk or judge in order to marry in the nation, but also added the stipulation that he swear an oath or provide some other evidence that he was not still legally married elsewhere. This part of the intermarriage law echoes the sentiments of the earlier 1849 prohibition of polygamous unions. Moreover, he had to present a "certificate of good moral character, signed by at least ten respectable Choctaw citizens by blood, who shall have been acquainted with him at least twelve months immediately preceding the signing of such certificate." The certificate requirement is illuminating in several respects. First, Choctaw legal authorities did not trust just any citizen to testify to the "good moral character" of a white male applicant for marriage: other intermarried white men, for instance, were not acceptable signatories. Thus, while these intermarried white men might have been Choctaw citizens legally, Choctaw authorities saw them as different in some way. Choctaw citizens by blood had to be willing to endorse an applicant for marriage. Second, the requirement that the signatories of the certificate know the applicant for at least twelve months reflects a desire to be certain about the applicant's character. Presumably those signatories knew the applicant because he had resided in the nation for those twelve months prior to seeking a marriage license. Choctaws, then, were wary of white men who moved into Choctaw territory and immediately sought Choctaw wives and therefore access to Choctaw citizenship.

The procedure for obtaining a marriage license did not end with demonstrating that one was not married elsewhere or presenting a certificate of good moral character: the applicant still had to pay a twenty-five-dollar fee and swear an oath of allegiance to the Choctaw government. The oath stated: "I do solemnly swear that I will honor, defend, and submit to the constitution and laws of the Choctaw nation, and will neither claim nor seek from the United Sates government or from the judicial tribunals thereof, any protection privilege, or redress incompatible with the same as guaranteed to the Choctaw nation by the treaty stipulations entered into between them, so help me God."[80]

The oath was an attempt to navigate the complications created by marriages between citizens of different sovereign nations. For instance, in the case of the commission of a crime, what court had jurisdiction to punish an intermarried citizen? To what court would an intermarried citizen submit a complaint or attempt to seek restitution? If the Choctaw Nation and the United States engaged in a war, a not so far-fetched prospect given the Trail of Tears or the Civil War, for whom might intermarried citizens fight? Choctaw legal officials hoped, through the oath, to transform outsiders into citizens, to provide a clear answer to these kinds of questions. In marrying Choctaw women white men made not only a financial commitment, for the license fee was not small, but a legal and civic commitment as well.

The gendered labor arrangements of the Choctaws provoke some consideration of how Choctaw men might have viewed the white men who married

Choctaw women and functioned as the primary agriculturalists in their house-holds. Choctaw men would likely have been perplexed by the determination of so many white men to farm, just as many white observers found the division of labor among natives unnatural. Indeed some white observers thought native men treated native women like slaves because native women performed so many tasks for the sustenance of their families and hard labor in the fields.[81] H. W. Gay, a Minnesotan who married a Choctaw woman stated, "In those days when a white man married an Indian woman, he was called squaw man and sometimes called galvanized citizen."[82] It is unclear from Gay's statement who was calling him a "squaw man," other white people or native people; either group might have used this phrase. White people might have used the term pejoratively to indicate dis-comfort with interracial marriage and the implication that the white husband was choosing to adopt an "Indian" rather than white lifestyle.[83] Native men, on the other hand, might have used the term to denigrate the white husband for per-forming agricultural labor, work perceived of as women's work. Or natives could have used the term to indicate that, because he lacked a matrilineally determined clan identity, the intermarried white man's connection to the tribe was through his wife.

While much of the intermarriage legislation applied to marriages between Choctaw women and "foreign" men, lawmakers did recognize that some Choctaw men married "foreign" women. According to the language of the act, however, the General Council did not oblige white women to obtain a marriage license, prove that they were not already married elsewhere, find Choctaws by blood to attest to their good character, or swear an oath of allegiance to the Choctaw government. Clearly Choctaw authorities found intermarried white women less threatening and saw less need to monitor carefully white women's access to Choctaw citizen-ship. Perhaps the long history of adopting non-Choctaw women into the nation explains the exemption of white women from the requirements of the intermar-riage law. Choctaws also likely realized that white women exercised few property rights upon marriage in American society and thus were unlikely to expect these rights upon marrying their Choctaw husbands. In contrast Choctaw authorities' careful circumscription of the property rights of white men who married Choctaw women indicates that white men did presume that they would have authority over their wives' property upon marriage.

Where white women do appear in this intermarriage act is as widows and absent partners.[84] A white woman preceded in death by her Choctaw husband continued to enjoy the privileges of Choctaw citizenship unless she remarried a white person "having no rights of Choctaw citizenship by blood." Marrying another intermarried white person, it seems, led to the loss of Choctaw citizenship for intermarried white women and men. Widowed intermarried white people presented a problem for Choctaw authorities: such individuals lacked clan affiliations and a connection to the nation but had not done anything to provoke a loss of citizenship except experience the misfortune of losing a spouse. These individuals also might be responsible for raising Choctaw children who did have clan membership and whom the Choctaws would want to keep in the nation. Widowed intermarried white people who then married each other presented a larger problem: they could produce children who would be Choctaw citizens but lacked clan membership and kinship ties, a prospect that many Choctaw would have found anathema given the importance of clan identity even as it experienced a nineteenth-century decline.

Abandoning one's Choctaw spouse also led to the loss of Choctaw citizenship, as well as a declaration of intruder status and removal from the nation, for both white women and white men. This provision attempted to prevent white people from marrying solely to gain citizenship rights in the nation and then quickly deserting their Choctaw spouses. It is also unclear from the statute if any kind of separation or divorce between a Choctaw Indian and a white person might qualify as abandonment. Thus the end of a long marriage might also result in the revocation of the white partner's legal citizenship and ejection from the nation.

Not long after the passage of this more detailed intermarriage act, a court decision would demonstrate the force of intermarriage laws and that the trend in changing social organization suggested by the passage of earlier laws about marriage and property inheritance continued. While the 1878 murder case against James E. Reynolds, an intermarried white man in the Choctaw Nation accused of murdering another intermarried Choctaw, focused on the issue of jurisdiction and who had authority in legal matters concerning intermarried white people in Indian Territory, the decision also established patrilineal descent as equal to matrilineal descent in determining Choctaw citizenship.[85] The court's decision regarding which judicial system, American or Indian, had the authority to hear the case depended on the citizenship of the wives: if the women were Choctaws by birth, their husbands obtained Choctaw citizenship through marriage, and the Choctaw courts would decide the case. The court found that the wives were in fact Choctaw based on their descent from a common male Choctaw ancestor; thus the Choctaw courts had jurisdiction over the prosecution of Reynolds. Many Choctaws had likely accepted the children of white women and Choctaw men, for instance, as citizens of the nation prior to this decision, but the decision validated the practice. The decision also confirmed that matrilineal descent and clan membership were no longer the central principle for social organization in the Choctaw Nation.

Marriage and the Forbidden Race

At the same moment that Choctaw officials were crafting increasingly complicated legislation to regulate marriages between Choctaw women and white men,
they were also prohibiting relationships between people of African descent and
Choctaw citizens. In 1838, just two years after the General Council began outlin-
ing the proper procedure for white men to marry Choctaw women, the council
also stated that "if any person or persons, citizens of this Nation, shall publicly
take up with a negro slave, he or she so offending shall be liable to pay a fine not
less than ten dollars nor exceeding twenty five dollars—and shall be separated."[86]
A second offense warranted between five and thirty-nine lashes on the bare back
as well as separation. The council did not stipulate a punishment for the "negro
slave" partner who violated this act. Perhaps the authorities thought that the
Choctaw partner was more culpable or assumed that the slave owner would punish the slave for violating this statute. The council also did not assume the gender
of the Choctaw offender. The language of this act alone does not indicate whether
it was the slave's status or race that lawmakers found unacceptable, but a slate of
other Choctaw legislation preventing people of African ancestry from holding
political office; prohibiting free black people from residing in the nation unless
they were also of Choctaw or Chickasaw descent; and preventing people of
African descent from gaining Choctaw citizenship through adoption or natural-
ization suggests that Choctaw lawmakers were beginning to think about race and
think about people of African descent negatively.[87]

The population of people of African descent in the Choctaw Nation at the
time of the passage of this prohibition was by no means insignificant. As early as
the 1720s European traders and settlers had introduced the Choctaws to African
slaves.[88] A little more than a century later in 1831, the federal government enu-
merated 17, 963 Indians, 151 white persons, and 521 slaves in preparation for
removing Choctaw Indians to Indian Territory.[89] The slave population more than
tripled the white population in Choctaw country. Eight years later there were
approximately 600 slaves of African descent living among the Choctaws.[90] And
by 1860 slaves of African descent comprised 14 percent of the population in the
Choctaw Nation.[91] Choctaw slave owners used their human property to perform
agricultural labor in the same manner as many of their counterparts in the American South. Slaves in the nation performed another important function when they
served as interpreters for their Choctaw masters because of their fluency in both
English and Choctaw languages.[92] The presence of this growing slave population
among the Choctaws led legislators to pass statutes like those found in slavehold-
ing states that prevented slaves from owning property or carrying guns without
permission from their owners and prohibiting the teaching of slaves to read or
write.[93]

The Choctaw legislature would not pass any further legislation regarding unions between people of African descent and Choctaws until 1885. In the interim the nation had experienced the trauma of the American Civil War, in which it sided quite earnestly with the Confederate States of America.[94] The nation also experienced its own Reconstruction as it negotiated peace terms with the federal government in 1866, which included a demand that the Choctaws accept their former slaves as citizens.[95] The Choctaws refused and requested that the federal government remove the former slaves from the Nation, a request that the federal government ignored.[96] For nearly two decades the Choctaw government then treated the Choctaw freedmen as American citizens but allowed the ex-slaves to farm in the nation.[97] Finally, in 1883 the Choctaw General Council passed the Freedmen Bill to explicate the status and rights of the freedmen. The bill granted freedmen civil, political, legal, and educational rights in the Choctaw Nation.[98] The freedmen did not have all of the rights of other Choctaws: they could not confer Choctaw citizenship on others through marriage.[99] Before the year was over the General Council would vote to revoke the freedmen's right to hold any political office in the nation, broadening the prohibition beyond that of the office of principal chief.[100]

The 1885 law regarding "Inter-marriage between Choctaws and Negroes" was quite clear: "It shall not be lawful for a Choctaw and a negro to marry." To do so was a felony punishable by fifty lashes on the bare back.[101] Thus the law declared an entire class of Choctaw citizens unmarriageable, though these people were no longer slaves and possessed some rights in the nation. This act clarified the target of the earlier antiamalgamation statute: the race, the African ancestry of the slaves, not their status, was what made relationships with them distasteful enough to be declared illegal.

Conclusion

The preoccupation of Choctaw legislators with regulating the marriages of Choctaw women and outsiders in particular demonstrates that the marital choices of Choctaw women were a matter of national consequence. And Choctaw women's marriages were so important to legal authorities because of the vital roles that Choctaw women played in society as landowners, as agriculturalists, and as producers of new clan members. Further, in marrying "foreign" men, mostly American, Choctaw women introduced a new citizen population that had very different perspectives on many aspects of Choctaw life: child custody, the gendered division of labor, governance, property inheritance, and national land policy. Though intermarried white women also represented a change because of their lack of clan ties in a society organized along lines of matrilineal kinship, the Choctaws did have previous experience successfully incorporating female

outsiders into the nation. And in light of the Choctaw Nation's institutionalization of the enslavement of people of African descent and its support of the Confederacy during the American Civil War, it is not surprising that Choctaw
authorities prohibited marriages between Choctaw citizens and people of African
descent throughout the nineteenth century.

While Choctaw women's marital choices grew increasingly important to
national authorities, these women lost some ground in arenas where they once
held power. First, the new system of government, formalized in written constitutions and legal statutes, left little official space for Choctaw women to participate
in the political process of managing the nation. Second, though legal authorities
protected women's traditional property rights even after marriage, they also
departed from clan determinations in reconfiguring rules of property inheritance.
Within families Choctaw women exercised less control over reproduction. Third,
the importance of clan relationships declined more generally, and legal officials, at
least, accepted patrilineal kinship on an equal basis with matrinlineal kinship in
determining legitimate members of the nation. A matrilineal connection to the
nation was no longer a prerequisite for membership. Finally, the introduction of
slave labor, the increased participation of Choctaw men in farming, and the growing population of white husbands who labored in fields encroached on the
authority that Choctaw women traditionally held because of their role as agriculturalists. Thus women's status did not simply decline within Choctaw society in
the nineteenth century, but rather the Choctaws accepted some elements of
American constructions of gender such as patrilineal inheritance and descent, but
also maintained important elements of their own cultural values and practices
such as women's property rights. Moreover, Choctaws were simultaneously con-
ceptualizing race as they refigured gender roles. "Civilization" for the Choctaw
Nation, as Americans and some Choctaws themselves termed it, the attempt by
Choctaws to reshape Choctaw practices into a more palatable form for Americans, led to a decreased role in political and family life for Choctaw women and
increased scrutiny of the marital choices they made.

Notes

1. For more on how native women might experience a decline in influence in one arena
and increased influence in others, see the work of Theda Perdue, *Cherokee Women: Gender
and Culture Change, 1700–1835* (Lincoln: University of Nebraska Press, 1998), or Carolyn
Ross Johnston, *Cherokee Women in Crisis* (Tuscaloosa: University of Alabama Press, 2003).

2. John R. Swanton, *Source Material for the Social and Ceremonial Life of the Choctaw
Indians* (Tuscaloosa: University of Alabama Press, 2001)*,* 77; Michelene E. Pesantubbee,
Choctaw Women in a Chaotic World: The Clash of Cultures in the Colonial Southeast (Albu-
querque: University of New Mexico Press, 2005), 10; H. B. Cushman, *History of the
Choctaw, Chickasaw and Natchez Indians,* ed. Angie Debo (Norman: University of Oklahoma

Press, 1999), 59, n. 14, and 87; Jesse O. McKee and Jon A. Schlenker, *The Choctaws: Cultural Evolution of a Native American Tribe* (Jackson: University Press of Mississippi, 1980), 29; and Patricia Galloway, *Choctaw Genesis: 1500–1700* (Lincoln: University of Nebraska Press, 1995), 2. Swanton's work was originally published by the Smithsonian Institution in 1931 as *Bureau of American Ethnology Bulletin 103.*

3. Galloway, *Choctaw Genesis,* 2.

4. Indian Pioneer History Collection, Roll IPH 3, vol. 7: 170. The Indian Pioneer History Collection is available at the Oklahoma Historical Society and will hereafter be cited in this manner: Roll IPH.

5. See Cushman, *History of the Choctaw, Chickasaw and Natchez Indians,* 194–95, or McKee and Schlenker, *The Choctaws,* 29, for more on Choctaw naming practices.

6. Swanton, *Source Material for the Social and Ceremonial Life of the Choctaw Indians,* 134. *Ogla* refers to family or clan. Swanton is quoting David I. Bushnell, Jr.

7. Both quotations from Richard White, *The Roots of Dependency: Subsistence, Environment, and Social Change among the Choctaws, Pawnees, and Navajos* (Lincoln: University of Nebraska Press, 1983), 38. See also Cushman, *History of the Choctaw, Chickasaw and Natchez Indians,* 157; Swanton, *Source Material for the Social and Ceremonial Life of the Choctaw Indians,* 104–7; or Angie Debo, *The Rise and Fall of the Choctaw Republic* (Norman: University of Oklahoma Press, 1934, 1982), 21–22.

8. Cushman, *History of the Choctaw, Chickasaw and Natchez Indians,* 203–6.

9. Pesantubbee, *Choctaw Women in a Chaotic World,* 46.

10. Cushman, *History of the Choctaw, Chickasaw and Natchez Indians,* 157, and White, *The Roots of Dependency,* 42.

11. Pesantubbee, *Choctaw Women in a Chaotic World,* 46.

12. Swanton offers the accounts of several observers who remarked on the reluctance of Choctaws to wage offensive wars but who fought valiantly when attacked. See *Source material for the Social and Ceremonial Life of the Choctaw Indians,* 164–70. The Choctaws' reluctance also stemmed from a desire for strategic advantage, and to be sure they attained it, they took the scalps of men, "which is a greater mark of valour" than "content[ing]" themselves with the scalps of women and children (see p. 164).

13. White, *The Roots of Dependency,* 108.

14. Cushman, *History of the Choctaw, Chickasaw and Natchez Indians,* 88

15. Galloway, *Choctaw Genesis,* 2, and Margaret Zehmer Searcy, "Choctaw Subsistence, 1540–1830: Hunting, Fishing, Farming, and Gathering" in Carolyn Keller Reeves's edited volume *The Choctaw before Removal* (Jackson: University Press of Mississippi, 1985), 32–54: 35.

16. See Debo, *The Rise and Fall of the Choctaw Republic,* 16.

17. Cushman, *History of the Choctaw, Chickasaw and Natchez Indians,* 88.

18. Swanton, *Source Material for the Social and Ceremonial Life of the Choctaw Indians,* 131, and see Debo, *The Rise and Fall of the Choctaw Republic,* 16.

19. Galloway, *Choctaw Genesis,* 2. See Fay A. Yarbrough, *Race and the Cherokee Nation: Sovereignty in the Nineteenth Century* (Philadelphia: University of Pennsylvania Press, 2008), 27–28, for more on the benefits of polygamous marriage for women in matrilocal households in the case of Cherokee Indians.

20. *Constitution, Treaties and Laws of the Choctaw Nation: Made and Enacted by the Choctaw Legislature* (Sedalia, Mo.: Democrat Steam Print, 1887): 155–56; reprinted

Fay. A. Yarbrough

(Wilmington, Del.: Scholarly Resources, 1975). Hereafter referred to as CTLCN XIX. It is unclear if the husband or the wives or all were liable for prosecution of the crime of polygamy.

21. McKee and Schlenker, *The Choctaws,* 29.

22. Galloway, *Choctaw Genesis,* 2.

23. McKee and Schlenker, *The Choctaws,* 29. See also White, *The Roots of Dependency,* 20.

24. Roll IPH 33, vol. 99: 394. Sofkey, also spelled sofke, is a sour corn drink or soup.

25. Roll IPH 22, vol. 65: 238.

26. Pesantubbee, *Choctaw Women in a Chaotic World,* 102.

27. Cushman, *History of the Choctaw, Chickasaw and Natchez Indians,* 174.

28. Roll IPH 17, vol. 51: 223.

29. Pesantubbee, *Choctaw Women in a Chaotic World,* 124.

30. Roll IPH 34, vol. 101: 488.

31. Roll IPH 15, vol. 46: 286–87.

32. See Debo, *The Rise and Fall of the Choctaw Republic,* 18, or Pesantubbee, *Choctaw Women in a Chaotic World,* 164.

33. Roll IPH 63: 136.

34. Cushman, *History of the Choctaw, Chickasaw and Natchez Indians,* 173–74, and Swanton, *Source Material for the Social and Ceremonial Life of the Choctaw Indians,* 37–38.

35. Pesantubbee discusses the various uses of corn in *Choctaw Women in a Chaotic World,* 124–25.

36. Cushman, *History of the Choctaw, Chickasaw and Natchez Indians,* 309–11, and Swanton, *Source Material for the Social and Ceremonial Life of the Choctaw Indians,* 127–38.

37. See Swanton, *Source Material for the Social and Ceremonial Life of the Choctaw Indians,* 161, or Cushman, *History of the Choctaw, Chickasaw and Natchez Indians,* 122.

38. Pesantubbee, *Choctaw Women in a Chaotic World,* 125.

39. Cushman, *History of the Choctaw, Chickasaw and Natchez Indians,* 174.

40. White, *The Roots of Dependency,* 21–22.

41. Swanton, *Source Material for the Social and Ceremonial Life of the Choctaw Indians,* 38.

42. Pesantubbee, *Choctaw Women in a Chaotic World,* 125.

43. Cushman, *History of the Choctaw, Chickasaw and Natchez Indians,* 214–16.

44. Swanton, *Source Material for the Social and Ceremonial Life of the Choctaw Indians,* 208–10.

45. Cushman, *History of the Choctaw, Chickasaw and Natchez Indians,* 174

46. Debo, *The Rise and Fall of the Choctaw Republic,* 18. Debo posits that these observers failed "to take into account the importance and difficulty of the chase" in assessing the division of labor in Choctaw society.

47. Glenda Riley, *Women and Indians on the Frontier: 1825–1915* (Albuquerque: University of New Mexico Press, 1984), 133.

48. Roll IPH 36, vol. 107: 239.

49. Pesantubbee, *Choctaw Women in a Chaotic World,* 54–55, and 96; Galloway, *Choctaw Genesis,* 201–2; and Peter H. Wood, *Black Majority: Negroes in Colonial South Carolina from 1670 through the Stono Rebellion* (New York: Norton, 1975), 38–39.

50. Pesantubbee, *Choctaw Women in a Chaotic World*, 53.

51. Ibid., 53 and 96.

52. Wood, *Black Majority*, 144, offers population data for South Carolina in 1708. See also Pesantubbee, *Choctaw Women in a Chaotic World*, 39.

53. *The Constitution and Laws of the Choctaw Nation*, vol. 13 of the Constitution and Laws of the American Indian Tribes Series (Park Hill, Cherokee Nation: John Candy, Printer, 1840): 3; reprinted (Wilmington, Del.: Scholarly Resources, 1975). Hereafter to be referred to as *CLCN* 13.

54. *CLCN* 13: 5–10, articles II–VI. These articles stipulate the distribution of powers as well as the duties of each branch of the government.

55. *CLCN* 13: 4–5, article I.

56. *CLCN* 13: 6, sections 7 and 5.

57. *CLCN* 13: 8, section 4.

58. *CLCN* 13: 9, section 5.

59. *CLCN* 13: 10, section 3.

60. *CLCN* 13: 12, section 13. For several early examples of laws passed by the General Council that carefully use "person or persons" in describing punishment, see *CLCN* 12: 13–15, sections 2, 3, 4, 5, 7, 8, 11, and 12.

61. Cushman, *History of the Choctaw, Chickasaw and Natchez Indians*, 88.

62. Ibid., 89.

63. *CLCN* 13: 15

64. *CLCN* 13: 14–15.

65. *CLCN* 13: 18.

66. *The Constitution and Laws of the Choctaw Nation*, vol. 14 of The Constitutions and Laws of the American Indian Tribes Series (Park Hill, Cherokee Nation: Mission Press, 1847), 63; reprint (Wilmington, Del.: Scholarly Resources, 1975). Hereafter referred to as *CLCN* 14.

67. *CLCN* 13: 17.

68. White, *The Roots of Dependency*, 127.

69. *Constitution and Laws of the Choctaw Nation: Together with the Treaties of 1855, 1865 and 1866* (New York City: Wm. P. Lyon & Son, 1869), 100. Hereafter referred to as *CLCN* 1869.

70. *CLCN* 1869: 100.

71. *CLCN* 1869: 100.

72. Roll IPH 35, vol. 104: 366–67. Cole had detailed knowledge of Choctaw marriage laws and offered a summary on pages 363–66. Quoted material comes from Cushman's account, *History of the Choctaw, Chickasaw and Natchez Indians*, 314–15.

73. Cushman, *History of the Choctaw, Chickasaw and Natchez Indians*, 315.

74. *CLCN* 13: 22.

75. *CLCN* 13: 22.

76. *CLCN* 14: 33–34.

77. *CLCN* 1869, 106.

78. *CLCN* 1869, 106.

79. *Constitution, Treaties and Laws of the Choctaw Nation, Made and Enacted by the Choctaw Legislature, 1887*, vol. 19 of The Constitutions and Laws of the American Indian

Tribes Series (Sedalia, MO: Democrat Steam Print, 1887), 171–72; reprint (Wilmington, Del.: Scholarly Resources, 1975). Hereafter referred to as *CTLCN* 19.

80. The oath duplicates the language of a similar oath required of white men seeking to marry Cherokee women in 1855. The Choctaw oath adds only "so help me God." See Yarbrough, *Race and the Cherokee Nation,* chapter 3, especially pp. 56–58.

81. Walter O'Meara, *Daughters of the Country: The Women of the Fur Traders and Mountain Men* (New York: Harcourt, Brace, and World, 1968), 45–47. See also Riley, *Women and Indians on the Frontier,* 133, and Richard White, *The Roots of Dependency,* 161.

82. Roll IPH 2, vol. 4: 8–10.

83. James Axtell, *The European and the Indian: Essays in the Ethnohistory of Colonial North America* (Oxford: Oxford University Press, 1981), 154–56.

84. *CTLCN* 19, 172, sections 5 and 6.

85. Cherokee National Records Microfilm Series, Roll CHN 73, vol. Cherokee (Tahlequah) Courts 1878: 12–28. Page numbering restarts in each year, and there are no volume numbers. This case appeared in Cherokee court at the request of Choctaw authorities. Indian courts assumed that because both the victim and alleged perpetrator were Choctaw citizens, Indian courts had the authority to prosecute the case and mete out justice; however, American courts might interpret the legal status of intermarried white people differently. Federal courts might attempt to exercise authority over this case because neither the accused nor the victim was a native Choctaw. See Yarbrough, *Race and the Cherokee Nation,* 56–57, for more on this case in the Cherokee context.

86. *CLCN* 13, 27–28.

87. *CLCN* 13: 12, section 14 and *CLCN* 13: 11, section 6. The Choctaw and Chickasaw Indians have a shared history, sometimes contentious, that includes an origin story that accounts for their separation into two nations. This history likely explains the exception made for Chickasaw Indians in this provision. See Arthur H. DeRosier, Jr., *The Removal of the Choctaw Indians* (Knoxville: University of Tennessee Press, 1970), 6–7; Tom Mould, *Choctaw Tales* (Jackson: University Press of Mississippi, 2004), 71–72; Cushman, *History of the Choctaw, Chickasaw and Natchez Indians,* 18–21; and Clara Sue Kidwell, *Choctaws and Missionaries in Mississippi, 1818–1918* (Norman: University of Oklahoma Press, 1995), 10. The Treaty of 1855 more clearly defined the relationship between the Choctaw and Chickasaw Nations so that each could establish a separate government; see Angie Debo, *The Rise and Fall of the Choctaw Republic,* 71–73; Kidwell, *Choctaws and Missionaries,* 173–74; and Grant Foreman, *The Five Civilized Tribes* (Norman: University of Oklahoma Press, 1934), 130–32. *CLCN* 13: 12, section 15.

88. Pesantubbee, *Choctaw Women in a Chaotic World,* 97. McKee and Schlenker find that most Choctaws were aware of enslaved Africans by 1750 (*The Choctaws,* 39).

89. DeRosier, *The Removal of the Choctaw Indians,* 137.

90. McKee and Schlenker, *The Choctaws,* 120–21.

91. William Loren Katz, *Black Indians: A Hidden Heritage* (New York: Atheneum, 1986), 135.

92. Mary Cole claimed to have learned the Choctaw language before she learned to speak English, Roll IPH 33, vol. 100: 56–59. Paul Garnett Roebuck's grandfather, a slave, acted as an interpreter for Choctaw and Chickasaw Indians in federal court at Paris, Texas, Roll IPH 27, vol. 81: 438–41.

93. *CLCN* 13: 19 and 20–21.

94. Debo, *The Rise and Fall of the Choctaw Republic,* chapter 4, especially pp. 80–83; Kidwell, *Choctaws and Missionaries,* 170 and 174; and Choctaw Nation Records Roll CTN 8, vol. 295: 32 and 229, and Roll CTN 8, vol. 297: 279. The Choctaw Nation Records are available at the Oklahoma Historical Society.

95. *Treaty with the Choctaw and Chickasaw, 1866,* Institute for the Development of Indian Law, *Treaties and Agreements of the Five Civilized Tribes,* American Indian Treaties Series (Washington, D.C.: Institute for the Development of Indian Law, 1974), 131–32, articles 3 and 4.

96. Debo, *The Rise and Fall of the Choctaw Republic,* 101.

97. Ibid., 102–4.

98. *The Freedmen and Registration Bills,* vol. 18 of The Constitution and Laws of the American Indian Tribes Series (Denison, Tex.: Murray's Steam Printing House, 1883), 1–4; reprinted (Wilmington, Del.: Scholarly Resources, 1975).

99. Ibid., 3, section 7.

100. *Laws of the Choctaw Nation,* vol. 18 of The Constitution and Laws of the American Indian Tribes Series (Denison, Tex.: Murray's Steam Printing House, 1883), 23

101. *Constitution, Treaties and Laws of the Choctaw Nation, Made and Enacted by the Choctaw Legislature, 1887* (Sedalia, Mo.: Democrat Steam Print, 1887), 156–57; reprint (Wilmington, Del.: Scholarly Resources, 1975).

Womanish Men and Manlike Women

The Native American Two-spirit as Warrior

> Roger M. Carpenter

In the first week of 1801 a young Anishinabe warrior appeared at Alexander Henry's fur trading post on the Park River.[1] The presence of yet another Indian usually attracted little notice at Henry's establishment, but this particular individual exhibited some oddly feminine mannerisms. Curious, Henry approached some of the Anishinabeg (Ojibwas) who made up the bulk of his employees and questioned them regarding the new arrival. As it turned out most of the Anishinabeg knew all about the young warrior, and they told Henry a tale that emphasized not the young man's strange, apparently effeminate day-to-day conduct but rather his prowess as a warrior, his extraordinary courage, his skill with arms, and his speed afoot.

One day not many years before, while traversing a section of prairie on foot, the young man and several of his companions found themselves pursued by a much larger party of Dakotas, who, like the Anishinabeg, were also dismounted.[2] Alarmed, the young man and his friends "ran a considerable distance" but soon realized that the "Scieux were gaining fast upon them." Thinking quickly, the young warrior took a bow and a few arrows from his companions and ordered them to keep running. He stopped, turned to face the onrushing Dakota war party, and unleashed several arrows in their direction, temporarily bringing them to halt and forcing them to return fire. Easily dodging the enemy's arrows, the young man quickly gathered them up and sped away when the Dakotas closed and attempted to encircle him. He soon caught up with his friends, with the enemy hot on his heels. As the pursuers began to narrow the distance between themselves and the Anishinabeg, the young man "again stopp'd and faced them with his bow and arrows and kept them at bay until his friends got a considerable distance when he again ran off to join them and the enemy after him." Over and over again, the young Anishinabe warrior repeated the stratagem of turning on the enemy as they closed, checking their advance with a hail of arrows, and retreating until he and his friends reached the protection of "a spot of strong wood [where] the Scieux dare not approach them."[3]

Alexander Henry could not help but be impressed by the young warrior's extraordinary courage, but at the same time he seemed flummoxed in his attempts to describe this amazing fighting man in his journal. In all likelihood Henry's difficulty stemmed from the fact that the man the Anishinabeg described to him seemed to have nothing in common with this same person whom he would now see on an almost daily basis. "This person," Henry wrote, "is a curious compound between a man and a woman. He is a man in every respect both as to members and courage but still he pretends to appear womanish and dresses as such. His walk and manner in sitting down, his manners and occupation, and language are that of a woman."

Nor should one assume that other Anishinabeg, despite the young man's prowess as a warrior, necessarily admired him. Some expressed disapproval of the young warrior's feminine dress and mannerisms, and Henry noted that the young man's own father "who is a great Chief among the Saulteaux cannot persuade him to act like a man." Indeed the name that Henry knew the young Anishinabe by, Berdash, identified his place in native society.[4] The reactions of Berdash's father and other Anishinabeg, however, cannot be taken as typical of native attitudes toward two-spirit persons, which varied greatly from one community to the next.

Historiography

The body of literature regarding the Native American berdache, or "Two-Spirit Persons," is rather small and sometimes contradictory and confusing. Most recent work suffers, as one historian of gender argues, from an unfortunate tendency of being imbued with current identity politics.[5] And yet that should not diminish its value. Gender, after all—and third or fourth genders especially—has been a category of academic inquiry for only a relatively short time and controversy is almost inevitable.[6] Ramón A. Gutiérrez has argued that current scholars of gender have used Native Americans as a way of romanticizing third and fourth genders.[7] Richard C. Trexler's *Sex and Conquest* sets out to examine native cross-gender roles in the context of—as justification for—the European conquest of the Americas. Most of Trexler's analysis employs European rather than indigenous conceptions of gender identity and tends to argue that native societies forced berdache status onto selected males. However, to reach that conclusion Trexler downplays that some males embraced their status as a berdache.[8]

The term *berdache* itself is somewhat controversial and is considered offensive by some. Persian or Arabic in origin, the term indicated the passive partner in male homosexual relationships.[9] While Europeans who encountered two-spirit people used it as a pejorative, there are few other terms—unless we wish to apply specific tribal terms—that are useful for this study.[10] Indeed native people in the past used this term or variations of it.

The sparse historical record indicates that, with the possible exception of the northeast, berdaches could be found in many, but by no means all, native communities throughout North America. Most frequently biological males, two-spirit persons often assumed the appearance and mannerisms of the opposite gender. Part of their absence from the historical record, however, may not be a simple case of scarcity. It may also be attributed to Europeans who did not quite comprehend what they witnessed, and in the case of writers promoting colonization ventures, they likely thought it best not advertise something distasteful or shocking to their readers.

Womanish Men

Curious Europeans usually received one of two explanations from native peoples as to how and why certain individuals became berdaches. These explanations, however, varied from one region and from one group of people to another. In some cases *berdache* status could be imposed on a male during his youth or boyhood if he demonstrated a propensity for playing with tools commonly used by women, such as hoes or looms. Another common explanation maintained that individuals became two-spirit persons through supernatural intervention, usually in the form of a dream or through other means of communicating with a deity or spirit. A man could, for example, have a dream in which a powerful supernatural being commanded him to "change his sex." A third, less commonly offered explanation emphasized that some berdaches self-selected the role, simply arguing "that is my road."[11]

Over the course of their lifetimes male berdaches, who seem to have been more numerous than their female counterparts, often crossed and recrossed the line between genders. However, for female berdaches, who seem to have been most common in the northern Plains and Plateau regions, choosing to live life as a man appears to have been an irreversible commitment. Yet this seems not to have been a hardship for female berdaches, who seem to have embraced life as a man, particularly in societies where being a male held definite advantages.

For Europeans, rooted in a worldview that permitted only two genders, encounters with Native American *berdaches* often provoked a range of reactions—mostly negative—that ran the gamut from bewilderment and bemusement to outrage and disgust. The sexual ambiguity of some two-spirit persons baffled Europeans, who variously referred to them as "male prostitutes," "sodomites," and "hermaphrodites."[12]

Some male *berdaches* did prefer the company of other men, but others were heterosexuals who married women and fathered children, all while performing women's day-to-day tasks, such as dressing hides and agricultural labor—except when they went to war. For a berdache, however, sexual preference did not stop with what Europeans regarded as the standard two choices. Some two-spirit people may have been bisexual, but others, cognizant of their spiritual power, believed it best to conserve that power by remaining celibate and were, to all outward appearances, asexual. Believing that intercourse dissipated their energies, they eschewed sexual relations in order to retain their spiritual power, which could be channeled to the benefit of their communities and give their warriors an advantage in battle.

As male berdaches shifted their shapes, traversing the gendered line from male to female and back, frequently altering their appearance and mannerisms as they did so, they confounded Europeans. The participation of berdaches in warfare baffled Europeans, primarily because they considered war an exclusively male occupation, and one reserved for manly men at that.

In many native societies male berdaches doffed their feminine attire in wartime, picked up their weapons, and accompanied the other men into battle. Warriors regarded a berdache's presence as beneficial, with whatever prowess he had with weapons or his other military skills as secondary benefits. A berdache's special connection with the supernatural and his ability to marshal spiritual power on their behalf held far more importance to members of a war party.

At first blush the notion of including an individual in a war party because of a supposed connection to the supernatural may seem preposterous. But in their earliest explorations of the Americas Europeans did just that—although they did not recognize the supernatural advantage as the reason for their action. Early Spanish expeditions often included Franciscan friars who, because of their order's rules, could not be used as military assets, but they accompanied conquistadores to offer them spiritual comfort and to convert native peoples to Christianity. While the friars could not be considered supernaturally charged beings on their own, they did represent a supernatural entity and could seek supernatural intervention to further the expedition's chances of success.

The rather common belief that two-spirit people could wield considerable supernatural power could have negative effects on their relationships with other people in their communities. Certainly most native people appreciated the supernatural, but they also recognized that such power cut both ways, being used for both good and evil. Playing it safe, other native people often thought it best to avoid berdaches, lest they somehow incur their ire. In all likelihood this sort of apprehension may have sharply reduced—and in some cases eliminated—the pool of potential sex partners of both genders.

Europeans encountered berdaches in their earliest explorations of North America. After leading the few survivors of the failed Narváez expedition through what is now Texas and the American Southwest from 1528 to 1536, Álvar Núñez Cabeza de Vaca later reported that he "saw something very repulsive, namely a man married to another." Cabeza de Vaca described these berdaches as "impotent and womanish beings, who dress like women and perform the office of women." However, Cabeza de Vaca also noted that they participated in warfare since they "use the bow." But Cabeza de Vaca seemed to be as perplexed as Alexander Henry would be two and a half centuries later. He observed that berdaches in east Texas tended to be "more robust than the other men, taller, and can carry heavy burthens."[13] Cabeza de Vaca's cultural blinders left him unable to reconcile the characteristics of individuals who, on the one hand, he deemed "impotent and womanish," while on the other he acknowledged as robust and endowed with physical strength.

European explorers who followed Cabeza de Vaca continued to be baffled by two-spirit people and by their participation in war. French explorer Jean Ribault encountered berdaches while exploring Florida in 1562, but he seems to have been confused as to their gender identity. In describing the Timucua peoples of Florida, Ribault wrote that "in all this country [there were] many hermaphrodites, which take all the greatest pain, and bear the victuals when they go to war." Ribault also noted that berdaches changed their appearance while at war, claiming that they "paint their faces much, and stick their hair full of feathers, or down, that they may seem more terrible."[14] Ribault's use of the term *hermaphrodite* reveals a certain level of confusion on his part, indicating that he seemed unable to ascertain the true biological identity of the *berdaches* he encountered. A few years later, during a subsequent exploration of Florida, Ribault again used the term, this time in an even more confusing manner, and in the space of a single sentence, when he credited an "Indian woman, of tall stature, which also was an hermaphrodite" with saving an expedition by giving the explorers a "great vessel, full of clear fountain water, wherewith she greatly refreshed us." Ribault would not be the last European unable to ascertain the gender of two-spirit people.

A little more than a century later three Frenchmen, two of them missionaries and the other a soldier, traveled, worked, and lived independently of one another among the Illinois peoples of the Upper Mississippi River Valley. All three men noted that there seemed to be a great number of berdaches among the Illinois, but they reached different conclusions about them, and while their writings complement each other in some respects, they also contradict each other.

Recollect missionary Louis Hennepin is perhaps best known for accompanying Robert de La Salle during his navigation of the Mississippi in the 1670s and 1680s and for attempting to claim credit as the discoverer of the river. La Salle paused during his southward journey at an Illinois village, and Hennepin took the opportunity to observe the native people. Like Ribault, Hennepin seemed confused as to the gender of two-spirit people among the Illinois, and, just as Ribault did with the Timucuas, he referred to them as hermaphrodites. Hennepin expressed surprise at the large number of male berdaches among Illinois people not only because he had "not observ'd any such thing amongst the other Nations of Northern *America,*" but also because he noted that most Illinois men had several wives, often marrying sisters on the theory that "they agree better than Strangers." However, Hennepin also noted that while Illinois men could "have several Wives, they are so lascivious as to be guilty of Sodomy, and keep Boys whom they cloath with Womens Apparel, because they make of them that abominable Use."[15]

French trader and soldier Pierre Liette spent the first few decades of the eighteenth century among native peoples in the Upper Mississippi River Valley, and, like Hennepin, he noticed that there seemed to be a large number of berdaches among the Illinois. According to Liette, despite having a skewed sex ratio of "four women to one man," the "sin of sodomy prevails more among" the Illinois "than in any other nation" Liette blamed Illinois women for this state of affairs, asserting that because they "retain some moderation," the young men could not satisfy "their passions as much as they would like." The solution that the Illinois hit upon—or at least Liette's interpretation of it—was to create a class of "men who were bred for this purpose since childhood." The Illinois did this, Liette claimed, by singling out young boys who played with women's tools, such as "the spade, the spindle, the axe," but not "the bow and arrows, as all the other little boys do" and dressed them as girls, "tattooed their cheeks" and breast "like the women." As they grew, these boys learned to mimic the female "accent, which is different from that of the men. They omit nothing that can make them like the women."[16] Illinois men, Liette claimed, were "sufficiently embruted to have dealings" with these berdaches as women. Despite their outward appearance as women, many Illinois two-spirits appear to have been bisexual, having relations with certain females, whom Liette referred to as "dissolute creatures."[17]

Hennepin and Liette made no effort to hide their disgust with the Illinois and the two-spirit people who lived among them. However, when Jesuit missionary Pierre Marquette traveled and worked among the Illinois people in the 1670s, he appeared to have taken a less judgmental approach. Marquette confirmed Liette's observations concerning Illinois women, noting that they "are always clad very modestly and very becomingly" and noted that the men did "not take the trouble to Cover themselves," which coincided with Hennepin's remark that Illinois men "go stark naked in Summer-time, wearing only a kind of Shooes made of the Skins of Bulls."[18] Like Hennepin and Liette, Marquette observed male berdaches among the Illinois who assumed "the garb of women and retain it throughout their lives they never marry and glory in demeaning themselves to do everything that the women do." However, Marquette also noted—unlike Hennepin and Liette—that two-spirit people among the Illinois commanded a good deal of respect, playing an important role in public life. Marquette also remarked that two-spirit people played a role in the governing of the community, often being "summoned to the Councils" where "nothing can be decided without their advice."

Marquette's description raises the intriguing possibility that Illinois society did not—Hennepin's and Liette's assertions to the contrary—always force berdache status on males at an early age. Some young men may have recognized the advantages of being two-spirit persons, such as their importance in public life, and made a conscious choice to assume the role of the other gender. Being a berdache, Marquette noted, allowed young men to follow the "profession of leading an Extraordinary life," and other Illinois regarded them as "Manitous,—That is to say, for Spirits,—or persons of Consequence."[19] While male berdaches carried out many of the daily tasks that Illinois women normally performed, such as hoeing corn and gathering firewood, they also took part in ceremonial life, but with some restrictions. Unlike other men, they could not dance in ceremonies, but they could participate by singing. They often accompanied men when they went to war but were allowed to use "only clubs and not bows and arrows," on the grounds that the latter were "the weapons proper to men."[20]

It is striking that the assessments that Hennepin, Liette, and Marquette made of Illinois berdaches vary so greatly. The three men lived and worked among Illinois people roughly within a decade of one another, yet their descriptions offer a glimpse of the differing prisms of European observers. Hennepin made little effort to understand the Illinois, and his account lacks the analysis present in Liette's and Marquette's. However, a lack of analysis did not prevent Hennepin from being judgmental. Despite his post as a missionary, Hennepin made no effort to convert the Illinois, arguing that since they were "brutish, wild, and stupid their Conversion is to be despair'd of, till Time and Commerce with the *Europeans* has remov'd their natural Ignorance."[21]

Liette, a soldier and a trader, did not consider that *berdaches* may have filled important societal and religious functions among the Illinois when he attempted to provide a (flawed) rationale for the many two-spirit people among them. For the most part his description of two-spirit people is just that—a description. Liette simply viewed the daily routine of Illinois two-spirits and seems to have decided that no male would willingly embrace such a status. In attempting to ascertain why there were berdaches among the Illinois, he first blamed women for not making themselves as sexually available as young men would like. This in turn—as Liette formulated it—resulted in Illinois men directing their lust elsewhere.

As a Jesuit missionary Marquette had a compelling interest—both religiously and intellectually—in attempting to ascertain how berdaches fit into native societies. Whereas Hennepin and Liette simply viewed two-spirit people as radical departures from the European sexual norm, Marquette realized that Illinois people regarded berdaches as important persons and powerful spiritual beings. Of course, although Marquette did far more to try and understand why the Illinois seemed to have so many two-spirit people, that did not mean he approved of the practice.

While the Illinois regarded *beredaches* as important personages, time and interactions with Europeans—as Hennepin hoped—may have prompted a change in their attitudes toward two-spirit people. When French Marine captain Jean Bernard Bossu met the Illinois in 1750, he found men among them dressed as women, but these individuals were not two-spirit people. At some point the Illinois began punishing men who fled in battle by forcing them to "let their hair grow, and to wear an *alkonan* like the women."[22] Another indication of a change in Illinois attitudes toward *berdaches* came when Bossu met with an elderly man who regaled him with tales of his visit to Paris thirty years earlier. The man entertained his tribesmen, listing the wonders he saw in France, such as the butcher shops, which impressed him with their "great abundance of flesh," the opera where "all the people are jugglers or sorcerers," and "the huts of the grand chief of the French, *i.e. Versailles* and *Louvre,* and that they contained more people than there are in their country."[23] However, "another *Illinois,* who had made the same voyage" spoke up and contemptuously described seeing "on the public walks men who were half women, having their hair dressed like women, wearing the same ear-rings, and great nose-gays on their breast; that he suspected they put *rouge* on their faces, and that he found they smelled like crocodiles." The Illinois man concluded his criticism of the French, stating that "such effeminate manners dishonor a respectable nation."[24] Bossu noted—perhaps with a little bit of chagrin—that the "half women" of whom the Indian spoke were "beaus, who are born with the weakness and the delicacy peculiar to women; nature seeming to have begun making them such, and afterward to make a mistake in the formation of their sex." Whereas the Illinois man saw the beaus as suffering from a character defect, Bossu blamed the fates—and to a degree, the fashions of the time—for their lack of "manliness."

For the most part there is little in the way of evidence regarding the sex lives of berdaches. However, there are clues here and there that suggest that male berdaches could be very forward in pressing their sexual demands on other men. Captured as a boy in the early nineteenth century, John Tanner spent most of his adult life among Anishinbeg peoples in the Western Great Lakes region. Adopted by an Anishinbe family, he acquired some renown as a hunter as an adult. One day a two-spirit person named Ozaw-wen-dib (Yellow Head) appeared at the lodge of Tanner's Indian mother. It is possible—but debatable—that Yellow Head may have been the same warrior known as Berdash whose exploits in war so confounded

Alexander Henry some years earlier.[25] "This man," Tanner later recalled, "was one of those who make themselves women, and are called women by the Indians." This is Tanner's only reference to Yellow Head as a male; for the rest of his discourse he referred to the berdache as "she." Tanner related that Yellow Head was about fifty years old—probably two to three decades older than Tanner at the time—and that she wasted no time in letting him know that she wanted a sexual relationship with him. "I do not know whether she had seen me, or only heard of me," Tanner recalled, "but she soon let me know she had come a great distance to see me, with the hope of living with me. She often offered herself to me, but not being discouraged with one refusal, she repeated her disgusting advances until I was almost driven from the lodge." Feeling, Tanner said, "embarrassment and shame whenever she addressed me," he did his best to avoid Yellow Head. His Indian mother, in contrast, seemed amused by her adopted son's discomfort. Indeed she seemed happy that Yellow Head had chosen to live with them for a while, since "she" "was very expert in the various employments of the women" and probably reduced the workload of Tanner's adoptive mother.[26] In the end matters turned out happily for Tanner. Yellow Head tired of pursuing him and instead married a chief who already had two wives. Tanner noted that the union "occasioned some laughter, and produced some ludicrous incidents, but was attended with less uneasiness and quarrelling" than if the new wife had been a female.[27] Much like Tanner's adoptive mother, the chief's wives were probably pleased to have another set of hands to help with their labors.

As Americans began to explore the Old Northwest and the trans-Mississippi west, they encountered berdaches, and, like the Europeans who preceded them, found them perplexing. Early-nineteenth-century American observers noted that native berdaches played a complex, and to them, confusing role in native societies. C. C. Trowbridge submitted a report to Michigan Territory governor Lewis Cass claiming that he saw men among the Miami "who assume the dress and character of women, and associate altogether with the females, taking an equal share in planting, hoeing & all the domestic drudgery." However, the White Face, as two-spirit people among the Miami were often called, did not limit themselves to drudgework. They often took "advantage of the liberty afforded them in their intercourse with the females" and frequently engaged in sexual relations with them. While Miami berdaches assumed the social and economic roles of women, they took on male roles in time of war. Before accompanying the other men to war, they exchanged their feminine dress for that of a warrior. Upon their return they reassumed their daily feminine roles and donned women's clothing again.[28] The ease with which two-spirit peoples of woodland and Great Lakes tribes shifted from their daily feminine economic and social roles to the all-masculine world of warfare suggests that, for males at least, berdache status had a permeable quality.

As nineteenth-century Americans began to explore the lands west of the Mississippi, they continued to encounter berdaches among native peoples. Artist George Catlin, who spent most of the 1830s painting the native peoples of the American West, regarded the existence of two-spirit people as "one of the most unaccountable and disgusting customs, that I have ever met in the Indian country." Catlin found berdaches so repulsive that he tried to say as little as possible about them, stating only that the practice involved "a man dressed in woman's clothes" who was "driven to the most servile and degrading duties." Catlin ended his very brief description by telling his readers that "for further account of it [the berdache custom], I am constrained to refer the reader to the country where it is practiced"—doubtless an impossibility for the vast majority of Catlin's reading audience—"and where I should wish that it might be extinguished before it be more fully recorded."[29] Like many white Americans and Europeans, Catlin expressed shock at the spectacle of a man dressing as, and assuming the role of, a woman. Perhaps worried that he might scandalize his Victorian reading audience, Catlin chose to limit his comments regarding *berdaches* to about a half page in his two volume tome. He did, however, include a painting entitled *Dance to the Berdash* among his body of work, but his notes describing the image dismiss the ceremony as an "unaccountable and ludicrous custom amongst the Sacs and Foxes, which admits not of an entire explanation."[30] Explanations for the custom did of course exist, but Catlin had little interest in finding out what they were.

Two-spirit peoples of the Great Plains tribes differed significantly from those of woodland peoples in some key respects. Whereas some woodland peoples imposed berdache status on individuals, plains societies often required some indication of supernatural intervention for one to become a two-spirit person. The permeable aspect of being a male berdache—the ability to go back and forth between the feminine role in times of peace and the masculine role in times of war—also seems to have been more pronounced among plains peoples.

Among the Hidatsa berdache status could be conferred on a male by being "blessed" by a female deity, although this was a particular divine favor that most parents tried to help their male offspring avoid. Because of their belief that a deity bestowed two-spirit status upon chosen individuals, the Hidatsa regarded them as blessed and viewed them as religious leaders. On a day-to-day basis they performed much of the same work as women, and usually more efficiently since they were usually bigger, stronger, and had none of the concerns of childbearing and rearing.[31] Parents made sure that their sons dressed like boys and encouraged them engage in boys' play and to avoid women's work, lest they be "blessed" and become berdaches.[32] Parents took an interest in their children's playtime activities, making sure that their sons did not develop an interest in playing with girls' toys such as dolls. However, Hidatsa parents showed little concern—possibly because of the rarity of female berdaches—if their daughters developed a fascination with bows and arrows.[33] Boys were forbidden to assist women in the hoeing of the corn, for fear if they engaged in this female activity, the Woman Above—a mysterious, malevolent deity—might cause them to dream of becoming a berdache.[34] If the Woman Above desired that a particular male should "change his sex," she would cause him to have dreams in which he saw himself dressed as a woman. A man could try to resist, but native people viewed dreams as foretelling the inevitable, and the Woman Above would not grant relief until the dream was fulfilled.[35] The efforts of Hidatsa parents to discourage their children from playing with the other gender's toys suggests that perhaps their society did impose two-spirit status on certain individuals. On the one hand, since their society made the transformation to a berdache a function of the supernatural, parents psychologically absolved themselves of responsibility if their offspring became two-spirit persons. On the other hand, the supernatural connection meant that berdaches occupied a special place in their society.

Two-spirit people sometimes fought in battle, and plains warriors, recognizing that they possessed significant supernatural power, gave them a wide berth whenever possible. In the 1930s elderly Hidatsas related to anthropologist Alfred Bowers that a Dakota berdache used this sort of mystical power that warriors feared to rout a thrity-man war party singlehandedly. Spying what they believed to be three Dakota women, the Hidatsas quietly approached intending to count coup—but not kill—the women. The Hidatsa leader struck all three Dakotas with his coup stick but found himself forced to retreat when one of the women turned out to be a berdache who struck back with his digging stick, saying, "You can't kill me for I am holy. I will strike coups on you with my digging stick." Singing a sacred song, he pursued the surprised Hidatsas. The Hidatsa leader turned and fired an arrow at his pursuer but looked on in dismay as it bounced harmlessly off the berdache's clothing. Realizing that he faced a powerful supernatural being—and knowing better than to trifle with the supernatural—the Hidatsa leader quickly ordered his war party to retreat.[36] The Hidatsa leader's actions may seem strange given that his thirty-man-strong war party could have easily killed the berdache and the two women had he instructed them to do so. But the presence of a spiritually powerful being—augmented by his seemingly invulnerable raiment—changed the dynamics of the encounter. The Hidatsa leader already had a long and successful record in leading war parties. An encounter with a two-spirit person—especially a losing encounter—might change his luck, and he ordered his men to withdraw.

While it may not have been customary for Dakota berdaches to fight, they sometimes accompanied warriors into battle. Using their supernatural powers, they predicted success for the warriors and the number of enemies they would kill or count coup on. During Red Cloud's campaign against Fort Phil Kearny in 1866, a two-spirit person named He e man eh' prophesied that the Dakota and Cheyenne would count coup on one hundred solders.[37]

While traveling through Osage country in 1839 and 1840, French artist Victor Tixier met a warrior known as "la Bredache," who lived with the "Head Chief" and his wife, the "Woman Chief." Tixier noted that only "a few years before" the Osage counted this man "as one of the most distinguished braves," but one day, he "suddenly gave up fighting and never left" the Head Chief, "except when the latter went to war." Much like Alexander Henry four decades earlier, Tixier had difficulty reconciling the valiant warrior whom the Osages told him about with the "extremely effeminate appearance of this man."[38]

Among the Omaha there is the story of a young man who led successful war parties, who was revealed, via supernatural intervention, to be a *mixu'ga*—a berdache: "On the way home he got up a dance in honor of his victory. As he was dancing, brandishing his weapons and praising himself, an owl hooted near-by in the woods. 'The leader is a *mixu'ga!*' The people listened in amazement, and at last the leader cried 'I have done that which a *mixu'ga* could never do!'"[39] Upon reaching home, believing he had been commanded by the moon to change his sex, the young man began to dress and speak like a woman.[40] However, he still married, fathered children, and remained a warrior, dressing as a man when he went to war and reassuming the garb of a woman when he returned home.

Among the Cheyenne it has been suggested that warriors considered the presence of berdaches favorable, thinking that because they abstained from sex they would have a reserve of virility—in short, just the sort of power required to win in battle. Even though they did not usually take part in battle themselves, their presence and their supernatural qualities, it was thought, would help the war party succeed.[41] There has been some question regarding this formulation of stored-up male essence as translating into spiritual power. Yet there is some precedent for the belief that abstaining from sex would make men more successful in war. Native peoples of the Eastern Woodlands—and the Cheyenne, prior to their moving onto the plains in the late eighteenth and early nineteenth centuries, were a woodland people—thought that by forsaking sexual intercourse men's spiritual power would increase. These beliefs had their groundings in social as well as spiritual concerns. Rape of female captives was extremely rare in woodland societies, and this has been attributed to the belief that men could dissipate spiritual power through sexual intercourse. But woodlands warriors had other practical reasons that kept them from violating female prisoners. Since a captive could be adopted, a female prisoner could become one's sister, cousin, or other close relative. Sexually assaulting a potential relative would have violated incest taboos. Even if a captive was assaulted and did not become part of her assailant's family, there remained the possibility that another clan could adopt her and could later seek revenge against the rapist.[42]

Manlike Women

As white Americans and Canadians began to explore the Northern Plains and Plateau regions in the early nineteenth century, they encountered female berdaches. While the evidence suggests that most two-spirit people were men who assumed the role of women, female berdaches, while by no means common, were not unknown in the northern Plains and Plateau.[43] However, they differed from their male counterparts in one key respect. While male berdaches recrossed the gender line several times over the course of their lives, a female two-spirit person rarely did so. Native females who chose to become berdaches took up the male roles of hunter and warrior and seemingly never looked back, primarily because being a male gave them certain advantages.

Raised in societies where women had little power, some northern Plains and Plateau women may have felt drawn to the prospect of being a two-spirit person—and hence a warrior. But becoming a berdache involved tradeoffs that many women would have found unacceptable. A successful female berdache usually could not attract a male mate. Males regarded them as difficult to control and unfit for marriage. Additionally most men did not want to risk being ridiculed if their wives turned out to be better hunters and warriors than they were.

Women engaging in combat was nothing new on the northern plains and in the plateau region. Jesuit missionary Pierre-Jean de Smet recalled how Flathead women seized weapons, tools, firewood—in short, whatever was handy—to repel a Crow assault on their camp. One of the women, "the celebrated Mary Quille, already distinguished in numerous battles," wielded an ax and pursued a Crow warrior for some distance. She returned to camp, disappointed that she could not run down her quarry, muttering, "I thought that these great talkers were men. I was mistaken: it is not worth while even for women to attempt to chase them."[44]

Other women engaged in combat on the Northern Plains. Late in life Crow medicine woman Pretty-shield recalled the exploits of a sixty-year-old woman, Strikes-two, who singlehandedly repelled a Dakota attack on their camp. Mounted on a gray horse, armed only with a root digger, Strikes-two instructed the men, women and children looking on to keep singing her song—"They are whipped. They are running away"—as she charged through bullets and arrows to attack the Dakotas and put them to flight. Pretty-shield recalled the pride she felt: "I *saw* her, I *heard* her, and my heart swelled, because she was a woman."[45]

In 1811 Canadian explorer and cartographer David Thompson noted the physical transformation that becoming a berdache could have on a woman. Approached by a couple he initially took to be a man and a woman, Thompson recognized the "man" as a woman who had been the wife of one of his servants three years earlier. Thompson banished the "man" from his trading establishment because "her conduct was then so loose."[46] Thompson learned that this person, now known as Qánqon or Boudash (sometimes rendered Bowdash) had become a "prophetess, declared her sex changed, was now a Man, dressed, and armed herself as such, and also took a young woman to Wife." According to Thompson, she suffered a few setbacks in her career as a prophetess. While living among the Chinook, "she predicted diseases to them, which made some of them threaten her life."[47]

Sir John Franklin, the Artic explorer, encountered Qánqon in the 1820s. Franklin claimed that she became a berdache when she "formed a sudden resolution of becoming a warrior." She shed her female attire, donned men's clothing, acquired "a gun, a bow and arrows, and a horse" and joined a war party. Franklin related that she "displayed so much courage which was so much heightened by her subsequent feats of bravery that many young men put themselves under her command" and became known as "the Manlike Woman."[48] Since she had "a delicate frame, her followers attributed her exploits to the possession of supernatural power." According to Franklin, Qánqon increased her following when she prophesied that native peoples would see "a great change take place in the natural order of things, and that among other advantages arising from it, their own condition of life was to be materially bettered." Her stock as a prophetess and faith in her predictions fell into disrepute when "she collected volunteers for another war excursion, in which she received a mortal wound." "The faith of the Indians," Franklin related, "was shaken by her death" at the hands of Blackfoot warriors.

Franklin was not the only one to comment on Qánqon's passing. American missionary William H. Gray recorded in his journal that "the Black Feet killed the Kootenie woman, or Bowdash, as she is called." When her Flathead war party found themselves surrounded by a larger force of Blackfoot, Qánqon went back and forth several times between the two parties, ostensibly attempting to negotiate a truce.[49] On her last trip the Flathead warriors slipped away as she stalled for time. When they realized that they had been deceived, the Blackfoot killed her.

However, the Blackfoot account of Qánqon's death at their hands emphasized her status as a powerful supernatural being. The Blackfoot wounded her several times with gunfire, but she still would not die. Realizing that they faced a supernatural being—and therefore should not trifle with her—the Blackfoot resorted to other tactics. Unable to kill her with gunshots, several Blackfoot warriors held Qánqon down in a sitting position while others slashed at her chest and abdomen with their knives. Her wounds, however, healed instantaneously. Finally one of the Blackfoot warriors cut out her heart. Unable to heal this wound, Qánqon died.

The Blackfoot, however, did not escape with impunity. Dissension racked the remainder of their expedition. One warrior directed an insult at the man who removed Qánqon's breechcloth. Another warrior mocked the man who killed her, and the two would have exchanged blows had the other members of the war party not intervened. The leader of the Blackfoot war party realized that "this woman's spirit continues to trouble us. We have killed a powerful woman." And, as a further testament to Qánqon's supernatural status, "no wild animals or birds disturbed her body."[50]

Qánqon was not the only one of her kind on the northern plains. American fur trader Edwin Thompson Denig encountered a female berdache known as Woman Chief among the Crows in the mid–nineteenth century. Taken as a captive from the Gros Ventures at about ten years of age, Woman Chief aspired to "acquire many accomplishments." Her adoptive father humored her by giving her a bow and arrows and permitted her to learn to ride. She grew to be taller and larger than most women, but she retained female dress, "with the exception of hunting arms and accoutrements."[51] Woman Chief found herself as a young woman a victim of her own prowess as a hunter. Not only did she fulfill the male role of killing game; she also had to carry out the female tasks of butchering the animals and carrying the meat home. In short, her success as a berdache doubled her workload.

After the death of her adoptive father, Woman Chief decided to take another woman as her wife. Denig alluded to no sexual attraction between Women Chief and her new wife. He may have been worried, like Catlin, that he would shock his reading audience, or he may have disregarded the sexual implications of the union completely. Denig emphasized the economic aspects of the marriage, stating that since Woman Chief succeeded as a "warrior and hunter, she could not be brought to think of female work." Indeed, attempting to perform both male and female labors would have involved an enormous amount of time and would have been impossible for the Woman Chief. Within a few years she had acquired three more wives.[52]

Her feats as a warrior made the greatest impression on Denig. When a Blackfoot party drove a Crow party into the refuge of a trading fort, she ventured out singlehandedly to confront the Blackfoot and escaped after killing three of them.[53] She later led horse-stealing raids against the Blackfoot, taking seventy horses, and personally killed and scalped two warriors who pursued the raiders. Woman Chief's career as a warrior and a hunter spanned twenty years. At one Crow encampment of 160 lodges, her accomplishments made her the third-ranked warrior. Ironically Woman Chief's life came to an end at the hands of the Gros Ventures, from whom she had been abducted as a child.

In the 1930s the elderly medicine woman Pretty-shield related the story of a Crow woman and a Crow berdache who served with General Crook and fought in the Battle of the Rosebud, a scrap that preceded the more famous Battle of Greasy Grass (Little Big Horn) by a week. Pretty-shield noted that Crow men did not like to discuss the woman and the berdache who fought on the Rosebud but declared she would "not be stealing anything from the men by telling the truth."[54] The woman, named The-other-magpie, had earned a reputation of being "both bad and brave" and a "wild one." The other Crow was a berdache named Finds-them-and-kills-them whom Pretty-shield described as "neither a man nor a woman. She looked like a man, and yet she had the heart of a woman." The-other-magpie fought armed only with a coup stick while Finds-them-and-kills-them carried a gun. Pretty-shield credited the pair with saving a Crow warrior. Much like other berdaches who normally wore woman's clothing, Finds-them-and-kills-them changed into a man's garb before going into battle. However, her reasoning (and Pretty-shield always referred to Finds-them-and-kills-them as "she" or "her") differed from that of other berdaches. Pretty-shield claimed Finds-them-and-kills-them did not want her enemies to "laugh at her, lying there with a woman's clothes on her. She did not want the Lacota to believe that she was a Crow man hiding in a woman's dress."[55]

Conclusion

Many Native American societies recognized that gender had a permeable quality about it and embraced the berdache—whether for their spiritual or military prowess—as an essential component of warfare. Berdaches, or two-spirits, remained important persons in many native communities until the late nineteenth and early twentieth centuries. By the beginning of the twentieth century Christian missionaries and government educators had achieved a great deal of success in imposing European notions of gender on native societies. Boys who dressed as females were punished, and in some cases boys who ran away from boarding schools were forced to dress as girls as a form of punishment, turning the outward appearance of the berdache into a form of humiliation.[56] For nearly three hundred years the very existence of Native American berdaches confounded and confused European and white American explorers, missionaries, and traders by presenting them with a third, and in some cases a fourth gender. But it was the berdaches' willingness to go to war—and their proficiency in battle—that most seemed to bewilder Europeans. For Europeans women did not have a place in war—except perhaps as camp followers—while the effeminate man had no place at all.

Notes

1. Henry's Park River post was located near the confluence of the Park and Red Rivers, in present day Minnesota, approximately eighty miles south of the present Canadian border.

2. Anishinabe are frequently referred to as Ojibwa, Ojibway, or Chippewa. Anishinabe is the proper name by which they refer to themselves and is gradually becoming the accepted term in academic literature. Anishinabe is the singular form and Anishinabeg the plural. See Gregory Evans Dowd, *War under Heaven: Pontiac, the Indian Nations & the British Empire* (Baltimore: Johns Hopkins University Press, 2002), 9.

3. Alexander Henry, *The Journal of Alexander Henry the Younger, 1799–1814,* ed. Barry M. Gough, 2 vols. (Toronto: Champlain Society, 1988–1992), 1: 105.

4. Ibid., 1: 104. *Saulteaux* or *Saulters* was a term that the French originally applied to Anishinabeg peoples living in the vicinity of Sault St. Marie. They later applied the term to all Anishinabeg peoples.

See Reuben Gold Thwaites, ed., *The Jesuit Relations and Allied Documents: Travels and Explorations of the Jesuit Missionaries in New France, 1610–1791; The Original French, Latin, and Italian Texts, with English Translations and Notes,* 73 vols. (Cleveland: Burrows Brothers, 1896–1901), 48: 75, 51:61, and 54: 133. Hereinafter cited as *JR.* See also Emma Helen Blair, *The Indian Tribes of the Upper Mississippi Valley & the Region of the Great Lake,* 2 vols. (1911; reprint, Lincoln: University of Nebraska Press, 1996), 1:109.

5. See for example, Richard C. Trexler, *Sex and Conquest: Gendered Violence, Political Order, and the European Conquest of the Americas* (Ithaca: Cornell University Press, 1995). For more on berdaches in current identity politics see Sue-Ellen Jacobs, Wesley Thomas, and Sabine Lang, eds., *Two-Spirit People: Native American Gender Identity, Sexuality, and Spirituality* (Urbana: University of Illinois Press, 1997). See also Richard C. Trexler, "Making the American Berdache: Choice or Constraint?," *Journal of Social History* 35, no. 3 (Spring 2002): 613–36.

6. Robert Fulton and Steven W. Anderson, "The Amerindian 'Man-Woman': Gender, Liminality, and Cultural Continuity," *Current Anthropology* 33, no.5 (December 1992): 605. Fulton and Anderson use a chart that shows references to the various terms applied to berdaches from the seventeenth century to the present, demonstrating that these references increased in the twentieth century as sexual identity became a field of academic inquiry.

7. Will Roscoe, *Changing Ones: Third and Fourth Genders in Native North America* (New York: St. Martin's Press, 1998), 189.

8. Roscoe, *Changing Ones,* 27.

9. Ibid., 7, and Fulton and Anderson, "The Amerindian 'Man-Woman,'" 603.

10. Roscoe, *Changing Ones,* 19, and Fulton and Anderson, "The Amerindian 'Man-Woman,'" 604.

11. Roscoe, *Changing Ones,* 27.

12. Ramón A. Gutiérrez, *When Jesus Came, the Corn Mothers Went Away: Marriage, Sexuality, and Power in New Mexico, 1500–1846* (Stanford: Stanford University Press, 1991), 72. See also René Goulaine de Laudonnière, "History of the First Attempt of the French (The Huguenots) to Colonize the Newly Discovered Country of Florida," in *Historical Collections of Louisiana and Florida, including Translations of Original Manuscripts Relating to Their Discovery and Settlement, with Numerous Historical and Biographical Notes,* ed. B. F. French (New York: J. Sabin & Sons, 1869), 172. Also see Louis Hennepin, *A New Discovery of a Vast Country in America,* 2 vols. (London, 1698), 1: 106.

13. Adolph Francis Bandalier, ed., *The Journey of Alvar Núñez Cabeza de Vaca and His Companions from Florida to the Pacific 1528–1536,* trans. Fanny Bandelier (New York: A. S. Barnes, 1905), 126.

14. Laudonnière, "History of the First Attempt of the French," 172, 291. See also Ian K. Steele, *Warpaths: Invasions of North America* (New York: Oxford University Press, 1994), 25–26.

15. Hennepin, *A New Discovery,* 1: 106.

16. Milo Milton Quaife, ed., *The Western Country in the Seventeenth Century: The Memoirs of Antoine Lamothe Cadillac and Pierre Liette* (New York: Citiadel Press, 1962), 112. Hereinafter cited as *Western Country*

17. *Western Country,* 113.

18. Hennepin, *A New Discovery,* 1:106.

19. *Mantiou* is an Algonquin term that is best translated "spirit." Speaking of a person as a *mantiou* indicated a spiritually and supernaturally powerful being. See James Axtell, *The Invasion Within: The Contest of Cultures in Colonial North America* (New York: Oxford University Press, 1985), 10, 16, and Frederic Baraga, *A Dictionary of the Ojibwa Language* (1878; reprint, St. Paul: Minnesota Historical Society Press, 1992).

20. *JR* 59:129.

21. Hennepin, *A New Discovery,* 1: 107.

22. Jean Bernard Bossu, *Travels through That Part of North America Formerly Called Louisiana,* 2 vols., trans. John Reinhold Forster (London, 1771) 1: 139–40. Bossu described an *alkonan* as a sort of short petticoat.

23. Ibid., 1: 142.

24. Ibid., 1: 143–44.

25. Elliot Coues, who edited some of Alexander Henry the Younger's journals for publication in the late nineteenth century, argued that Berdash and Yellow Head were one and the same person. See Elliot Coues, ed., *New Light on the Greater History of the Early Northwest: The Manuscript Journals of Alexander Henry, Fur Trader of the Northwest Company, and David Thompson, Official Geographer of the same Company 1799–1814: Exploration and Adventure among the Indians on the Red, Saskatchewan, Missouri, and Columbia Rivers,* 3 vols. (New York: F. Harper, 1897), 1:53–54. Coues cited the name of Berdash's father as evidence that the two were one and the same person. However, Alexander Henry noted that Berdash lost an eye in a fight, while Tanner mentioned no such physical deformity.

26. John Tanner, *A Narrative of the Captivity and Adventures of John Tanner, (U.S. Interpreter at the Saut. de Ste. Marie) during Thirty Years Residence among the Indians in the Interior of North America* (New York, 1830), 105.

27. Ibid., 106.

28. C. C. Trowbridge, *Meearmeear Traditions,* ed. Vernon Kinietz, Occasional Contributions from the Museum of Anthropology of the University of Michigan, no. 7 (Ann Arbor: University of Michigan Press, 1938), 68.

29. George Catlin, *Letters and Notes on the Manners, Customs and Conditions of the North American Indians: Written During Eight Years' Travel amongst the Wildest Tribes of Indians in North America, in 1832, 33, 34, 35, 36, 37, 38, and 39,* 2 vols. (London, 1841), 2: 215.

30. Ibid., 1: 286.

31. Ibid. 166–68.

32. Alfred W. Bowers, *Hidatsa Social and Ceremonial Organization* (Washington, D.C.: U.S. Government Printing Office, 1965), 105.

33. Ibid., 115.

34. Ibid., 132.

35. Ibid., 326.

36. Ibid., 255–56, 259–60.

37. George Bird Grinnell, *The Fighting Cheyennes* (New York, 1915; reprint, Norman: University of Oklahoma Press, 1956), 237–38.

38. Victor Tixier, *Tixier's Travels on the Osage Prairies,* ed. John Francis McDermott, trans. Albert J. Salvan (Norman: University of Oklahoma Press, 1940), 234.

39. Alice C. Fletcher and Francis La Flesche, *The Omaha Tribe,* 2 vols. (Washington, D.C., 1911; reprint, Lincoln: University of Nebraska Press, 1992), 1: 133.

40. The Omaha referred to *berdaches* as *mixu'ga,* literally, "instructed by the moon." See ibid., 1: 132. The belief that the moon was a female spirit who could instruct men to be berdaches was also common among the Winnebago. See Nancy Oestreich Lurie, "Winnebago Berdache," *American Anthropologist,* new series, 55, no. 5, part 1 (December 1953): 708–12.

41. E. Adamson Hoebel, *The Cheyennes: Indians of the Great Plains* (New York: Holt, Rinehart and Winston, 1960), 77.

42. Axtell, *Invasion,* 310–11.

43. Charles Callender and Lee M. Kochems, "The North American Berdache," *Current Anthropology* 24, no. 4 (August–October 1983): 446. Although I exclude the northeast, it is possible that berdaches did exist in these societies. However, there is no mention of them in the documents left by explorers, missionaries, traders, and others who dealt with native peoples extensively.

44. Pierre-Jean de Smet, *Oregon Missions and Travels over the Rocky Mountains, in 1845–46* (New York: E. Dunigan, 1847), 302.

45. Frank B. Linderman, *Pretty-shield: Medicine Woman of the Crows* (New York, 1932; reprint, Lincoln: University of Nebraska Press, 1974), 116–17.

46. David Thompson, *David Thompson's Narrative of His Explorations in Western America, 1784–1812,* ed. Joseph Burr Tyrrell (Toronto: Champlain Society, 1916), 512.

47. Ibid., 513.

48. Sir John Franklin, *Narrative of a Second Expedition to the Shores of the Polar Sea, in the Years 1825, 1826, and 1827* (London: J. Murray, 1828), 305–6.

49. Claude E. Schaeffer, "The Kutenai Female Berdache: Courier, Guide, Prophetess, and Warrior," *Ethnohistory* 12, no. 3 (Summer 1965): 215–16.

50. Ibid., 216.

51. Edwin Thompson Denig, *Five Indian Tribes of the Upper Missouri: Sioux, Arickara, Assiniboines, Crees, Crows,* ed. John C. Ewers (Norman: University of Oklahoma Press, 1961), 196.

52. Ibid., 199.

53. Ibid., 197.

54. Linderman, *Pretty-shield,* 131.

55. Ibid., 132.

56. Roscoe, *Changing Ones,* 36, 100–101.

Two-spirit Histories in Southwestern and Mesoamerican Literatures

⟳ Gabriel S. Estrada

This critical review of existing Greater Southwestern and Mesoamerican historical and contemporary literatures regarding two-spirit roles interrogates the discrepancies in findings across indigenous, U.S., and Latino borders. While U.S.
Southwestern-centered writings often affirm the value of historical two-spirit genders, Eurocentric histories focused on Hispanic writings and Mesoamerican
indigenous nations tend to designate very low status to two-spirit sexualities. For
example, while Walter Williams documents the ceremonial importance that sur-
rounds Pueblo two-spirit peoples,[1] Richard C. Trexler theorizes that these same
roles were only the most degrading products of sexual abuse and dominance.[2]
Primary documents upon which Southwestern and Mesoamerican two-spirit histories are based were often written centuries apart, and the interpretations of these
documents are often ideologically opposed. American Indian Southwestern scholarship mostly relies upon oral traditions, exploration narratives, and ethnographic
accounts of the 1800s and 1900s in order to suggest vibrant two-spirit roles in
earlier centuries and precolonial cultures.[3] Paula Gunn Allen's *The Sacred Hoop* is
one of many two-spirit historical revisions that defends these traditions.[4] These
positive two-spirit histories contrast starkly with many geographically overlapping
Mestiza/o and U.S. Euro-American writings that find homophobia, to use a modern term, throughout the Southwest and Mexico.[5] Eurocentric writings mostly
rely on primary documents from first-contact, Inquisition, and colonial accounts
from the Spanish in the sixteenth, seventeenth, and eighteenth centuries and do
not consider contemporary indigenous methodologies that could help reinterpret
the homophobia of colonial documents. This essay argues that two-spirit historians are rightly critical of accepting Spanish and Eurocentric voices as the sole
authorities on their cultures' sexual and gender traditions.

Throughout this essay the contemporary term *two-spirit* is employed because
American Indian scholars and activists made convincing spiritual and cultural
arguments for using this term at the seminal third annual intertribal Native
American First Nations gay and lesbian conference held near Winnepeg, Canada,

in 1990. Within a growing body of two-spirit creative works,[6] Qwo-Li Driskill embraces the spiritual eroticization of diverse two-spirit bodies as resistance to historical sexual, political, and cultural colonization.[7] Despite white queer-positive representations of historical American Indian berdaches,[8] most Native American and conscientious scholars refuse to use the term berdache, noting its Eurocentrism and roots in historical Old World and Arab concepts of "male prostitution."[9] While two-spirit roles include queer sexuality, they are more often linked with mixed-gender roles reflected in work or other relations. First Nation Native American scholars often reject sexually leaning gay, lesbian, bisexual, transgender, and queer (GLBTQ) identities in favor of two-spirit identities that reflect various indigenous nation affiliations as well. Brian Joseph Gilley reports that some two-spirit groups feel that only those who practice two-spirit ceremonies or reconstruct two-spirit traditions can self-identify as two-spirit.[10] Others prefer to use gender and sexual terms in their own language. For example, Diné author Carolyn Epple attests that only the term *nádleehí* can truly represent a mixed gender role specific to her Navajo people and cosmology.[11]

Two-spirit Historiography of the Greater Southwest

Deborah Miranda's article "Extermination of the Joyas: Gendercide in Spanish California" offers key insights into the usage of Spanish colonial documents for contemporary two-spirit cultural reconstruction. Based upon Sandra Holliman's gender reconstructions published in *Handbook of Gender in Archaeology* and Miranda's own familial research, Miranda's description of California Indian *joyas* is worth quoting at length because it forms the core of her scholarly reclamations of these traditions. Miranda makes important definitions of broad California Indian two-spirit undertaker roles, especially focusing on the male-bodied, two-spirit roles of the Chumash *'aqi:* "The journey to the afterlife was known to be a prescribed series of experiences with both male and female supernatural entities, and the *'aqi,* with their male-female liminality, were the only people who could mediate these experiences. Since the female (earth, abundance, fertility) energies were so powerful, and since the male (Sun, death-associated) energies were equally strong, the person who dealt with that moment of spiritual and bodily crossing over between life and death must have specially endowed spiritual qualities and powers, not to mention long-term training and their own quarantined tools."[12] In other words the mixed-gender *'aqi* would have to draw upon their development of both male and female spiritual qualities to guide the Chumash dead successfully. Miranda notes that the extermination of this sacred role would have caused *joyas*. Before missionization, *joyas* often sexually partnered with normative Chumash men. Spanish priests routinely imposed physical, spiritual, and social punishment and exile to exterminate all *joya* practices.[13]

Miranda not only considers the methods the Spanish used to exterminate third-gender people and the impact of that extermination upon California natives, but also traces adaptations and the survival of these colonial two-spirit peoples. From 1775 to 1832 Spanish priests documented the existence of the *joya* traditions they worked to oppress as new waves of California native converts replaced the many who fell ill to the abuses and diseases of mission life. Miranda suggests that *joyas* probably survived by splitting their spiritual and sexual roles by either covertly sexually partnering with men or by leading single lives that centered around being "caretakers and grave-tenders of Native culture." She reviews the life of linguist and ethnologist John Peabody Harrington's primary Chumash ethnographic consultant, Kitswpawit Fernando Librado, born in 1839, as an example of a two-spirit survivor very much interested in spiritual and caretaking matters of his culture, often researching both male and female roles among the Chumash. She notes that while Librado did not act as an actual undertaker, "he did, in many ways, act as an undertaker for his culture, gathering indigenous cultural knowledge and caring for its scattered pieces what culture the dead had left behind."[14] Chumash informant Maria Solares of Santa Ynez told Harrington that Librado indeed "stayed with men and would go crawling to other men at night," strengthening Miranda's speculation that Librado was adapting the old *'aqi* roles to new colonial realities.[15] As the mission system weakened and eventually was replaced by U.S. colonization and the genocides that accompanied California statehood in 1848 and the 1849 gold rush, the loss of Chumash *'aqi* and other California native *joya* roles would not begin to be restored until the twentieth century. From Librado's story Miranda moves on to trace the "emergence of the spiritual and physical renewal of California Indian Two-Spirit individuals."[16] She points to the contemporary two-spirit Tongva/Ajachmen author, painter, artist, soapstone carver, and weaver L. Frank Manriquez as a reincarnation of the older *joya* roles of caretaking of the knowledge and objects of the dead. As a lesbian "with the energy of two genders balancing within her," Manriquez describes her experiences recovering California Indian artifacts at Musée de L'Hommé saying: "I walked into this room where there were boxes and boxes and boxes and boxes of my people's lives, and they were like muffled crying coming from these shelves and these boxes, and it was just heart-breaking but these pieces and I became friends. *I tried to touch as many of them as I possibly could.*"[17] Miranda explains how this act of touching the dead's objects is spiritually dangerous in California Indian culture and a sign of Manriquez's revitalization of older two-spirit undertaker ways. Miranda succeeds in tracing an indigenous reading of the traditional *'aqi* roles into contemporary times for California native two-spirit peoples with the lesbian and undertaker figure of L. Frank Manriquez and her regeneration of ancient two-spirit ways.

Because of the repression of two-spirit roles, many American Indians and people of indigenous descent look to the past and present for traces of these roles or for inspiration that could help to re-create two-spirit ways. I trace my matrilineage to the seminomadic Rarámuri of my grandmother's pueblo, Namiquipa, Chihuahua, and have noted that contemporary Rarámuri ethnography confirms continued two-spirit roles, such as that of the *na'wi* or man-woman.[18] Concho, Apache, and Pueblo Nations also held sway over northern Chihuahua and likely interacted with the Rarámuri.[19] The Rarámuri may have also made use of the trade routes that reached far into the Southwest and into Central Mexico from Paquimé centuries after the turn of the first millennium.[20] Some archaeological records indicate a complementary rather than a hierarchical gender system at Paquimé from 1200 to 1450 C.E. and at other ancient pueblos of the Southwest.[21] While Christine S. VanPool and Todd L. VanPool suggest that these complementary genders may have been echoed among ancient Paquimé dwellers, they find no decisive archaeological proof that speaks for or against two-spirit presence at Paquimé. What do the direct descendants of related ancient Pueblo cultures have to say about two-spirit ways?

Contemporary Native American historiographical debates help explain why Mexican and Spanish-era Southwestern literatures do not record the two-spirit traditions that later U.S. oral ethnographies show. Referring to Pomo survival of historical Russian, Spanish, and Euro-American attempts at genocide on the Pomo Nation, queer Pomo scholar Greg Sarris interrogates both historical relationships of non-native authors with their native subjects and the relationship of contemporary readers with these texts. Whether the author is a Spanish priest of the sixteenth century or a gay white activist recovering "his" gay American roots through Native American experience, Sarris reminds readers that "representatives from the dominant culture exploring the resistance of subjugated people are likely to see little more than what those people choose or can afford to show them."[22] For this reason contemporary indigenous authors may provide gender insights that could not have been shared easily during more homophobic periods of colonization. Historical native informants were sources of wildly clashing narratives about "sodomy" and transgendered ways. Depending upon the methodology and political stance writers choose, two-spirit histories can be interpreted as being nonexistent, oppressed, or exalted.

Working from oral tradition, Laguna Pueblo author Leslie Marmon Silko makes positive two-spirit statements that would have been very difficult to make during Spanish colonization. Silko confirms that Pueblo history is based upon stories and that "a great deal of the story is believed to be inside the listener; the storyteller's role is to draw the story out of the listeners. The storytelling continues from generation to generation."[23] In this sense Pueblo history is ultimately best understood inside a storied Pueblo cultural context not available to non-Pueblo peoples and researchers. While Silko demonizes two gay characters in *Almanac of the Dead: A Novel,* she articulates her own enthusiastic version of Laguna Pueblo two-spirit peoples in *Yellow Woman and a Beauty of the Spirit:* "Before the arrival of Christian missionaries, a man could dress as a woman and work with the women and even marry a man without any fanfare. Likewise, a woman was free to dress like a man, to hunt and go to war with the men, and to marry a woman. In the old Pueblo worldview, we are all a mixture of male and female, and this sexual identity is changing constantly. In sacred kiva ceremonies, men mask and dress as women to pay homage and to be possessed by the female energies of spirit beings."[24]

A key element in this discourse is to note that all Pueblo are a mix of masculinity and femininity. Therefore it is not abnormal for anyone to express both masculinity and femininity in appropriate community arenas. By expressing complementary genders in one body, two-spirits exercise flexible gender rights that everyone can utilize as well when the need arises. Silko further notes that Pueblo men in sacred kiva spaces can become possessed by female spirits, momentarily and appropriately embodying mixed gender energy. Although Christianity and colonial laws made these fluid gender realities difficult to express publicly, this fluidity survives in oral traditions and among some Pueblo traditionalists. Given Silko's celebration of the power and honor of female creativity in her Laguna Pueblo tradition, it is not surprising that men who commit to female ways would also be honored or that reversed female to male identification could also find a home in the Pueblo world. Community and partnership, not gender stratified domination and submission, are the values that she transmits about Pueblo marriage, noting that married people were free to have sex with other people if they so chose. Again Silko's sources are mainly the oral traditions that she has gleaned from her own family and her medium of transmitting this two-spirit history is storytelling.

Paula Gunn Allen, Silko's cousin, is another Laguna Pueblo woman who makes strong statements on lesbian and gay roles among Native Americans, although through comparative western and Native American methodologies. Allen states that "it is my contention that gayness, whether female or male, traditionally functions positively within tribal groups," but qualifies her statement, noting that "much of my discussions of lesbians I have gathered from formal study, personal experience, and personally communicated information from other Indians as well as my own knowledge of lesbian culture and practice."[25] She suggests that "same-sex relationships may have been the norm for primary pair-bonding" before opposite-sex bondings would occur.[26] Allen notes how lesbian traditions among her own Pueblo peoples and other Native Americans were hidden from history and suppressed through Christianization. Allen asserts that to bring back respect for gynocentric and lesbian spirituality is essential, since "for American Indian people, the primary value was relationship to the Spirit World." Like Silko, Allen cites the female-centered creatrix "Thought Woman" as the spiritual source of these fluid gender traditions that changed during colonization. She emphasizes that the loss of valued lesbian roles is part of the patriarchal colonization that suppress all women's roles and those of traditional men as well.[27]

Thomas A. Foster's *Long before Stonewall: Histories of Same-Sex Sexuality in Early America* provides two sharply contrasting Eurocentric views of historical two-spirit Pueblos. Tracy Brown's treatment of the Pueblo relies upon civic records of court cases in New Mexico during eighteenth-century Spanish colonization. Brown admits her conclusions are based upon scant court evidence and focus on only one civil case of homosexuality that targeted two Pueblo men in 1731. Throughout the entire eighteenth century, it is the only case of male-male sex to be tried, and as such a case that perhaps provides more insight into homophobic Hispanic civic codes than into Pueblo culture.[28] She writes: "There is very little evidence of Pueblo perspectives on sexuality and sex in the New Mexican documentary record . . . the evidence on 'berdache' in New Mexico is sparse until the mid–nineteenth century" as the U.S.-Mexican War ends.[29] Once Mexico ceded most of its Southwestern claims to U.S. imperialism in 1848, anthropologists such as Matilda Cox Stevenson began to arrive to study New Mexican tribes for U.S. interests. Stevenson documents the acceptance of the two-spirit Zuni *lhamana* We'wha, who played important ceremonial, civic, and artistic roles in "her" community as a third-gendered person. In 1916 the anthropologist "Elsie Clews Parsons, too, noted that she encountered positive attitudes toward berdache at Zuni."[30] Herein lies the great methodological problem for many western historians. It is risky to presume that acceptance of two-spirits of the late 1800s and early 1900s replicates those traditions that existed earlier or prior to European contact. At the same time it is illogical to imagine that transgressive gender and sexual roles could have gained widespread Pueblo support given Hispanic and American colonial laws against transgender institutions. Brown decides, "assuming that attitudes concerning berdache would most likely have declined (rather than improved) with time and increased contact with Europeans, there is at least some reason to believe that Pueblo communities did not denigrate berdache at the time of investigation," in 1731.[31]

In contrast Chicano gender historian Ramón A. Gutiérrez argues that berdache activity in the Americas reflects captured and sodomized warriors, a position that necessitates deconstructing accounts of flourishing berdache peoples. He concludes: "When facts are misinterpreted with the goal of finding gay models of liberation where they do not exist, we perpetuate on We'wha . . . and all berdache that once existed yet another level of humiliation while shrouding their enslavement and rape, their pimping and pandering in romantic webs of obfuscation."[32] While some would laud Gutiérrez 's article for going beyond simplistic structural analysis to a poststructural critique of sexualized power, some of the methods and sources used for his articles are not sound.

What is surprising is that Gutiérrez 's 2007 article is virtually the same article he wrote almost twenty years earlier for a 1989 issue of *Out/Look,* an article that thoroughly criticized Will Roscoe, one of the foremost anthropological scholars on two-spirits.[33] Gutiérrez later openly questioned Spanish colonial texts during a panel discussion at the 2001 Gender in the Borderlands Conference in San Antonio; his new article does not voice these historiographical concerns. In fact he attacks Roscoe's queer-friendly approach to We'wha as being an unsubstantiated "gay liberationist" white projection of idealizing and imposing queer freedom onto Native American pasts. In contrast to Roscoe's long-standing partnership with gay native scholars and activists, Gutiérrez's own research takes an isolated Hispanic approach with a privileging of texts written by Spanish conquistadors and priests. It is Eurocentric.

In chapter 9 of *Changing Ones: Third and Fourth Genders in Native North America,* Roscoe monitors instances in which Gutiérrez edits and misrepresents the anthropological data, the same data that logically convinced Brown that two-spirits had centuries of acceptance in Pueblo culture. For example, Gutiérrez intimates that Zuni two-spirits such as U'k have the lowest status and are ridiculed by their people. He quotes the anthropologist Parsons: "Did you notice them laughing at her [U'k]; she is a great joke to her people."[34] Roscoe easily provides a next line for Gutiérrez: "she is a great joke to her people not because she is lha'-mana but because she is half-witted."[35] In fact the two-spirit U'k had just stumbled during a dance because she was mentally slow and also clumsy, a far cry from We'wha who by all accounts was an extremely accomplished potter, weaver, ceremonial participant, and cultural diplomat to the United States. Again misrepresenting the anthropological data, Gutiérrez suggests that the two-spirit We'wha was of the lowest social caste of sexual slaves. However, anthropologists Stevenson, Parsons, David Wilcox, Ruth L. Bunzel, John Adair, and Triloki N. Pandey all confirm from non-*lhamana* that the two-spirit was an accepted role in Pueblo society.[36] In fact, one of Roscoe's Zuni informants recently confirmed religious support for two-spirit ways in the Zuni Nation "because we still have Ko'lha'ma [the berdache kachina] and so it's still respected."[37] Roscoe contrasts the low level of Zuni homophobia with a northern Tewa-speaking Pueblo where the two-spirit kachina spirit was no longer honored and gay youth faced intense harassment.

Although Roscoe notes that Pueblo two-spirit traditions extend back to creation stories, evidenced by the ancient Laguna-Acoma story that recounts the victory of two-spirit Sto-ro-ka over the kachina spirits,[38] many Pueblo simply choose not to retell these sacred narratives to a public or anthropological audience. As a Taos Warm Springs Pueblo trained in anthropology, Terry Tafoya does not bring anthropological evidence into his discussion of two-spirit terminology. Instead he explains: "As one whose paternal relatives reside in a pueblo that banned all anthropologists in the 1920s after Elsie Clews Parsons published unauthorized ethnographic materials of our village, I know all too well that research does not exist in a political vacuum."[39] Tafoya emphasizes the need for community or national permissions to release stories, a dynamic that non–Native American researchers rarely consider once a story has been written down in previous literature. Tafoya affirms that ethnographic accounts of Pueblo two-spirit peoples tend to say much more about the ethnographer's culture than they say about Pueblos themselves.

As a Navajo/Oneida defined by her ancestral clans, Carrie House makes stronger assertions against both non-native and native interpreters of Navajo culture for a popular audience in her article "Navajo Warrior Women: An Ancient Tradition in a Modern World." She not only remarks how nonnative ethnographers have "misunderstood or failed to grasp many meanings in our lives,"[40] but also criticizes her fellow Navajo scholar Carolyn Epple for having profaned sacred knowledge regarding their cosmological beliefs and sacred entities. She scolds: "Use of the words of this sacred entity should not be heard or seen in an analytical academic context. It is not appropriate to have our creation stories and mythology challenged with Western scientific theories."[41] From many traditional Pueblo and Navajo perspectives, the less said about two-spirit histories and ways in academic print and the more these ways are practiced in private ceremony, the better. In this traditionalist light the controversy surrounding the scientific validity of Parsons, Clews, and other sources that Trexler, Brown, Gutiérrez and Roscoe debate are highly marginalized discourses.

While male-bodied two-spirit peoples receive more attention in the colonial literature, warrior women also embodied the two-spirit traditions. One historical warrior woman was Lozen, an Apache two-spirit person who resisted Mexican invasions in the 1840s and continued to fight for her Apache people when white people intensified their wars against the Apache after the 1848 Mexican-American War.[42] The war leader Victorio was her brother, and she was also the "right hand" of Geronimo in his famous resistance against the U.S. Army that ended in 1886. Apache veteran James Kaywaykla recounts: "The people knew her wisdom and respected her ability as a warrior, but most of all they respected her Power for locating the enemy." It was her locating power that allowed Geronimo and other Apaches to escape capture many times. Kaywaykla's grandmother confirmed that Lozen never married, capping her statement with a hint: "She had no husband.

You are too young to understand."[43] Roscoe fills in the gaps by reporting the Lozen probably had a female partner, Dahtetse, with whom she is photographed along with Geronimo's warriors. These were likely the two women reported to enjoy "sexual relation together" at Fort Sill where they were interned.[44] Lozen is but one of many historical two-spirit figures accepted by the majority of nations in the Southwest. Roscoe reports twenty-eight nations, such as the Shoshone, Tipai, and Papago, that honored these "women's" traditions involving hunting, men's work, going to war, cross-dressing, relations with women, and shamanism.[45] Xicana lesbian Cherríe Moraga states that Xicana origins include the "Apache, Yaqui, Papago, Navajo, and Tarahumara from the border regions as well as dozens of native tribes throughout México,"[46] yet she does not clearly identify their two-spirit warrior women traditions and their potential impact on Xicana/Mestiza sexual decolonization.[47] Northern Mexico is also home to many indigenous nations with two-spirit roles, such as the Pueblo, O'odham, Yuma, Kickapoo, Apache, and Pai Pai, which all extend over the current U.S.-Mexico border.[48] Moraga's formulation of a Xicana/o "Queer Aztlán" is clearly based on Roscoe's anthology *Living the Spirit,* which documents this tradition[49] but cites Gutiérrez's article as evidence of widespread indigenous homophobia.[50] Moraga's Xicana-Indigena resistance to Spanish imposition of heterosexual-centered patriarchy (heteropatriarchy) is intriguing,[51] but there needs to be much more dialogue between queer Xicana/o and two-spirit discourses. While Gloria Anzaldúa's complementary cosmological discussions of Nahua culture are useful,[52] she also mutes non-Mexica history in a Tejana context and could have commented much more on Apache, Carrizo, Coahuilteco, Comanche, Kickapoo, and other two-spirit genders. Despite Moraga's and Anzaldúa's ambiguous relationship to northern Mexican indigenous nations, two-spirit traditions of Northern Mexico and the Southwest are ancestral to many Xicanas/os and Native Americans and hence integral to our diverse gender and sexual decolonizations.

Cherríe Moraga's *Heroes and Saints & Other Plays* ambiguously relates contemporary indigenous relationships to Xicanas and and thus does not make a strong case for her actual Xicana/Indigena activism.[53] Although Moraga does mention transnational Runa and Tarahumara people as part of the farm-working communities that struggle against poisoning and sexual and labor oppressions along with Chicanas,[54] Linda Margarita Greenberg notes that the racial tension in the evocation of *indigenismo* in *Heroes and Saints* at times "risks placing the Indian in the past, turning the Indian into a visual cue and religious icon while effacing the historic and continuing violence against Indian populations undertaken by Spanish and mestizo peoples in the Americas."[55] Rafael Pérez-Torres concurs: "If, then, mestizaje in Mexico represents a flight from the Indian, we might think of Chicana mestizaje as a race *toward* the Indian. Although this does not necessarily

Gabriel S. Estrada

make Indian subjectivity any more present within the cultural discourse of Chicana mestizaje."[56] The danger of co-optation of indigenous voices of today exists within Moraga's Xicana discourse, as does the opportunity to create dialogue or alliance with contemporary indigenous peoples. Moraga acts in the forefront of indigenous Xicana activism through La Red Xicana Indigena, a network that recognizes contemporary Xicana and indigenous women's politics of various nations of the Americas.[57] Perhaps her subsequent writings will reflect a new standard of indigenous diversity within and outside of Xicana identity and again raise consciousness regarding decolonizing indigenous and Xicana genders and sexualities.

Mesoamerican Sexual Histories

In contrast to the relatively plentiful descriptions of two-spirit gender roles and spiritualities in the U.S. ethnographies of the late 1800s and early 1900s, the earliest Spanish Empire documents of the 1500s, 1600s, and 1700s represent two-spirit sexuality as either rampant or heavily suppressed sin. Mesoamerican two-spirit voices are heavily muted by Catholic persecution of homosexual penetrative sex that is bereft of a sense of two-spirit spirituality or communities outside of sexual context. In the 1500s Fray Bartolomé de las Casas denied that Caribbean and Mesoamerican Indians engaged in the rampant homosexuality as charged by Spanish priests such as Gonzalo Fernández de Oviedo and conquistadors such as Hernán Cortés. For example, he stresses that the natives of Hispaniola are "without malice or guile" and ready for Christianization, completely undeserving the torture they receive from the Spanish.[58] While Las Casas' rhetoric may have succeeded in limiting some of the harsher methods of genocide, outright extermination or eternal enslavement offered by some conquistadors and priests in the Valladolid debates of 1550 and 1551, he may have succeeded only in creating a safer route to assimilation into a heterosexist Spanish colonial system in which many racial and gender abuses continued.

Wrestling with the specter of colonial gendercide, Miranda recounts that Vasco Núñez de Balboa fed forty two-spirit peoples to his dogs in 1513. She relates an English version of the atrocities: "The Indians turned to the Spaniards 'as if it had been to Hercules for refuge' and quickly rounded up all the other third-gender people in the area, 'spitting in their faces and crying out to our men to take revenge of them and rid them out of the world from among men as contagious beasts.'"[59] Balboa's narrative makes it appear as if Panamanian natives welcomed him with joy as a moral leader who would rid them of their indecency. Miranda's argument that the natives were terrorized and converted to the Spanish view for fear of their lives makes more sense. Although Miranda believes that this account documents clear internalized gendercide, neither conquistadors nor Spanish priests are reliable sources of information because both are clearly

174

motivated by intense political considerations. If Miranda's own California native people could flee persecution early in colonization, what prevented these two-spirit peoples from fleeing Balboa and returning at a later time? To what extent is Balboa's narrative fabricated or changed for rhetorical purposes? Miranda is completely aware that Spanish documents must be approached very cautiously. A more accurate methodology is to find contemporary indigenous peoples who relate their own two-spirit histories and cultures rather than to rely on the early Spanish narratives that were often rewritten and retranslated years after the events they described purportedly occurred.

Contemporary Zapotec gender and sexual narratives go above and beyond mere tolerance for two-spirit peoples. Beverly N. Chiñas finds that Isthmus Zapotecs almost appear to have a preference for transgender males, known as muxe. She writes: "Isthmus Zapotecs believe that muxe are the brightest and most gifted children. Muxe have recently become heavily involved in local politics, even to the point of being elected president of some of the municipios."[60] Lynn Stephen emphasizes that muxe do not represent the low-status sexual passivity found in some Eurocentric mestizo communities, noting interactions in terms of gendered work, food, dress, speech, and ritual as central to muxe identity.[61] In fact these narratives may even demonstrate more openness to two-spirit peoples than the narratives of contemporary Pueblos. How these contemporary Zapotec narratives relate to homophobic Spanish documents of past centuries is unclear. It is highly unlikely, though possible, that indigenous cultures only formed two-spirit genders in resistance to Spanish heterosexism. The word *muxe* does appear to derive from the Spanish *mujer*, meaning woman. However, those who work with oral tradition can imagine how two-spirit traditions may have been hidden over the centuries from the flames and judgments of Mestizo and Spanish cultures. One possible answer for the continued presence of two-spirit roles among Zapotecs has to do with differing class expectations. Stephen suggests that "the persistence of a third gender role among contemporary Zapotecs for bodies that are sexed as male suggests that state societies such as the Zapotec and the Mexica may have had overlapping gender systems that included not only elite gender complementarily but also other systems that allowed for three or more genders."[62] In other words elites who had significant wealth holdings experienced more pressure to assume complementary heterosexual gender roles than common people. The common muxe practices may have outlived the Zapotec elite who were largely replaced by Spanish and mestizo elite. Stephen admits that this is speculation, unlike many other researchers who vehemently make arguments based upon the most fragmentary colonial manuscripts.

Nobel Peace Prize laureate Rigoberta Menchu makes a point of contrasting Maya Quiché acceptance of two-spirit peoples with the more homophobic

Ladino population of Guatemala: "We don't have the rejection of homosexuality that Ladinos [Mestizos] do; they really cannot stand it."[63] In contrast Antonio Gaspar Chi, a Yucatec Maya of the late 1500s, asserted that a Yucatec Mayan lord Tutul Xiuh had outlawed homosexuality prior to the arrival of the Spanish. Chi writes: "These natives did not eat human flesh, nor did they know the nefarious sin as in other parts of the Indies. It is said that in the time of a Xiuh lord, they had punished this sin by casting those found guilty in a burning furnace."[64] It is probably more than a coincidence that the Mayan laws of burning "sodomites" matched Spanish law. In fact, given the colonial oppressions of Diego de Landa—who burned Mayan manuscripts and then used the "confessions" of the Maya he illegally tortured to rewrite Mayan history—the burning of two-spirit Maya seems highly unlikely. Although Pete Sigal believes that Maya saw homosexuality as a corruption of military abilities, he also comments that Xiuh's pronouncement had heavy political motivation for the Maya to reflect Spanish sexual law. Fellow conquistador Bernal Díaz del Castillo made claims of finding clay idols in the Yucatan that "showed Indians committing acts of sodomy with each other" as did Francisco López de Gómara, who wrote: "Among the trees, we came upon an idol of gold and many of clay; forming the position of two men mounted one over the other in the act of sodomy."[65] Supposedly these idols were destroyed or melted down. Rhetorically the message is clear that indigenous gold and human labor would find better religious use by the "highly moral" Catholic Church and Spanish Empire that condemned homosexuality. These narratives of conquest present themselves as somewhat dubious rhetorical statements meant to justify colonization by any means and provide a stark contrast to las Casas' and Chi's highly political writings that deny any indigenous toleration of "sodomy."

The Spanish destruction of preconquest Nahua written texts makes ascertaining the nature of precontact sexuality extremely difficult, if not impossible. As a result "scholars have understandably been drawn to theoretical models of gender and sexuality," Martin Nesvig confirms.[66] Nesvig explains that the homosexual connotations of Aztec heteropatriarchy, the only model that many mestizo Mexicans such as Octavio Paz have been able to articulate, are based on the belief that the macho Aztec sexually gains power "through the penetration of a passive body," male or female.[67] Aztec heteropatriarchy, a natural result of the increasing importance of male warrior roles in an expanding empire, is a common model of gender and sexuality that researchers utilize in Mesoamerica. What complicates an understanding of historical Aztec heteropatriarchy is the lack of written preconquest documents, the vagueness of stone sculptures, and the limited nature of heteropatriarchy as the dominant gender and sexual theory.

Even preconquest stone sculpture offers debatable two-spirit and gender histories, especially when the narratives that accompany them are filtered through colonial experiences and Spanish translations as in the case of the stone sculpture of the woman warrior Coyolxauhqui. While Cecelia Klein sought to overcome the lack of preconquest documents by interpreting the remains of the sculpture, she used established models of gender to conclude that Coyolxauqui represents the "archetypal" vanquished cross-dressed warrior woman who was the basis for ascending male Aztec patriarchy.[68] For Klein and for Moraga the preconquest placement of the stone sculpture of the decapitated Coyolxauhqui at the base of the Aztec Templo Mayor was meant to symbolize the subsequent defeat of all feminized enemies who were sacrificed and then thrown down from the temple, just as Huitzilopochtli threw the dismembered Coyolxauhqui down from the Aztec temple Coatepec where she mythically attempted to kill their mother, Coatlicue, in order to prevent Huitzilopochtli's birth.[69] In contrast Michel Graulich argues that Huitzilopochtli's rise to power represents the ascendancy of youth over age, the younger sibling over the elder, just as the recent immigrant Aztecs were able to ascend above the older established civilizations of Central Mexico.[70] Xicana historian Ana Castillo concludes that the era of young Aztec male dominance succeeded a historical period in which women had greater power, thus combining the sexual and age variables.[71] Clearly stone sculpture cannot replace what the burned Mexica libraries could have explained about Coyolxauqui's symbolic meaning, especially since no Nahuatl language oral traditions remain to provide further explanation.

Sigal contends that "as the Nahuas at the time of the conquest connected male homosexuality with ritual and sacrifice, these conceptions clearly diverged from the European discourse of sodomy and sin."[72] From the *Florentine Codex,* Sigal quotes a man cursing the deity Tezcatlipoca for having tricked him by fate from the retention of a slave: "Great *cuiloni,* Titlacauan! Curses upon you for giving me a captive only so that you could mock me."[73] *Cuiloni* can refer to a passive homosexual, but rather than noting the linkage with homosexuality, trickery, and spiritual power as Geoffrey Kimball does, Sigal refers to Trexler in order to assume that *cuiloni* is merely an epithet meant to control the deity, to subvert the greater power that Tezcatlipoca would normally have over human fate. What limits Sigal's research is that it interprets fragmentary postconquest non-two-spirit transgender rituals based upon the deeply homophobic and racist work of Trexler as well as the Eurocentric and phallocentric writings of Jacques Lacan. As Roscoe points out, Trexler's furious insistence that all "berdache" roles are a result of rape, usually by pedophiles, is based upon what Trexler, in his own words, can "imagine" rather than what is actually written in Nahua documents.[74] When Sigal cites various colonial texts, laws, and confessionals prohibiting two-spirit activities or condemning two-spirit people to death, he suggests there was little resistance to purported oppressions and offers few criticisms of colonial sources. More historiographies of Spanish sources with different methodologies are required before the Nahua fragments can offer a more critical analysis of Nahua two-spirit histories.

Sigal's interpretations make one wonder what kind of resistance to homophobia or transphobia Nahua two-spirits were able to muster before and after colonization. Kimball provides critical insight into the largest compilation of any indigenous language and culture, the *Florentine Codex,* mostly compiled by Nahuas under the editorial hand of Fray Bernardino de Sahagún in the mid-1500s. The *Florentine Codex* documents evil and good behavior as a way to control Nahua society. Kimball notes that the phrase "Tlatiloni/tlatlani/chichinoloni/ tlata/chichinolo" seems to be oddly inserted as a condemnation of effeminate male-bodied peoples who were to be burned to death. It translates as "He is one who is burned, he is one who burns, he is one who is burned up, he burns, he is burned up."[75] Kimball suspects that Sahagún took liberties to ensure that Aztec Empire codes would exactly match the sentencing to burning for homosexuality that had only relatively recently been adopted in Spain under changing Inquisition laws. Kimball also notes that the Nahua sign for transgender recognition was to chew gum conspicuously. If the sentence was so harsh, Kimball wonders, why was the signal of gum chewing so conspicuous? Kimball opens up a discourse of resistance by speculating that private two-spirit sexual encounters may have been permissible even if Nahua or Catholic colonial civic laws inhibited outright two-spirit sexual relationships and gender roles.

My own initial reading of ancient Nahua cosmology in "The 'Macho' Body as Social Malinche" allows for an understanding of internal gender dualities that would permit an acceptance of two-spirit peoples as normative within a more complementary gender system.[76] I was most influenced by Carolyn Epple's brilliant argument for an internal and broadly cosmological gender duality reflected by Navajo traditions of nádleehí.[77] I also borrowed heavily from Xicana-Nimipu author Inés Hernández-Ávila and her Nahua-influenced formulation of an activist "Social Malinche" who ceremonially and politically defends her indigenous and mixed-blooded people. My previous work interweaves western language, feminist and other cultural forms with contemporary Navajo, Nahua, Xicana lesbiana, and Nimipu influences, which is more appropriate than using the phallocentric, homophobic, and Eurocentic theories that so wholly guide Sigal's analysis. Moreover, the impact of Sigal's homophobic writings may not be evident to him as a white scholar. Even while I was writing this essay, my participation in a 2010 Chicana Feminist Conference at California State University, Long Beach, was attacked by a neo-Mexica Chicano's commentary in the online campus newspaper. Although my name did not appear in the blog, the writer cited the need to bring back the "traditional" Mexica ways of destroying gay "jotos" that Sigal enthusiastically endorses as historical fact. It was a virtual death threat. At the same time these kinds of oppressive linguistic events cannot motivate me simply to create an oppositional identity to homophobia. If anything, my relationship to being a two-spirit person has been a bit of a rabbit dance, two steps forward and one step back. In this historiography I am taking a step back and listening to scholars who have a different relationship to their Native American nations and two-spirit histories.

New developments in indigenous civilization mark a trend toward understanding differences in gender within complementary frameworks that defy the heterosexist norm that Trexler and Sigal purport rule Maya, Aztec, and all American Indian cultures.[78] This language of complementary gender is also beginning to make inroads in the literature on Mexican Indian women of various nations, especially as more women and feminists have become involved in the study of Mesoamerica. Louise Burkhart states: "Women in Aztec Mexico occupied a symbolic and social domain that was separate from and complementary to that of men."[79] However, Nahua women's power to bequeath land and home to their daughters and sons diminished over the course of Spanish colonization and is an index of a patriarchal shift that occurs after rather than before colonization.[80] Lisa Sousa documents the fact that preconquest and sixteenth-century Mixtec codices evidence a complementary gender system in which political power was shared by a ruling female/male couple who were often shown facing each other seated on a mat. The strong roles for Zapotec and Mixtec women help to balance the presumption that all Mesoamerican societies were as patriarchal and heterosexist as the Spanish were.[81] Burkhart notes that even if some Aztec male warriors taunted their enemies as being "cuiloni," sexually penetrated, one cannot assume that this reflected an overarching fear of femininity that could intrude into the domestic realm in which women had property rights and symbolic power of the battle of childbirth.[82] Moreover, such a negative use of the word would not necessarily apply to nonwarrior two-spirit Nahuas in a complementary gender system. These complementary roles neither suggest a true equality among multiple genders nor do they prohibit investigating gender inequalities; they do put forth a dynamic process of struggle to maintain valued gender differences. While the authors of *Indian Women of Early Mexico* do not comment on two-spirit genders, their lengthy documentation of complementary gender roles make Sigal's homophobic and phallocentric theories even more questionable. Two-spirit roles were honored prior to colonization, which may be evidenced by contemporary practices by Zapotec muxe and other indigenous nations across Mesoamerica and the Southwest.

Conclusion

U.S. American Indian historiographies of two-spirit peoples have much to contribute to a pan-American understanding of gender and sexuality. The work of

Miranda should push others to look to two-spirit writers who offer key insights into the Spanish sexual colonization that individuals survived in diverse ways with great effort. Rooted in oral narratives, Chumash, Tongva, Ajachmen, Pueblo, Navajo, and Apache stories offer provocative statements about historically inclusive gender systems. Recent two-spirit writings also support the acceptance of two-spirit peoples in the Southwest that historical documents often fail to record. The strength of these gender traditions defies the notion that indigenous cultures simply evolved from patriarchal or homophobic nations. This historiography questions the veracity of Spanish colonial historical records with their conflicting narratives of indigenous homosexuality being either rampant or severely prohibited. While Xicana lesbianas fight to imagine creative resistance to Aztec heterosexism, one questions why Aztecs should remain central, given the diverse indigenous ancestry of Xicanas/os throughout the Southwest and Northern Mexico. Zapotec muxe and new writings on complementary Nahua genders can spark new analyses of historical two-spirit genders in Mesoamerica. Much work on two-spirit traditions in Latin America remains to be written. Although Rigoberta Menchu speaks of two-spirit tolerance among the Maya, her voice echoes in an international publishing world that excludes most indigenous peoples of Guatemala and Mexico from publishing widely on issues of sexuality, politics and history. While this historiography could create debates in academic circles interested in two-spirit histories, a desired outcome is that indigenous, indigenous-descended, and multicultural peoples know that there are options when it come both to understanding sexual histories and to listening for two-spirit voices in a Spanish colonial context. Clearly this is an exciting time to exchange new knowledge of ancient two-spirit peoples.

Notes

1. Walter L. Williams, *The Spirit and the Flesh: Sexual Diversity in American Indian Culture* (Boston: Beacon Press, 1992), 32.

2. Richard C. Trexler, *Sex and Conquest: Gendered Violence, Political Order, and the European Conquest of the Americas* (Ithaca: Cornell University Press, 2005), 116.

3. Will Roscoe, "Strange Country This: Images of Berdaches and Warrior Women," in *Living the Spirit: A Gay American Indian Anthology,* ed. Will Roscoe (New York: St. Martin's, 1988), 48–76.

4. Paula Gunn Allen, "Hwame, *Koshkalaka,* and the Rest: Lesbians in American Indian Cultures," in *The Sacred Hoop: Recovering the Feminine in American Indian Traditions* (Boston: Beacon Press, 1992), 245–61.

5. Pete Sigal, ed., *Infamous Desire: Male Homosexuality in Colonial Latin America* (Chicago: University of Chicago Press, 2003).

6. Sophie Mayer, "This Bridge of Two Backs: Making the Two-Spirit Erotics of Community," *Studies in American Indian Literatures* 20, no. 1 (Spring 2008):1–26.

7. Qwo-Li Driskill, "Stolen From Our Bodies: First Nations Two-Spirits/Queers and the Journey to a Sovereign Erotic," *Studies in American Indian Literatures.* 16, no. 2 (Summer 2004): 50–51.

8. Walter Williams, *The Spirit and the Flesh,* 32.

9. Sue Ellen Jacobs, et. al., "Introduction," in *Two-Spirit People: Native American Gender Identity, Sexuality, and Spirituality,* ed. Sue-Ellen Jacobs, Wesley Thomas, and Sabine Lang (Urbana: University of Illinois Press, 1997), 6.

10. Brian Joseph Gilley, *Becoming Two-Spirit: Gay Identity and Social Acceptance in Indian Country* (Lincoln: University of Nebraska Press, 2006), 95.

11. Carolyn Epple, "Coming to Terms with Navajo Nádleehí: A Critique of 'Berdache,' 'Gay,' 'Alternate Gender,' and 'Two-Spirit,'" *American Ethnologist* 25, no. 2 (May 1998): 268.

12. Deborah Miranda, "Extermination of the Joyas: Gendercide in Spanish California," *GLQ: A Journal of Lesbian and Gay Studies* 16, no. 1–2 (2010): 266; and Sandra Holliman, "The Archaeology of Nonbinary Genders in Native North American Societies," *Handbook of Gender in Archaeology,* ed. Sarah Milledge Nelson (Lanham, Md: Altamira Press, 2006).

13. Miranda, *Extermination of the Joyas,* 263–64.

14. Ibid., 270–71.

15. Ibid., 271.

16. Ibid., 256.

17. Ibid., 275.

18. John G. Kennedy, *The Tarahumara: Survivors at the Canyon's Edge* (Pacific Grove, Calif.: Asilomar Press, 1996), 132.

19. Ana Alonso, *Thread of Blood: Colonialism, Revolution and Gender on Mexico's Frontier* (Tucson: University of Arizona Press, 1996).

20. Beatriz Braniff, "Paquime: Origen de una Nueva Tradición Cerámica," *Cerámica de Mata Ortiz: Artes de Mexico* 45 (1999): 14.

21. Christine S. VanPool, and Todd L. VanPool, "Gender in Middle Range Societies: A Case Study in Casas Grandes Iconography." *American Antiquity* 71, no. 1 (January 2006): 54.

22. Greg Sarris, quoted in Terry Tafoya, "M. Dragonfly: Two-Spirit and the Tafoya Principle of Uncertainty," in *Two-Spirit People: Native American Gender Identity, Sexuality, and Spirituality,* edited by Sue-Ellen Jacobs, Wesley Thomas, and Sabine Lang, 192–200 (Urbana: University of Illinois Press, 1997), 197–98.

23. Leslie Marmon Silko, *Yellow Woman and a Beauty of the Spirit* (New York: Simon and Schuster, 1996), 50.

24. Miranda, "Extermination of the *Joyas,*" 263–64.

25. Allen, *The Sacred Hoop,* 246

26. Ibid., 256.

27. Ibid., 247.

28. Tracy Brown, "'Abominable Sin' in Colonial New Mexico: Spanish and Pueblo Perceptions of Same-Sex Sexuality," in *Long before Stonewall: Histories of Same-Sex Sexuality in Early America,* ed. Thomas A. Foster (New York: New York University Press, 2007), 51–52.

29. Ibid., 66.

Gabriel S. Estrada

30. Ibid., 67.

31. Ibid.

32. Ramón A. Gutiérrez, "Warfare, Homosexuality and Gender Status among American Indian Men," in *Long before Stonewall: Histories of Same-Sex Sexuality in Early America,* ed. Thomas A. Foster (New York: New York University Press, 2007), 29.

33. Ramón A. Gutiérrez, "Must We Deracinate Indians to Find Gay Roots?" *Out/Look* 1, no. 4 (1989): 61–67.

34. Gutiérrez, "Warfare, Homosexuality and Gender Status," 25.

35. Will Roscoe, *Changing Ones: Third and Fourth Genders in Native North America* (New York: St. Martin's Press, 1998), 191.

36. Ibid., 193.

37. Ibid., 113. That gay white anthropologist Will Roscoe glosses the Zuni kachina as berdache instead of two-spirit is at odds with his rhetoric of maintaining friendly relationships with two-spirit communities. Again, most two-spirit writers find that term to be culturally offensive and prefer two-spirit terms in their own language.

38. Will Roscoe, "Ever since the World Began: Berdache Myths and Tales," *Living the Spirit: A Gay American Indian Anthology,* ed. Will Roscoe, (New York: St. Martin's Press, 1988), 86–87.

39. Terry Tafoya, "M. Dragonfly," 194.

40. Carrie House, "Navajo Warrior Women: An Ancient Tradition in a Modern World," in *Two-Spirit People: Native American Gender Identity, Sexuality, and Spirituality,* ed. Sue-Ellen Jacobs, Wesley Thomas, and Sabine Lang (Urbana: University of Illinois Press, 1997), 224.

41. Ibid., 226.

42. Peter Aleshire. *Warrior Woman: The Story of Lozen, Apache Warrior and Shaman* (New York: St. Martin's, 2001), 2.

43. Eve Ball, *In the Days of Victorio* (Tucson: University of Arizona Press, 1970), 14–15.

44. Roscoe, *Changing Ones,* 90–91.

45. Ibid.*,* 213–22.

46. Cherríe Moraga, *The Last Generation: Prose and Poetry* (Boston: South End Press, 1993), 166.

47. According to Ana Castillo, *Xicana* refers to an activist and feminist identity for Mestizas, women of mixed Mexican Amerindian heritage living in the United States outside their indigenous nations of origin. While *American Indian* usually refers to aboriginal nations internal to the United States and *indigenous* more often refers to aboriginal peoples of Latin America, I will use the terms interchangeably while acknowledging here the legal distinctions that demarcate American Indian nations from other indigenous peoples. Xicanas may be of American indigenous or American Indian origin. Anna Castillo, *Massacre of the Dreamers: Essays on Xicanisma* (New York: Plume Books, 1994), 11.

48. Roscoe, *Changing Ones,* 213–22.

49. Moraga, *The Last Generation,* 194

50. Ibid., 164.

51. Gabriel S. Estrada, "The 'Macho' Body as Social Malinche," in *Velvet Barrios: Popular Culture & Xicana/o Sexualities,* ed. Alicia Gaspar de Alba (New York: Palgrave Macmillan, 2003), 48.

182

52. Gloria Anzaldúa, *Borderlands/La Frontera: The New Mestiza* (San Francisco: Spinsters/ Aunt Lute Books, 1987).

53. Cherríe Moraga, *Heroes and Saints & Other Plays: Giving Up the Ghost, Shadow of a Man, and Heroes and Saints* (Albuquerque: West End Press, 1994).

54. Linda Margarita Greenberg, "Learning from the Dead: Wounds, Women, and Activism in Cherríe Moraga's *Heroes and Saints,*" *MELUS: Multi-Ethnic Literature of the U.S.* 32, no. 1 (Spring 2009): 176.

55. Ibid., 180.

56. Ibid., quoting Rafael Pérez-Torres, *Mestizaje: Critical Uses of Race in Chicano Culture* (Minneapolis: University of Minnesota Press, 2006), 16, 74–75.

57. La Red Xicana: Xicana Indigenous Woman's Network, accessed July 19, 2009 at http://www.laredxicanaindigena.com (July 19, 2009).

58. Bartolomé de las Casas, *A Short Account of the Destruction of the Indies* (London: Penguin Books, 1992), 9.

59. Miranda, "Extermination of the *Joyas,*" 259.

60. Beverly N. Chiñas, "Isthmus Zapotec Attitudes towards Sex and Gender Anomolies," in *Latin American Male Homosexualities,* ed. Stephen O. Murphey (Albuquerque: University of New Mexico Press, 1995), 295.

61. Lynn Stephen, "Sexualities and Genders in Zapotec Oaxaca," *Latin American Perspectives, Special Issue: Gender Sexuality and Same-Sex Desire in Latin America* 29, no. 2 (March 2002): 55.

62. Ibid., 48.

63. Rigoberta Menchu, *I, Rigoberta Menchu* (New York: Verso, 1987), 60.

64. Pete Sigal, "Gender, Male Homosexuality, and Power in Colonial Yucatán," *Latin American Perspectives, Special Issue: Gender Sexuality and Same-Sex Desire in Latin America,* 29, no. 2 (March 2002): 27.

65. Clark Taylor, "Legends, Syncretism, and Continuing Echoes of Homosexuality from Pre-Columbian and Colonial Mexico," in *Latin American Male Homosexualities,* ed. Stephen O. Murphey (Albuquerque: University of New Mexico, 1995), 84.

66. Martin Nesvig, "The Complicated Terrain of Latin American Homosexuality," *Hispanic American Historical Review* 81, nos. 3–4 (August–November 2001): 689.

67. Ibid., 691.

68. Cecilia Klein, "Fighting with Femininity: Gender and War in Aztec Mexico," *Estudios de Cultura Nahuatl* 24(1994): 227.

69. Moraga, *The Last Generation,*74–75.

70. Michel Graulich, "Más sobre La Coyolxauhqui y las mujeres desnudas de Tlaltelolco," *Estudios de Cultura Nahuatl* 31 (2000): 87.

71. Castillo, *Massacre of the Dreamers,* 64.

72. Pete Sigal, "The Cuiloni, the Patlache, and the Abominable Sin: Homosexualities in Early Colonial Nahua Society," *Hispanic American Historical Review* 85, no.4 (2005): 593.

73. Ibid., 573.

74. Will Roscoe, *Changing Ones,* 194.

75. Geoffrey Kimball, "Aztec Homosexuality: The Textual Evidence," *Journal of Homosexuality* 26, no. 1 (1993):18.

76. Estrada, "The 'Macho' Body as Social Malinche," 41.

Gabriel S. Estrada

77. Carolyn Epple, "A Navajo Worldview and *Nádleehí:* Implications for Western Categories," in *Two-Spirit People: Native American Gender Identity, Sexuality, and Spirituality,* ed. Sue-Ellen Jacobs, Wesley Thomas, and Sabine Lang (Urbana: University of Illinois Press, 1997), 224.

78. Michael J. Horsewell, "Toward an Andean Theory of Ritual Same-Sex Sexuality and Third-Gender Subjectivity," in *Infamous Desire: Male Homosexuality in Colonial Latin America,* ed. Pete Sigal (Chicago: University of Chicago Press, 2007), 58.

79. Louise Burkhart, "Mexica Women on the Home Front: Housework and Religion in Aztec Mexico," in *Indian Women in Early Mexico,* ed. Susan Schroeder, Stephanie Wood, and Robert Haskett (Norman: University of Oklahoma Press, 1997), 25.

80. Susan Schroeder, "Introduction," in *Indian Women in Early Mexico,* ed. Susan Schroeder, Stephanie Wood, and Robert Haskett (Norman: University of Oklahoma Press, 1997), 17.

81. Lisa Sousa, "Women and Crime in Colonial Oaxaca: Evidence of Complementary Gender Roles in Mixtec and Zapotec Societies," in *Indian Women in Early Mexico,* ed. Susan Schroeder, Stephanie Wood, and Robert Haskett (Norman: University of Oklahoma Press, 1997), 201.

82. Burkhart, "Mexica Women on the Home Front," 26.

Suggested Readings

The subject of Native American women and gender is incredibly vast. In an effort to encourage additional readings, the following categories are offered, representing just a few of the foundational texts as well as the more recent contributions. This list is not comprehensive by any stretch of the imagination, but we feel that these works represent the best of historical works on the subject of gender and sexuality in native communities through the first half of the nineteenth century.

Comparative and Methodological Works

Jaffary, Nora, ed. *Gender, Race and Religion in the Colonization of the Americas*. Burlington, Vt.: Ashgate Publishing, 2007.

Klein, Laura F., and Lillian A. Ackerman, eds. *Women and Power in Native North America*. Norman: University of Oklahoma Press, 1995.

Kugel, Rebecca, and Lucy Eldersveld Murphy. *Native Women's History in Eastern North America before 1900: A Guide to Research and Writing*. Lincoln: University of Nebraska Press, 2007.

Richter, Daniel K. *Facing East from Indian Country: A Native History of Early America*. Cambridge: Harvard University Press, 2001.

Woodworth-Ney, Laura E. *Women in the American West*. Santa Barbara: ABC CLIO, 2008.

Colonial New England

Felsenstein, Frank, ed. *English Trader, Indian Maid: Representing Gender, Race, and Slavery in the New World*. Baltimore: Johns Hopkins University Press, 1999.

Little, Amy M. *Abraham in Arms: War and Gender in Colonial New England*. Philadelphia: University of Pennsylvania Press, 2007.

Mann, Barbara Alice. *Iroquoian Women: The Gantowisas*. New York: Peter Lang, 2000.

Plane, Ann Marie. *Colonial Intimacies: Indian Marriage in Early New England*. Ithaca: Cornell University Press, 2000.

Great Lakes / New France Gender and Sexuality

Anderson, Karen L. *Chain Her by One Foot: The Subjugation of Women in Seventeenth-Century New France*. London: Routledge, 1991.

Fur, Gunlög. *A Nation of Women: Gender and Colonial Encounters among the Delaware Indians*. Philadelphia: University of Pennsylvania Press, 2009.

Greer, Allan. *Mohawk Saint: Catherine Tekawitha and the Jesuits*. Boston: Oxford University Press, 2006.

Sleeper-Smith, Susan. *Indian Women and French Men: Rethinking Cultural Encounter in the Western Great Lakes*. Amherst: University of Massachusetts, 2001.

Suggested Readings

Sleeper-Smith, Susan. *Rethinking the Fur Trade: Cultures of Exchange in an Atlantic World.* Lincoln: University of Nebraska Press, 2009.

Van Kirk, Sylvia. *Many Tender Ties: Women in Fur Trade Society, 1670–1870.* Norman: University Oklahoma Press 1980.

Viau, Roland. *Femmes de personne: Sexes, genres et pouvoirs en Iroquoisie ancienne.* Montréal: Boréal, 2000.

The American Southwest and Texas Borderlands

Barr, Juliana. *Peace Came in the Form of a Woman: Indians and Spaniards in the Texas Borderlands.* Chapel Hill: University of North Carolina Press, 2007.

Gutiérrez, Ramón A. *When Jesus Came, the Corn Mothers Went Away: Marriage, Sexuality, and Power in New Mexico 1500–1846.* Stanford: Stanford University Press, 1991.

Hurtado, Albert L. *Sex, Gender, and Culture in Old California.* Albuquerque: University of New Mexico, 1999.

Irwin, Mary Ann, and James F. Brooks, eds. *Women and Gender in the American West.* Albuquerque: University of New Mexico, 2004.

Kanter, Deborah E. *Hijos del Pueblo: Gender, Family, and Community in Rural Mexico, 1730–1850.* Austin: University of Texas Press, 2009.

Viqueira, Juan Pedro. *Propriety and Permissiveness in Bourbon Mexico.* Translated by Sonya Lipsett Rivera and Sergio Rivera Ayala. Wilmington, Del.: Scholarly Resources, 1999.

Two-spirited Peoples and Sexuality

Forgey, Donald G. "The Institution of Berdache among the North American Plains Indians." *Journal of Sex Research* 11, no. 1 (February 1975): 1–15

Gilley, Brian Joseph. *Becoming Two-Spirit: Gay Identity and Social Acceptance in Indian Country.* Lincoln: University of Nebraska Press, 2006.

Jacobs, Sue-Ellen, Wesley Thomas, and Sabine Lang, eds. *Two-Spirit People: Native American Gender Identity, Sexuality and Spirituality.* Urbana: University of Illinois Press, 1997.

Lang, Sabine. *Men as Women, Women as Men: Changing Gender in Native American Cultures.* Austin: University of Texas Press, 1998.

Roscoe, Will. *Changing Ones: Third and Fourth Genders in Native North America.* New York: St. Martin's Press, 1998.

Williams, Walter L. *The Spirit and the Flesh: Sexual Diversity in American Indian Culture.* Boston: Beacon Press, 1992.

Southeastern Indians

Perdue, Theda. *Cherokee Women: Gender and Culture Change, 1700–1835.* Lincoln: University of Nebraska, 1998.

Saunt, Claudio. "'Domestick . . . Quiet being broke: Gender Conflict among the Creek Indians in the Eighteenth Century." In *Contact Points: American Frontiers from the Mohawk Valley to the Mississippi, 1750–1830,* edited by Andrew R. L. Cayton and Fredrika J. Teute. Chapel Hill: University of North Carolina Press, 1998.

Yarbrough, Fay A. "Legislating Women's Sexuality: Cherokee Marriage Laws in the Nineteenth Century." *Journal of Social History* 38, no. 2 (Winter 2004): 385–406.

Contributors

Roger M. Carpenter received his doctoral degree in Native American and early American history from the University of California, Riverside. He is an assistant professor at the University of Louisiana, Monroe, and is the author of *The Renewed, the Destroyed, and the Remade: The Three Thought Worlds of the Huron and the Iroquois, 1609–1650*.

Gabriel S. Estrada received his doctoral degree in comparative cultural and literary studies from the University of Arizona at Tucson. He is an assistant professor in the American Indian Studies Program at California State University, Long Beach. He is author of "Two-Spirit Film Criticism: Fancydancing with Imitates Dog, Desjarlais and Alexie" in *Post Script* and "Victor Montejo's El Q'anil: Man of Lightning and Maya Cultural Movements" in *Latin American Indian Literatures Journal*.

M. Carmen Gomez-Galisteo holds a B.A. in English with honors and a Ph.D. (*sobresaliente cum laude*) in American studies, both from the Universidad de Alcalá. She has published in a number of journals, including *AdAmericam, Contemporary Legend, Clepsydra,* and *RAEI.* Her first book, a study on intertextuality, parodies, and sequels, will be published by McFarland in early 2011. She is currently teaching at ESNE–Universidad Camilo José Cela (Madrid).

Dawn G. Marsh earned her doctoral degree in Native American history from the University of California, Riverside, where she also received training in anthropology and archaeology and a certificate in Museum Studies. She is an assistant professor in the history department at Purdue University. Marsh has articles forthcoming in *Ethnohistory* and the *Journal of Indigenous Policy.*

Jan V. Noel received her doctoral degree in Canadian history from the University of Toronto. She teaches at the University of Toronto in Mississauga and holds the rank of associate professor. She is the author of *Canada Dry: Temperance Crusades before Confederation* and is currently working on a book-length project concerning Canadian gender history in the pre-Confederation period.

Sandra Slater received her doctorate in American history from the University of Kentucky. She is an assistant professor of history and an affiliate faculty member of the Women's and Gender Studies and the Carolina Lowcountry in the Atlantic World programs at the College of Charleston. She is currently completing a manuscript, "Meeting of Men: Comparative European Masculinities in the New World."

Dorothy Tanck de Estrada received her doctoral degree from El Colegio de México. She is a professor at the Centro de Estudios Históricos of El Colegio de México in Mexico City.

She is the author of six books, including *Historia de la lectura en México, La educación primaria en la ciudad de México,* and *Pueblos de indios y educación en el México colonial, 1750–1821,* which was awarded the 2001 Howard F. Cline Memorial Prize for the best work of ethnohistory by the Conference on Latin American History of the American Historical Association.

Fay A. Yarbrough received her doctorate in American history from Emory University. She is an associate professor at the University of Oklahoma. She is the author of *Race and the Cherokee Nation: Sovereignty in the Nineteenth Century* and is currently researching a project considering Choctaw Indians and the American Civil War.

Index

Index

Index

Index

Malinche, 16, 178

manliness. *See* masculinity

Mann, Barbara Alice, 57, 59, 63, 64, 67, 68, 72n32, 74n41

Manriquez, L. Frank, 167

Maori of New Zealand, 4

Marie de l'Incarnation, 63, 64

Marmolejo, María de, 13

Marquette, Pierre, 151–53

marriage: between black people and Choctaws, 138–40; in Choctaw Nation, 123, 124–26, 128, 131–40; European gender roles in, 31; and husband as cuckold, 37; of Illinois Indians, 151; infidelities in, 39; intermarriage in Choctaw Nation, 132–37, 144n80; intermarriage of Native American women to European men generally, 27n31; of Iroquois, 59, 60, 66, 67; and polyandry, 60, 66; polyandry and polygamy, 60, 66, 126, 141–42n20; and property rights in Choctaw Nation, 124, 131–32, 136, 140; and property rights of white women, 136; and Pueblo Nation, 169; in Querétaro, New Spain, 91; of Seneca, 66; separations of Choctaw husbands and wives, 125–26, 128, 134, 137; of Spanish, 19, 25n9; and two-spirits/hermaphrodites/berdaches, 148, 154, 157, 158, 160; between white people and Choctaws, 132–37, 139–40; and women's responsibility for sins of their husbands, 39

Marsh, Dawn G., 1, 2, 5, 6, 102–22, 187

Marshall, Abraham, 104

Marshall, Humphrey, 104, 115

Marshall, Moses, 6, 102–5, 114

masculinity: of Aztecs, 43–45, 179; basis of, 5; of Cabeza de Vaca, 17; conflicts between Native American and European men over, 1, 30–53; and conquistadors' description of conquest and physical land, 4, 5; and courage of explorers, 31–32, 41–42, 50n3; definition of, 30–31; emasculation of Native American men as power for Europeans, 36–37; of Englishmen, 32–34, 37–38, 45–46; of

European men, 4–5, 31–34, 36–38, 41–42, 50n3; of female berdaches/two-spirits, 28n50, 148, 156, 158–61, 169, 171–74; of Frenchmen, 36–37; and honor of Englishmen, 37–38; of Native American men, 39–46; natives and, 4–5; in New England, 38–39; and Pequot War, 45–46; of Spaniards, 36; superiority of European males as stereotype, 17, 43; theory of hypermasculinity, 35; and two-spirits, 46–49; virtues of European men, 19, 31–32, 37, 41–42, 50n3; and warfare, 5, 41–46

Massachusetts Bay Colony, 46–47

matrilineage and matriarchy: and Choctaw Nation, 6, 124–26, 131, 132, 137, 140; and Iroquois, 57, 59, 60, 61, 66, 67, 69, 71n15, 73n38

Maura, Juan Francisco, 16, 17

Maya Quiché, 175–76, 179, 180

Mead, Elizabeth Kemp, 124

Menchu, Rigoberta, 175–76, 180

Mendieta, Gerónimo, 48–49

Mesoamerican sexual histories, 174–80

mestizos/as, 7, 89, 91, 173–74, 175–76, 182n47

Mexico, 36, 47, 75–96. *See also* Aztecs; Querétaro, New Spain; Salvadora de los Santos Ramirez

Miami Indians, 62, 154

Miles, Tiya, 3

Millet, Pierre, 63, 72n29

Miranda, Deborah, 166–67, 174–75, 180

miscegenation, 16

Mixtec codices, 179

Mohawks, 63, 64, 65, 67

Moltolinía, 48–49

Montagnais, 42–43

Montrose, Louis, 26n20

Moraga, Cherríe, 173–74, 177

Morgan, Lewis H., 58, 61, 63, 70n13, 73n37

Morris, Robert, 62

Mosher, Donald L., 35

Mother Nature, 34

motherhood, 16, 17, 41, 60

Index

Index